MOLLY E. HOLZSCHLAG
AND JASON PELLERIN

Perl
web site workshop

SAMS   201 West 103rd Street, Indianapolis, Indiana 46290

Perl Web Site Workshop

Copyright © 2002 by Sams Publishing

International Standard Book Number: 0-672-32275-7

Library of Congress Catalog Card Number: 00-109235

Printed in the United States of America

First Printing: December 2001

04   03   02   01   4   3   2   1

Trademarks

Warning and Disclaimer

Acquisitions Editor
Mark Taber

Managing Editor
Charlotte Clapp

Project Editor
Angela Boley

Indexer
Chris Barrick

Technical Editor
Clinton Pierce

Team Coordinator
Amy Patton

Media Developer
Dan Scherf

Cover/Interior Designer
Gary Adair

Contents at a Glance

Table of Contents

About the Authors

There is little doubt that in the world of Web design and development, **Molly E. Holzschlag** is one of the most vibrant personalities around. With twenty Web development book titles to her credit, Molly is also an engaging speaker and teacher, appearing regularly at such conferences as Comdex, Internet World, Web 2001, and Web Builder.

Honored as one of the Top 25 Women on the Web, Molly is an advisory board member to the World Organization of Webmasters, a member of the Web Standards Project, and spent a year as Executive Editor of WebReview.com. For more about Molly's books, articles, events, and Web-related activities, drop by (where else?) http://www.molly.com/.

Jason Pellerin is Senior Web Applications Developer at Playboy.com, which involves far less nudity, and far more Perl, than you might think. Before that, he was the SysAdmin at the late, lamented Bungie Software, where he was responsible for keeping the online carnage humming on bungie.net, and selling inappropriate t-shirts to minors through the Bungie Store. Jason has a BA in philosophy from Yale University, two cats, and a strange affection for cursed baseball teams.

Dedication

For F.
— Jason

For Randal, Perl amongst Perls and my best heckler
— Molly

Acknowledgments

A special thanks to Mark Taber for all the support in getting this book published. Clinton A. Pierce valiantly jumped into the fray to help out, and we are grateful for his help. David Fugate at Waterside helped with the particulars and peculiars (agent specialties) and did, as always, a phenomenal job.

INTRODUCTION

Many Web designers are finding out that to add solid functionality to their sites, they need to learn to integrate design goals with server solutions. Perl is an extremely powerful and flexible way to help designers achieve their goals.

In this book, we've created a Web site workshop that provides all the scripts and programming you need to put Perl into action right away. Whether you are a designer, or anyone interested in adding functionality to a site using Perl, this book takes a very practical approach.

Instead of starting out by learning the language, the book is divided into chapters that focus on different applications that a Web developer might want to include on his or her site: forms, games, and more advanced techniques. These scripts are ready to go, and the reader need only follow step-by-step instructions to help install and then modify them to individual tastes.

Along with the book comes a CD, chocked full of Perl, Perl modules, and the book's scripts.

The book works as a practical device to empower readers with the ability to add multiple levels of functionality, doing so while keeping cross-browser and platform concerns in mind. But, ideally, the workshop will serve also to inspire the reader to want to learn more about Perl so as to empower him or her to grow in skill and understanding of the role of Perl in Web design.

Perl on the Web

Web designers are naturally focused on client-side design and technology. Often, they are wary of the complexity they perceive involved with server technologies. Compounding their concern is that many books and articles geared toward the Web designer gloss over the details regarding server technologies, preferring to recommend a visit to the systems administrator or Internet service provider (ISP) instead of providing straightforward details.

The plain truth is that designers can use Perl to create fantastic interactivity for site designs. Granted, you might not become the next Perl programming guru (well, you can if you want to!), but certainly you can put Perl to practical work enhancing your designs. We've written *Perl Web Site Workshop* to help you accomplish just that. Our goal is to give designers access to one of the best, most powerful, and widely available scripting languages on the Web.

Perl is responsible for strengthening many of the behind-the-scenes features of the Web. Most of today's cutting-edge Web sites, such as Yahoo! and Amazon, use Perl in some way or another to maintain sites, connect to databases, process forms, or allow for customization of pages.

Perl is extremely accessible and powerful. As you'll learn in upcoming chapters, you don't have to be a Perl programmer to make Perl work. You just have to understand some basics, which we're going to provide you with, step-by-step.

If you're concerned that Perl is out of your grasp because you're not a computer programmer, don't worry! We've designed this book with the non-programmer in mind. We'll walk you through all you need to know to get the scripts in this book working on your Web sites quickly and with ease.

Furthermore, Perl scripts are fairly easy to modify (we'll show you how to do that, too). And, if you should become inspired to actually learn Perl, it's a fun language to be involved with—endorsed by passionate supporters and contributors who have made and continue to keep Perl available to all who are interested.

To help you understand just why Perl is the language of choice for many Web programmers, we're going to provide in this chapter:

- A basic description of Perl

- A discussion of the main differences between browser technology and server-side technology

- An explanation of Perl's critical partner in Web adventures: the
  Common Gateway Interface (CGI)

We'll also take a look at which servers support Perl, and then give you
a taste of what this book has to offer in terms of Perl on the Web.

About Perl

Perl's accessibility is in large part due to the altruism of its father,
Larry Wall. Its technical origins are varied, and include the programming language known as C, and a Unix scripting application called
awk. Larry Wall was challenged by the limitations he found in the
Unix tool environment, so he set about creating Perl.

Wall then thrust his newborn language out into the wild frontier of
the Usenet Internet newsgroups, where it met up with countless bits
of commentary and feedback—much of which has since been incor-
porated into the language, currently in its fifth version. At this
writing, the stable version is 5.6.1 and the experimental developer
version is 5.7. This development version is not recommended for
standard production environments.

Supporters of Perl have a tight-knit community and an entire culture
has grown up around it. It's kind of hard to believe that a computer
technology is responsible for inspiring such devotion. It happens,
though—look at the enthusiasm of Macintosh users!

Perl is another great example of such enthusiasm. There are many
fine books on Perl, Web resources and free script repositories
abound, and extremely active newsgroups are available to help
others get involved with and use Perl to its fullest and best. The best

You can install Perl right off
the CD included with this
book—we've included
versions for Microsoft
Windows, Macintosh, and
Unix. Or you can download
the absolute latest version of
Perl from
**www.perl.com/pub/language/
info/software.html**

place to begin is at **http://www.perl.com**. You'll also want to visit **http://www.perl.com/CPAN/** to get Perl, Perl documentation, and plenty of FAQs.

About Open Source

Open source is a term used to describe software that is developed to be freely shared, possibly improved, and redistributed by others. Open source software has been around for some time, but it has recently gained an increase in awareness, particularly through recent industry recognition of Linux.

Two of the important premises of the open source movement are that open source software must be redistributed without restriction, and that any source code changes to the software itself must be made available to the community. Perl strongly adheres to both these principles.

Perl, to the delight of all, is free. It's a very democratic language, really. It's supported by its users, and its modules and documentation (not to mention aspects of the language itself) have all been written by volunteer enthusiasts. It conforms, if to anything, to the concepts and beliefs of *open source.*

Perl was created with Unix in mind. However, the language has been ported to just about every popular platform, including Windows, Macintosh, VMS, MS-DOS, and even Amiga.

Server Versus Browser

To understand the way Perl works on the Web, it's important to understand the difference between server-side programming and browser-, or client-side programming, as well as the general relationship between Web servers and Web browsers.

Web designers who have been around for a few years will remember server-side imagemaps. These maps required the server to process the map's coordinates to enable them to work—this is a familiar example of server-side programming.

A bit later came JavaScript, which opened up scripting on the client, or browser, side. These days we can choose a variety of methods to achieve an end goal, but the fact remains that Web servers and Web browsers rely on one another in an increasingly complex and integrated relationship.

Web servers and Web browsers work hand-in-hand to deliver the information that ultimately ends up on a Web page visitor's screen.

When a Web site visitor makes a request by typing in a Web URL address or by clicking on a link, the browser sends the requested document to the server. In the simplest and most common of situations, the server sends this request to the browser, which then interprets and displays it on the visitor's screen. Requests are usually for HTML documents or graphic files.

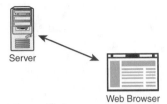

Server

Web Browser

Figure 1.1
*Illustration of server-browser
relationship.*

To extend and enhance the capabilities of the Web, server-side
programming and browser-side programming were added to this
method of exchange.

When a browser makes a request to a server, the request can be for a
document, or it can trigger a server-side program such as a Perl
script to run on the server. If a program is triggered on the server
side, the browser maintains a connection with the server while the
program runs. Once the program is complete, the results are sent to
the browser, all ready to go.

In the case of browser-side programming, such as JavaScript, the
browser sends and receives a request from the server as usual. If the
requested document contains a browser-side program, this program
is executed within the browser.

So, a server-side program runs on the server, whereas a browser-side
program runs within the browser.

At one time, server-sided programming wasn't only a preference, it
was the only choice. Browsers simply weren't sophisticated enough
to manage complex tasks on their own. Their job was merely to
provide a window with which to view a Web-based document.

The past few years have seen enormous changes in browser technologies. Ferocious competition and a hungry public have caused
browser developers to expand the browser's power. Now, developers
and designers have a growing range of choices to make about where
and how to run applications.

There's ongoing debate as to which is better. When browser-based
technologies came on the scene with some force, as was the case
with JavaScript, professional opinion swayed to the browser side
advantage.

Advantages of Server-Side Programs

- **Unlike client-side programs, server-side programs will always run.** Older browsers do not support many browser-based programs such as JavaScript, and newer browsers allow you to disable browser-based programs. This is not a concern when using server-side programs, because they run on the server and are independent of the browser.

- **Server-side programs allow you to read and write to databases, or local files on the server.** With server-side programs, you can save information about visitors, query databases, and create custom pages among other activities. Browser-side programs do not allow for these applications.

However, the use of browser technologies such as JavaScript means that each time upgrades to the language occur, upgrades to the interpreter—which resides in the browser—must occur as well.

Server technology doesn't have this problem; when a new version of a language becomes available server side, browsers can still deal with the output because the technology isn't relying on the browser's intelligence.

So which is better, and which do you want to use? The answer really depends on your needs. Each method has pros and cons, and you may even need to use both methods to achieve your particular goal. Because this book is about Perl and specific to programs that run on the server, we will focus almost exclusively on server-side programming.

Perhaps most significantly, browser-based technologies rely on specific browsers and specific browser versions to perform well—if the browser supports those technologies at all.

This creates the greatest challenge faced by Web designers today: how to make sites perform in interesting but consistent ways between platforms, browsers, and browser versions. As a result, many professionals are looking back to the server to provide the stability necessary to accommodate the needs of today's best sites.

Perl and CGI

Most of the scripts in this book are designed to run as CGI programs (or just "CGIs" for short). CGI, which stands for Common Gateway Interface, is not a language like Perl; it's a protocol for how a Web server interacts with outside applications or scripts. CGI is the oldest, and most broadly compatible, way of adding interactivity to a site, and can be used with programs or scripts written in any language, and is "spoken" by almost every Web server. (There are other ways of running applications that offer higher performance—some of those, like Apache/mod_perl, can be used with the scripts in this book; others, such as PHP or JSP, require languages other than Perl, and will not work with our scripts.)

The technical details of how CGI passes information to and from your scripts are not important to delve into here. The point to keep in mind is that a CGI, unlike a static HTML page or image, is a program that runs on the server each time it is requested by a user. It receives, from the Web server, all the form input and cookies that the user enters (or her browser sends), and the output of the program is sent back to the user by the Web server, just as the contents of an HTML page are sent. But unlike that static page, what is sent back may differ for each user, or each time the CGI is requested.

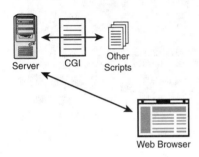

Figure 1.2
CGI and the client/server environment.

CGI Resources

Use these selected CGI sites if you'd like to learn more about CGI.

The Common Gateway Interface Overview:

- **http://hoohoo.ncsa.uiuc.edu/cgi/intro.html** (introduction)
- **http://hoohoo.ncsa.uiuc.edu/cgi/primer.html** (primer)

CGI City

- **http://www.icthus.net/CGI-City/references.shtml** (references)
- **http://www.icthus.net/CGI-City/books.shtml** (books)

CGI Resources.Com

- **http://www.cgi-resources.com/Documentation/** (tutorials and help)
- **http://www.cgi-resources.com/Books/** (books)
- **http://www.cgi-resources.com/Magazine_Articles/** (helpful articles)

Figure 1.3

This form is processed using Perl.

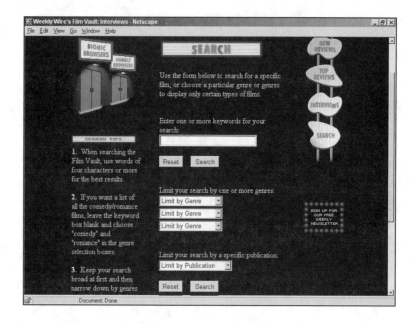

Is Perl the only language that can be used with CGI? The answer is no. Other languages, such as C, are also used at the end of the CGI pipe. However, Perl remains the most flexible, easy to use, and common language utilized for this purpose.

Check out Chapter 4, "Working with Forms," for how to use Perl to set up a variety of functional and attractive forms for your Web pages.

What's in Store

Forms might be the most familiar way Perl is used on the Web, but Perl can do a *lot* more than just manage forms. Let's take a look at the various things you'll learn from this book in terms of making Perl work for you.

Features and Functions

To help you manage your scripts, and your Web site more effectively, we've provided you with some very helpful management tools. You'll find scripts that help you manage other scripts on your site, utilities to rename files behind the scenes, check links, squash bugs, and validate code.

Customizing Sites

Perl can help the Web designer add a range of customized features to the pages that site visitors see.

Perl enables you to create time and date stamps. This is helpful in greeting visitors, and giving your pages the appearance of being lively and fresh.

It's very likely you've seen comments on Web pages such as "page last updated on . . ." This, too, can be done with a Perl script, and also serves to keep audiences aware of a site's timeliness.

Cookies play an enormous role in helping a user track activity within his browser. We will introduce you to a simple cookie and show you how to use it to make a customized guestbook.

Would you like to offer a different graphic selected at random from a list each time an individual visits your Web page? As with time-based functions, this will give the appearance of custom material. Moreover, this effect can be used with great creativity, offering playful or intriguing effects for your site visitors. Randomization can be achieved using server-side includes. We've added all of these techniques and related issues to Chapter 6.

Fun Stuff

Certainly, the Web has been and will probably always be a tool. We use it for many reasons, but honestly, if the Web weren't fun, would we really be here? The appeal of the Web is not just about shopping and information convenience. We have a good time there!

If you're looking to create a little rest and relaxation for your site visitors, we'll show you how to add fun stuff such as polls and interactive stories to your pages. Just drop by Chapter 7, "Fun and Games," for the necessary scripts and modifications.

You can find scripts for Web site management tools in Chapter 5, "Features and Functions."

Much of customization relies on browser detection and routing, which we teach you how to do with CGI and Perl in Chapter 6, "Customizing Pages."

Using Perl to Publish Entire Web Sites

Publishing entire Web sites is no small task, which is why it takes up two entire chapters! We begin by teaching you how to work with templates, and then show you how to use Perl to actually manage and publish a complete, customizable Web site. We begin in Chapter 8, "Designing with Templates," and carry the concept through to Chapter 9, "Creating Your Own Portal."

Managing a Web Site

In Chapter 10, "Web Site Publishing Wizard," we'll put together a tool box which will allow you to manage your Web site through your browser. This will give you the tools you need to publish content without having to worry about the details of how it's installed and organized.

Toward Learning Perl

While the majority of the focus in this book is to get you using Perl quickly and easily, we do hope we'll inspire some of you to go on to explore Perl as a language. To that end, we've included a chapter on Perl basics. Chapter 11, "Getting Ready to Learn Perl," gets those of you interested in being able to write your own custom scripts a leg up on how to do just that.

What's Up Next

You should now have a clear idea as to what Perl is, how it relates to CGI, and how it works on the Web. In Chapter 2, "Getting Ready to Design with Perl," we get you set up with the skills and tools necessary to work with the scripts in *Perl Web Site Workshop*.

Getting Ready to Design with Perl

With an understanding of what Perl is, and a general sense of how you can use it to enhance your Web sites, it's time to make sure you have the knowledge and software necessary to work with the scripts in this book. In this chapter, we'll let you know what skills you'll need and what tools you'll want to have. Then, we'll provide you with questions to ask your Internet Service Provider (ISP) so you can make sure your server and account is set up to support CGI and Perl.

Readers of this book will undoubtedly come from a variety of backgrounds. Some of you have programming experience, and are using this book primarily for the scripts and assorted tips it contains. Some of you are working designers who don't have enough time in the day to dedicate to learning programming, yet want to put the power of programming to work on your Web sites. Still others are trying to find ways to enhance personal or business-related sites, but have no interest in learning how to program.

Because most readers will likely be using Windows or Macintosh computers to create Web sites, we have presented the information in this chapter (and this book) from that perspective.

Although we will be spending time in the Unix environment, Unix skills are not required. For those of you who might be a little intimidated by the Unix environment, we promise to provide plenty of descriptions and easy help get you comfortable. And, for those of you who want to work in a Unix environment, we've naturally included information that will be helpful to you.

Skills You'll Want

In this section, we'll let you know exactly what skills you'll need for this book, and at what level. This way, no matter your current skill level, you'll know how to make the most of *Perl Web Site Workshop*.

HTML

We expect you to have a good understanding of HTML in order to best use this book. You don't need to be an HTML guru, but you do need to know how to get around an HTML document and how to code HTML properly.

If your familiarity with HTML is based on What-You-See-is-What-You-Get (WYSIWYG) Web authoring tools like Microsoft FrontPage and Adobe GoLive, we believe your design skills will be significantly enhanced if you do seek out some basic HTML skills. Without strong HTML skills, your ability to work with Perl on the Web will be greatly restricted. Fortunately, there are a lot of good books and Web sites on learning the basics of HTML.

Unix

If you're unfamiliar with Unix, worry not! We're going to walk you through what you do need to know. We'll have detailed instructions wherever necessary, and plenty of sidebars offering power commands and resources to help you out.

Unix skills are a plus, of course. If you're an old pro at Unix, stick with what you know. But, if you're more familiar with the Windows or Macintosh environments, use the tools with which you are familiar, or select from those we recommend. We've made it a point to include sidebars offering power commands and additional resources wherever applicable.

FTP

Most of you probably have HTML experience, so you already know that FTP means File Transfer Protocol. FTP allows you to transfer files from one computer to another computer on the Internet. For our purposes, FTP will be used primarily to move your scripts from your desktop workstation to the Web server where they will reside.

Telnet

Telnet allows you to log in to a Unix shell account, where you'll have immediate access to your Web server. From there, you can edit files on the server, test your Perl scripts from the command line, or move, copy, and delete files.

Telnet is simple to use, but because it's the interface you'll use to access what is most likely a Unix-based server, we're going to tell all. Anything that happens at the shell (Unix command prompt) level will be described in detail, and, as with FTP, we're providing you with some FAQs and tutorials so you can feel more sure of your skills in this area.

We step you through the process of editing and managing files using a Telnet connection in Chapter 3, "Scripting Basics."

HTML and Web Design Tutorials

Well, there are so many of these it's almost impossible to tell you where to go, but we've named a few of our favorites for your use.

- **Web Review** has the latest in design and developer tools, events, resources, and intelligent columns from industry leaders, **http://www.webreview.com**

- **Builder.Com** is C|NET's developer central, and has a lot of great articles on HTML, **http://www.builder.com**

- **WebDeveloper.Com** has excellent, up-to-date articles and references for Web developers, **http://www.webdeveloper.com**

- **The World Wide Web Consortium (W3C)** is the standards association and has extensive tutorials, FAQs, and resources on HTML in its current and historic versions, **http://w3c.org/**

- **Ziff-Davis** offers a range of everything from developer tools to online education. Try **http://www.devhead.com** for articles and script archives, and **http://www.zdu.com** for instructor-led courses and online tutorials.

- **IBM DeveloperWorks** presents high-end developer information. Begin at **http://www.developerworks.com**

Unix Help

This is also a vast area, but we've selected a few choice gems:

- **Unix FAQ.** Questions and answers gathered from Usenet,
  http://www.cis.ohio-state.edu/hypertext/faq/usenet/unix-faq/faq/top.html

- **UNIXhelp for Users**. This is an excellent beginner's resource, well
  organized and informative, **http://www.geek-girl.com/Unixhelp/**

- **FTP FAQ.** Overview of FTP, software, and general FTP topics,
  http://hoohoo.ncsa.uiuc.edu/ftp/faq.html

- **Telnet FAQ.** This helpful overview of Telnet offers links to software
  downloads and other resources, **http://mist.cit.cornell.edu/telnet.html**

Tools You'll Need

If you don't have the right tools for a job, that job is certain to take
longer and cause more frustration. Fortunately, the tools you need to
make the most out of this book are very straightforward. And, unlike
the gifts you might be considering for your favorite handy-person,
the tools we discuss and recommend are either quite affordable or
downright free.

ASCII Text Editor

An ASCII text editor is simply a plain word processor. You're going
to use it to edit and modify the Perl scripts and HTML found in
upcoming chapters.

You can use any text editor you want, as long as it is ASCII
compliant. This means that the editor must have an option to save
the text as raw, unformatted text.

Let's take a look at some ASCII editors, by platform, that we have
found to be particularly useful.

Windows

For Windows users, we recommend Windows Notepad or Allaire's
HomeSite.

Even though word processors
such as Microsoft Word or
WordPerfect offer text-only
options for saving, you
shouldn't use them. The
potential risk of introducing
extraneous or unreadable
characters in your file is
high. We recommend
avoiding word processors and
sticking with straightforward
ASCII editors.

Notepad comes with all versions of Windows and can be found on your hard drive. Users of Windows 95 or above simply click the Start button, choose Run, and then type **notepad.** It's a very straight-forward editor with few confusing commands or extras on the interface. You simply start to type, and save your text when you're ready.

Allaire's HomeSite is a powerful editor used primarily for working with HTML documents. However, because the editor is ASCII compliant, it is easily used for working with Perl scripts as well as HTML. HomeSite will be especially useful for those of you who want some great power tools within your editing interface.

Macintosh

Macintosh users should consider using SimpleText or BBEdit.

As with Windows Notepad, SimpleText is a plain text editor included with the Macintosh operating system. It's easy to access, and easy to use.

BBEdit (short for Bare Bones Edit) is similar to Allaire's HomeSite in that it's primarily an HTML editor. It will appeal to those individuals wanting HTML tools integrated into the interface, while the ASCII-compliant format saves information without any formatting codes.

Unix

For Unix, we recommend vi or pico. Both of these editors are enabled from the Unix command prompt, by typing vi or pico.

pico is a great place to start for relative newcomers to Unix. It looks very much like pine, a popular Unix e-mail program. Commands are available at the bottom of the interface window for easy access.

vi is widely used, particularly by programmers. It has an interface that works using modes (command and insert), and relies on the individual to use the keyboard rather than use keystroke combinations or a mouse to maneuver the interface. It is usually the default visual editor on a Unix-based system. See Figure 2.1.

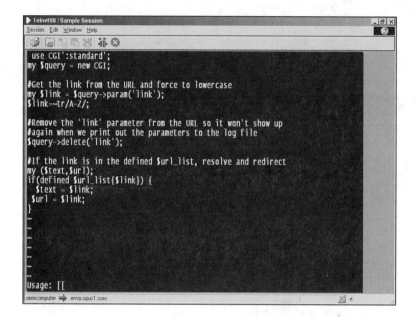

Figure 2.1
Editing Perl in vi.

Where to Get ASCII Editors

Many of the editors mentioned are available within your operating system. Try these Web sites for more information on non-resident editors:

- HomeSite: **http://www.macromedia.com/**

- BBEdit: **http://www.barebones.com/**

For support when using resident editors, try these FAQs:

- vi FAQ: **http://www.uni-konstanz.de/misc/faqs/Computer/ msg00097.html**

- pico tutorial: **http://www2.ncsu.edu/ncsu/cc/pub/tutorials/pico_tutor/ pico_intro.html**

FTP Client

An FTP client is a software program that allows you to transfer files from one computer to another computer over the Internet. In this section, we discuss our recommendations for FTP software.

Windows

Most Windows users who have experience with a high volume of file transfers prefer to use a program known as WS_FTP. (See Figure 2.2.)

This program, from Ipswitch, is very affordable and well worth the money. It's extremely flexible and customizable, as well as having an easy-to-use interface.

Figure 2.2

Using WS_FTP to transfer files.

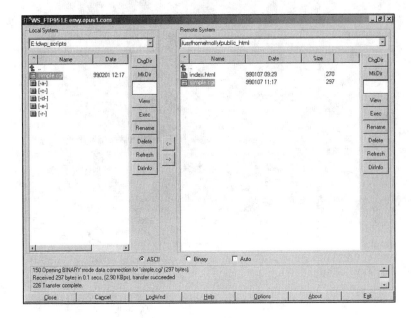

Macintosh

For Mac, Fetch is our recommendation. It's a fun, easy program that is freely available. Commercial users will have to purchase an appropriate license, but will find the license fee extremely affordable.

Fetch lets you point and click or drop and drag files to be transferred (Figure 2.3).

Finding FTP Clients

You can find the recommended FTP clients for demo, download, and purchase at the following Web sites:

- WS_FTP: **http://www.ipswitch.com/**
- Fetch: **http://www.dartmouth.edu/pages/softdev/fetch.html**

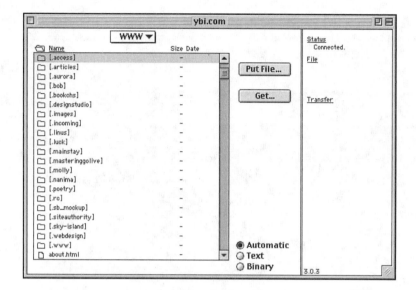

Figure 2.3

Fetch is our Macintosh FTP client choice.

Unix

For those of you comfortable with Unix, you can do all your edits directly on the server and not need to use an FTP client.

Telnet Client

If you're not working directly on a Unix machine, you'll want a Telnet client to log in to your shell account.

Windows

There are many Telnet clients for Windows, and we'll mention a few here. You can always try out your own by visiting a shareware and demo software repository such as **http://www.download.com/**.

Windows comes with a Telnet client simply called "Telnet." You can access it by clicking the Start button, selecting Run, and typing in the word **telnet**. The program will start.

However, users wanting a little more power might want to try WinTel. This shareware program combines Telnet with FTP, too! A nice feature is crash recovery, so if you lose a connection during a file transfer, you can pick up where you left off without having to upload the file all over again.

Perl Web Site Workshop

If you want full customization, check out Eric's Telnet. This Telnet client is growing in popularity due to the amount of options available. (See Figure 2.4.)

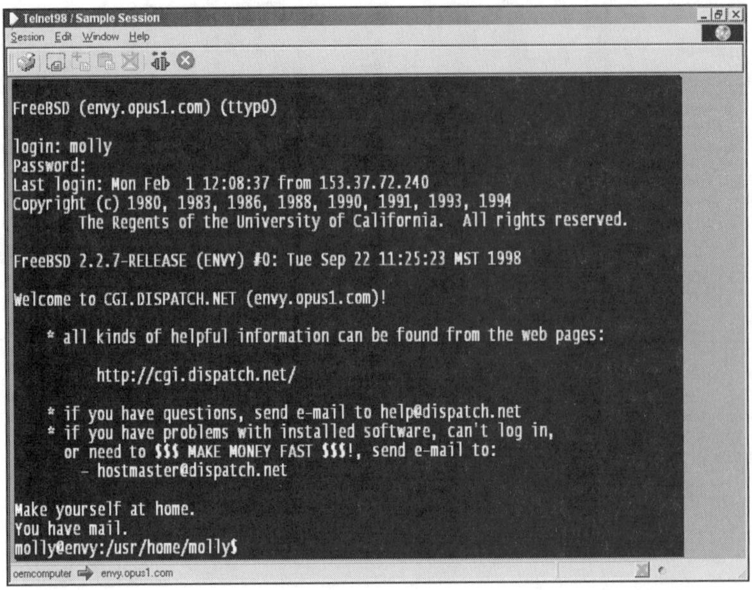

Figure 2.4

Using Eric's Telnet to access a shell account.

Macintosh

For Macintosh, we recommend NCSA Telnet. Although the product is no longer in development and is not supported, its ease of use and popularity make it the first-stop choice for Macintosh computer users.

How to Get a Telnet Client

If you don't have or don't want to use a Telnet client residing on your operating system, visit these links to find the appropriate software:

- WinTel: **http://members.aol.com/smehr/wintel.html**

- Eric's Telnet: **http://www.telnet98.com/**

- NCSA Telnet for Macintosh: **http://www.ncsa.uiuc.edu/SDG/ Homepage/telnet.html**

Web Browser

Everyone has a favorite Web browser. In fact, Jason prefers Galeon, a Mozilla-based browser for the GNOME desktop, while Molly tends to work with Microsoft's Internet Explorer more frequently.

Any Web designer worth his or her salt knows that no matter the favored browser, staying current with browsers as well as having several types on which to test the way your designs look, feel, and function is not a frivolity—it's a necessity.

You'll be using your Web browsers to run the many scripts provided in this book. So, if you don't have the most recent version of your favorite Web browser, we advise getting it. We also highly encourage you to have access to other browsers and versions of those browsers so you can test your work under a variety of circumstances.

Keep Your Browser Up to Date!

Be sure to keep your Web browser current. Here's where to find the browsers you'll need:

- Galeon: **http://galeon.sourceforge.net**
- Netscape (all available platforms):
  http://home.netscape.com/computing/download/
- Microsoft Internet Explorer (all available platforms):
  http://www.microsoft.com/ie/

Serving It Up

Your skills are in place. You've downloaded your tools. You're confident and ready to take the next step. What do you need?

Access to a server that supports CGI and Perl.

To help you make sure your ISP is CGI and Perl enabled and ready to accommodate the scripts you'll be using from this book, we've provided the following list of questions to ask your ISP.

- **What Web server and operating system does your ISP have?**
  The scripts contained within this book have been tested on a Unix-based system running Apache, and a Windows NT–based system running Microsoft's IIS.

If your current ISP isn't able to provide access to CGI and Perl for you, you're going to have to look for an ISP who will. The scripts in this book *require* CGI and Perl in order to work.

- Will you be allowed to run your own CGI programs and Perl scripts from your Web account? This is a critical concern. Some ISPs do offer CGI, but they only allow you to access scripts that they have made available. You must be able to add your own Perl scripts in order to accomplish the features and functions provided in *Perl Web Site Workshop.*

If the general rule of thumb for your ISP is to not accept user-run scripts, is there a way that you can submit scripts for approval? Some ISPs will be flexible on the issue if you ask them specifically to approve a script. This is not the ideal scenario because you will have to run each change and new script by your ISP, which can become frustrating! We feel the better choice is to find a more accommodating ISP.

- Is Perl installed on this system, and if so what version of Perl is it? At the time of writing, the current version of Perl is 5.6.1.

- Where is Perl located on your system? Specifically, you want the path to where Perl resides. A path will look very much like this: /usr/bin/perl. Specific path information will be needed for all the scripts in this book.

- Are any additional Perl modules installed on this system, and if so, what are they and what is the path where they are they located? Perl modules are a collection of functions (mini-programs).

- Where will your CGI programs reside, and do they require a specific extension? In general, most ISPs create a specific directory for CGI programs such as /cgi-bin or /htbin. However, some ISPs allow you to place them wherever you want. The standard extension for CGI is .cgi, and for Perl, .pl. Depending upon how your server is set up, you may also need to name your CGI programs with a specific extension.

We've prepared a helpful form that you can use to identify what your ISP has to offer. This form will also help you as you work your way through this book.

Server Information Form

Your CGI Environment

Web Server:

Web Server Operating System:

Perl Version:

Perl Path:

Additional Perl Modules and their path:

1.

2.

3.

Others:

File Extension for CGI Programs:

Location to place CGI Programs on your Web Server (path):

Moving Right Along

At this point, you should have a clear idea of the skills, tools, and
server access you will require. That's great! We're ready to move on
to actually working with scripts, looking at guidelines for selecting
them, learning how to place them on a server, test the scripts, and
make modifications.

Scripting Basics

Before we dig into working with Perl scripts, there are some basic concepts you'll need to know. First, it's a good idea to find out whether Perl is installed on the server with which you'll be working—and if it is, which version of Perl is installed.

There are a number of file types you'll be using throughout this book. Some of these file types may be familiar; others will be new to you. We'll cover what these file types are, how they're named, and any custom or convention regarding the file types that you'll need in order to use them properly.

Once you're certain that Perl is set up properly, and that you understand the various file types you'll be using, it's important to set up file directories. If you're not already accustomed to doing this—particularly in the non-graphical terrain known as Unix—we encourage you to get some practice with this. Set up files, delete them, set them up again until you've got the hang of it.

File permissions play a critical role in the way the various scripts in this book work. If you set file permissions improperly, you may end up with scripts that function incorrectly, or don't work at all. We'll help you understand how to set up file permissions and use them appropriately.

The Comprehensive Perl Archive Network (CPAN) is an online resource that will be invaluable to you as you work through this book—and as you make your way on your own with Perl. We'll discuss what its role is, where you can find it, and some of the features that make it such an essential part of any Perl user's toolbox.

Finally, because Perl is so often connected with Unix, we're going to provide a number of Unix resources and Web site addresses that will help you understand more about Unix, what it is, and how to use it effectively.

Checking for Perl on Your Server

Let's begin by finding out whether Perl is resident on your server, and if so, what version is running. To do this, log on to your server or your ISP account using a Telnet connection and type

```
perl -v
```

from the command prompt. The version of Perl that is resident on your server will appear (see Figure 3.1).

```
molly@envy:/usr/home/molly$ perl -v

This is perl, version 5.005_02 built for i386-freebsd

Copyright 1987-1998, Larry Wall

Perl may be copied only under the terms of either the Artistic License or the
GNU General Public License, which may be found in the Perl 5.0 source kit.

Complete documentation for Perl, including FAQ lists, should be found on
this system using 'man perl' or 'perldoc perl'.  If you have access to the
Internet, point your browser at http://www.perl.com/, the Perl Home Page.

molly@envy:/usr/home/molly$
```

Figure 3.1

Checking for Perl on a server.

The most recent Perl version, as of this writing, is 5.6.1. Perl 5.005 is perfectly acceptable in most cases, but if you find that you have an earlier version on your server, you should consider upgrading, or asking your server administrator to do that for you.

If you want to get the most recent, stable version, visit http://www.perl.com and follow the instructions there for upgrading the Perl software on your server.

Understanding File Types

There are many file types that you can encounter in your development travels. In this section, we'll hone in on those you'll be using specifically with this book. We'll also let you know the general permissions recommended for the file type, and give you an idea where certain files reside already, or should be placed in order for the scripts in this book to run properly.

.pl

This is the file extension for a Perl script. Perl files are run from the command line or called from other operations such as CGI (see the next section). Perl files *must* be made executable by the owner—we'll show you how to do this in the upcoming section of this chapter titled "Setting File Permissions." You can also have Perl files be executable by others, but Perl files should be writable by only the owner. Perl files must also be made readable.

.cgi

These are Common Gateway Interface (CGI) script files. Visitors to your Web site can access these directly using their Web browsers, or from within the context of an HTML page.

These should be readable and executable for all users, but writable for only the owner.

.pm

Perl modules are libraries of code that you can include in .cgi or .pl scripts to add functions to those scripts. Modules can also define classes for use in object-oriented programming. Modules that come with Perl are generally found already in residence in the /usr/lib/perl directory on your server. Modules that you install yourself will go in either /usr/lib/perl/site_perl, or into a Perl library directory that you create yourself.

Unlike Perl files, Perl module files are not executable scripts, and don't need any special permissions beyond being readable for all users, and writable for only the owner.

.html, .htm

These are HTML files and are in most cases publicly accessible. Typically, HTML files reside in the root directory and any appropriate subdirectories on your server.

Note that the .html extension is the one that we use. The .htm extension came about as a result of Microsoft's early limitations on file suffixes. Although you can use either depending upon your server configurations, we recommend sticking to the .html convention unless your systems administrator requires you to do otherwise.

Creating File Directories

File directories are the locations where files are stored on a server. The "root" directory is the first directory in the tree, and subdirectories are created beneath it.

At a minimum, you'll need two directories to run the scripts in this book—one in which to keep your CGI scripts, and another in which to keep command-line scripts. If you don't have root access—which sometimes occurs when you're one of many members on a large service provider's server—you'll need to create a third directory for modules and other library files.

About the CGI Directory

The cgi-bin directory is where you'll place the majority of your CGI scripts. This directory, like the others, should *not* be placed in your regular HTML documents tree. One common setup is to keep your regular HTML documents under /home/htdocs/html, and your CGI scripts in /home/htdocs/cgi-bin.

You'll have to follow the configuration directions for your Web server to set up the cgi-bin directory to allow execution of scripts.

If you use Apache, make sure the following appears in your main server configuration file. This file is named httpd.conf and is originally generated by Apache upon installation to the conf directory under the Apache installation prefix.

```
ScriptAlias /home/htdocs/cgi-bin /cgi-bin
<Directory /home/htdocs/cgi-bin>
options +ExecCGI
</Directory>
```

Many ISPs give you access to their cgi-bin directory, the directory where CGI scripts go. If you have access to this, you won't need to create one of your own. You will need to record the correct path and add that to your scripts wherever necessary.

If you want to keep some CGI scripts in directories other than cgi-bin, you'll have to configure your Web server to recognize all files that end in .cgi as scripts.

If you're using Apache, you can do this by making sure these lines appear in your httpd.conf:

```
(1)AddHandler cgi-script .cgi
```

Setting Up a Perl Script Directory

CGI scripts are only half of the story of Perl on the Web. Perl is also tremendously useful on the back end, and in this book there are several utility scripts that you'll run from the command line on the server.

Do *not* put command line Perl scripts in your cgi-bin directory. If you do, you open up your server to potentially dangerous hacker activity. Think security!

A good choice for a utility script directory is the bin directory in your home directory. If you have root access, you could choose instead to put scripts in /usr/local/bin. Because a lot of other software installs itself there, wading through a bunch of other programs to find yours may be confusing. Therefore, we recommend using the subdirectory ~/bin underneath your home, or root, directory.

Making a Perl Module Library

The Perl library is where you'll keep the modules you create yourself following our examples, and any outside modules you install.

If you have root access, put all your modules in the pre-existing /usr/lib/perl/site_perl.

If you don't have root access, or you don't want to put your modules in site_perl, you'll need to create a Perl library directory.

If your Web document root is /home/htdocs/www, a good choice for this would be /home/htdocs/lib/perl.

Setting File Permissions

You need to learn a few commands and concepts that will help you keep your site secure, and make it possible for you to allow site visitors to do exactly (and *only* exactly) what you want them to be able to do when they access your site.

If you're unfamiliar with Unix, the information in this section may seem confusing at first. But bear with us—we show you how to do this step-by-step as we take you through the scripts, so you'll learn to get the hang of it. But we still feel that some background is of great importance here.

Unix is a multi-user operating system, and as such, it has the concept of the "owner" of a file built into it. Generally, the owner is the creator of the file.

Because Unix was designed to allow multiple users (who might not know or trust each other) to work together on the same computer, it also includes the concept of file "permissions," which allow you to determine who can do what with your files.

For more help with Unix, see the resource list at the end of this chapter.

chmod

Change mode, or chmod is the command you use to change the permissions (or mode) of a file. You can only use it on files that you own, unless you have root permissions.

From the command line, you'll type **chmod mode filename**, where **mode** is either a numeric or symbolic setting for the permissions you want to give the file, and the **filename** is the name of the file for which your are setting the permissions.

The numeric modes are three- or four-digit octal (base 8) numbers, like 0640 or 755. The first digit from the left (if present) sets special bits, making the file execute SUID or SGID (Set User ID and Set Group ID). The second sets permissions for the owner of the file, the third for the owning group, and the last for all other users. The numbers are a combination of three bits, with values of 4, 2, and 1. If a number has a 4 in it, the user can read the file. If it has a 2, he can write to (and delete) the file. If it has a 1, she can execute that file as a program.

For example, **chmod 777 file.pl** gives all users all permissions for the file. **chmod 744 filename** means that the owner can read, write, and execute, but every body else can only read. **chmod 755 filename** (the mode you'll use for your CGI scripts) means that the owner can do anything, and all other users can only read and execute the file.

u+x means *user execute* and is a symbolic way of saying that the user is allowed to execute the program. Similarly, **a+x** means *anyone execute* and means, literally, that anyone can execute the program.

Setting modes symbolically is easier for most beginners than dealing with octal numbers. The form of the symbolic mode is **[user][+/-] [permission]**. For example, a symbolic set would be typed out **chmod u+x filename** (see Figure 3.2). This allows the owner to execute the file; **chmod a+x filename** allows anyone to write the file; **chmod g-w filename** takes write permission away from the owning group.

We'll use the symbolic process in this book, but if you'd like to try the numeric approach, feel free to do so—just be certain you're setting up public files with appropriate permissions!

Figure 3.2

Changing mode using the symbolic approach.

```
molly@envy:/usr/home/molly/public_html/cgi-bin$ ls
better_oo.cgi*           first_func.cgi*        guestbook_2.cgi~*
browser_detect.cgi*      first_oo.cgi*          magic_soothsayer.cgi*
browser_detect.cgi~*     guest_1.cgi*           mail_form.cgi*
clock.cgi*               guestbook.cgi*         mailform1.cgi*
echo_date.cgi*           guestbook_1.cgi
first_example.cgi*       guestbook_2.cgi*
molly@envy:/usr/home/molly/public_html/cgi-bin$ chmod a+x guestbook_2.cgi
```

Read the chmod man page (type **man chmod** at the command line on your server) for a more detailed explanation.

chown

This is "change ownership," or **chown**. You'll use this command to change ownership of a file. You can do this *only* if you have root permissions. For the most part, you will probably not have to use this command—but it's good to know about.

The basic command is **chown owner filename**.

If you need to do more complex operations, consult the manual (type **man chown**) for instructions (see Figure 3.3).

SUID Scripts

Sometimes in the course of human events you may need to allow a user to execute a script with more permissions than he normally has. One example would be to allow an individual to write a file to a directory that the general public does not have write access to.

```
CHOWN(8)              FreeBSD System Manager's Manual            CHOWN(8)
line 1
NAMEhtml              first_cgi.html            mailtest.html
    chown - change file owner and group        mailtest.html~
chap_05/             games/                    mailtest2.html
SYNOPSIS             good.html                 mailto.html
    chown [-R [-H | -L | -P]] [-f] [-h] owner [:group] file ...
    chown [-R [-H | -L | -P]] [-f] [-h] :group file ...
date.shtml           images/
DESCRIPTION/usr/home/molly/public_html$ cd cgi-bin
    Chown sets the user ID and/or the group ID of the specified files.
better_oo.cgi*       first_func.cgi*           guestbook_2.cgi~*
    The options are as follows:.cgi*           magic_soothsayer.cgi*
browser_detect.cgi~* guest_1.cgi*              mail_form.cgi*
    -H      If the -R option is specified, symbolic links on the command line
            are followed.  (Symbolic links encountered in the tree traversal
            are not followed).ok_2.cgi*
molly@envy:/usr/home/molly/public_html/cgi-bin$ chmod a+x guestbook_2.cgi
    -L      If the -R option is specified, all symbolic links are followed.
Formatting page, please wait...Done.
    -P      If the -R option is specified, no symbolic links are followed.
```

Figure 3.3

Consulting the manual for chown *help.*

To do this, you will need to create a Set UID (User ID), or SUID, script. This is a script that always runs as if it were being run by its owner, regardless of who actually runs the script. You make a script SUID with the command **chmod +sx filename**.

All About CPAN

CPAN stands for Comprehensive Perl Archive Network. It's a network of mirrored Web and FTP sites that contain the biggest collection of cool and useful Perl modules around.

CPAN is updated frequently with new modules and new versions of existing modules. Before you start to write a module of your own, it's a good idea to check CPAN for similar modules. This can save you a lot of time, and, because all modules include their full source code, you can learn a lot in the process as well. Where is CPAN?

The easiest way to find a CPAN server near you is to go to http://www.perl.com/CPAN (see Figure 3.4). You'll be redirected to an appropriate CPAN site, which you can then bookmark for future returns. Of course, you can always go back to **http://www.perl.com** each time. A searchable version of the CPAN is maintained at http://search.cpan.org.

Do *not* make any of the scripts SUID root. Doing this would grant the script all privileges on your system. If you make a programming error in such a circumstance, the results could be catastrophic. The other critical concern is security. If someone does manage to crack your code, she can gain control over your entire system.

Figure 3.4

CPAN is your one-stop shop for modules and other helpful Perl files.

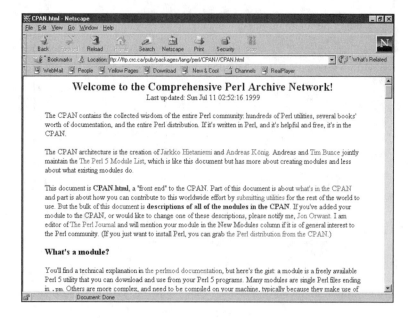

Getting Modules from CPAN

You can get modules from CPAN using your usual Web or FTP client. If you use a Web browser, you can search the module listings, and browse them by name, author, and category.

Once you find the module you want, use your browser or FTP client to transfer the file to your server, or to your home/office machine and then to your server—depending upon what your setup is.

Using the CPAN Module to Get Modules from CPAN

You can also use the CPAN.pm Perl module to make installing other modules from CPAN much easier. On newer versions of Perl, this module is installed by default—if it's not, you'll need to download and install it yourself. Once you've retrieved and installed the CPAN module and the libnet bundle—a very useful package of Perl modules—you can install additional modules very easily. To do so:

1. Download the CPAN module from
   http://www.perl.com/CPAN/modules/by-module/CPAN/CPAN-
   1.57.tar.gz and save the file to your computer.

2. Untar the file by typing `cd name_of_directory tar -zxvf`
   `CPAN-1.57.tar.gz`

3. Go to the new directory just created, `cd CPAN-1.57`

4. Build the makefile by typing `perl Makefile.PL`
   `[LIB=/path/to/private/library]` at the command prompt.

5. If you answer 'no' to manual configuration, the module will try
   to autoconfigure its settings.

6. Build the module by typing `make` at the command prompt.

7. Test the module by typing `make test` at the command prompt.

8. Install the module. Type `make install` at the prompt.

> If you are installing to the standard location, you must be root (or have write permission in /usr/lib/perl5). Read the README file included in CPAN-1.57 for more information, or simply type **perldoc CPAN** at the command prompt.

Installing other modules is as simple as typing `perl -MCPAN -e`
`shell` to get into the CPAN shell, and from there typing `install`
`[module]`. For example, to install the FastTemplate (which you'll be
using in Chapter 8, "Designing with Templates") module using this
system, you'll type `install CGI::FastTemplate`, at the `cpan>`
command prompt. The CPAN module will automatically download,
build, and install the latest version of the named module.

Installing Modules by Hand

To install Perl modules by hand, follow this process:

1. Download the module to your build directory. This is the directory where you build scripts/modules that you download, as
   opposed to a library directory, which is where they install
   themselves once they're built.

2. Untar with `tar -zxf filename` (if you have GNU tar) or `gunzip`
   `filename | tar -xf` (if you don't). (If you are running Linux,
   you have GNU tar.)

3. Type `cd` (change directory) to the newly created module source
   directory.

4. Enter these commands, in order, on the command line:

You will need to be root for the install step, if you are installing to the default location. If you are not root, you cannot install to the default location, so you'll install to a non-standard location, add **LIB=/path/to/library** (replace /path/to/library with the actual path) to the perl Makefile.PL line.

```
perl Makefile.PL
```

make (this builds the module)

make test (optional – this runs the modules self-test routines, to make sure that the module is working)

make install (this installs the module)

Unix Resources

Because many readers will be unfamiliar with the Unix environment, we've provided these recommended resources for you.

- *Unix in a Nutshell* by Daniel Gilly. This book is a must-have for anyone using Unix. It is an excellent desktop reference of Unix commands and guidelines..

- **UNIXhelp for Users.** A great place to begin—tasks, Unix commands, concepts, and helpful utilities, **http://www.mcsr.olemiss.edu/unixhelp/**.

- **A Basic Unix Tutorial.** Another great place for newcomers to Unix, this Web site walks you through logging in and logging out, understanding the Unix shell, all about files and directories, customization, editing, and good resources for more advanced users or those of you interested in digging deeper, **http://www.isu.edu/departments/comcom/unix/workshop/unixindex.html**

- **The Unix Reference Desk, http://www.geek-girl.com/unix.html**. This Web site is a very thorough information center with links to all things Unix—FAQs, tutorials, programming, servers—even Unix humor for when the going gets tough!

What's Up Next

You've got the basics down and your tools in place. It's time to take a deep breath and get ready to begin scripting! Don't worry, we'll start out gently. Chapter 4, "Working with Forms," will contain a lot of methodology familiar to HTML coders. You'll get a taste of how to write and modify your files, as well as set permissions and generally get into the swing of using Perl and CGI to create dynamic Web pages.

Working with Forms

Forms work by combining standard HTML and, most often, CGI with associated scripts.

The HTML is used to create a form's display elements, such as text fields and boxes, check boxes, radio buttons, and submit and reset buttons. The HTML also contains information that sends the inputted data to the server upon submit. At this point, CGI takes over, and introduces the input data to the script for processing.

In this chapter, we're going to take a look at the behind-the-scenes processing. We'll start small, with a simple script, and then show you how to make the form and resulting script process more complex and functional.

Before we move on to look at forms, we want to point out some basic programming conventions used in upcoming scripts. This will help you familiarize yourself with the script's contents and navigate them more efficiently.

Some Programming Basics

#	This is a comment. Use comments to clarify what you're doing at any given point within the code.
;	A semi-colon indicates the end of a line of code.
{}	Brackets indicate groups of code.
$,@,%	These indicate variables. We discuss these in greater depth in Chapter 11, "Getting Ready to Learn Perl."

This script makes use of the object-oriented interface to CGI.pm. CGI.pm is a Perl module that helps provide Perl coders with CGI scripts by reading CGI input and writing out HTML pages. CGI.pm is included in the standard Perl distribution. You can easily find out if you have it: type `perldoc CGI` at the command line; if you get the documentation, you've got it, if not, you can download it from CPAN (see Chapter 3, "Scripting Basics").

A Simple Gateway Script

This script is a very simple gateway script that either displays a form, or echoes the form's input back in a simple page. The script is self-contained, meaning that you will not create an HTML form with input fields in order for it to work. However, you will create an HTML page to access it.

How to Use

1. Copy the script into your text editor.

2. Save the script as first.cgi.

3. Place the form in your cgi-bin directory on your server.

4. Change the permissions to make executable by all users:

   ```
   chmod a+x first.cgi
   ```

first.cgi

```perl
#!/usr/bin/perl -w

use CGI;            # import the CGI.pm module

$q     = new CGI;   # create a new CGI object, $q,
                    # which will automatically read
                    # any input and format it for
                    # easy access.

$self = $q->url;    # and get our own url

# start the page by printing a standard
# HTTP header ("Content-type: text/html")
print $q->header;
# If we've gotten some input, display the result page.
# Otherwise, display the input form.
if ($q->param){

  # Make the name look nice by capitalizing the
  # first letter
    $name = ucfirst( $q->param('name') );

  # This is a 'here document': everything down to the
  # label specified (in this case, 'HTML') will be
  # printed.  The closing HTML label must be the first
  # word on its line.
  print <<HTML;
  <html>
    <head>
      <title>My First CGI</title>
    </head>
```

first.cgi (continued)

```
  <body>
    <h1>My First CGI</h1>

    <p>Hello, $name! This is my first CGI!</p>

  </body>
</html>

HTML

} else {

  # Another 'here document' -- note that
  # it's not a good idea to have two with the
  # same label in one script.
  print <<FORM;
<html>
  <head>
  <title>What's your name?</title>
</head>

<body>
  <h1>What is your name?</h1>

  <form action="$self" method="post">
    <p>Your name: <input type="text" name="name"/></p>
    <p><input type="submit"/></p>
  </form>

</body>
</html>

FORM

}
```

Other Files Needed

You'll want to create a simple HTML file so you can see the script in action. To do so:

1. Open your text editor.

2. Create a standard HTML document with a link to first.cgi.

3. Save the file as first.html.

4. Upload the HTML to the appropriate directory on your server.

first.html

```
<html>
<head>
<title>Simple CGI Script</title>
</head>

<body>
<p>
<br/>
<br/>

<div align="center">
<a href="/cgi-bin/first.cgi">Simple CGI Script Test</a>
</div>

</body>
</html>
```

Once you've got the HTML file loaded onto the server, test the file using your browser. In Figure 4.1, we've clicked the link to our script test, and the script goes into action, giving us our input form.

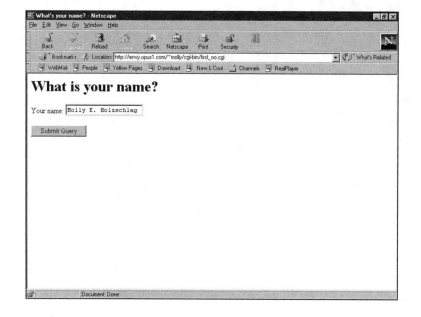

Figure 4.1
The form.

Go ahead and input your name, and click the Submit button, and the results will be a customized welcome (see Figure 4.2).

Figure 4.2

The form results.

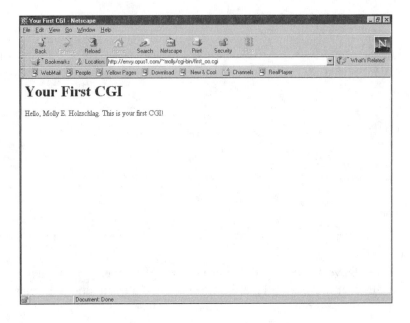

Modifying the Script

The easiest and most obvious modification is to format the HTML
output to your tastes. To do this, simply modify the HTML that
appears within the script. In this version, I've made the background
color black, with cream text. The affected lines are shown in bold.

first_example.cgi

```perl
#!/usr/bin/perl -w

use CGI;          # import the CGI.pm module

$q    = new CGI;  # create a new CGI object
$self = $q->url;  # get our own url

# start the page by printing a standard
# HTTP header ("Content-type: text/html")
print $q->header;

# If we've gotten some input, display the result page.
# Otherwise, display the input form.
if ($q->param){

  # Make the name look nice by capitalizing the
  # first letter
  $name = ucfirst( $q->param('name') );
```

first_example.cgi (continued)

```
print <<HTML;
<html>
  <head>
    <title>Your First CGI</title>
  </head>

  <body bgcolor="#000000" text="#FFFFCC">
    <ht>Your First CGI</h1>

    <p>Hello, $name! This is your first CGI!</p>

  </body>
</html>

HTML

} else {

  print <<FORM;
<html>
  <head>
    <title>What's your name?</title>
  </head>

  <body bgcolor="#000000" text="#FFFFCC">
    <h1>What is your name?</h1>

    <form action="$self" method="post">
      <p>Your name: <input type="text" name="name"/></p>
      <p><input type="submit"/></p>
    </form>

  </body>
</html>

FORM

}
```

You can get more complex with your modifications, too! Let's say you have a clever idea to customize this form. You want to put a Magic Soothsayer up on your site, and the site visitor types in a question to get the answer of the day.

You can customize the form by simply changing the HTML within it. In this case, the title, the background, background color, text color, and input fields are all customized. Note that we've added a value to the input type, which allows us to personalize the submit button.

Customizing the Input

```html
<html>
   <head>
   <title>Molly's Magic Soothsayer</title>
  </head>

  <body background="../images/soothsayer_bak.gif" bgcolor="#333333"
text="#CC3300">
   <h1>What is your question?</h1>

   <form action="$self" method="post">
     <p>Your name: <input type="text" name="name"/></p>
     <p>Your question: <input type="text" name="question"/></p>
     <p><input type="submit" value="ask the soothsayer"/></p>
   </form>

  </body>
</html>
```

When the script is complete, the input results will appear with your customization (see Figure 4.3).

Figure 4.3

The customized input.

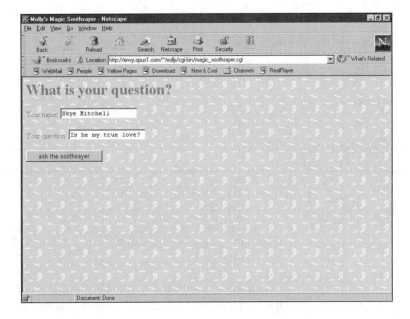

The output needs to be customized, too.

Customizing the Output

```html
<html>
    <head>
      <title>Molly's Magic Soothsayer</title>
    </head>

    <body background="../images/soothsayer_bak.gif" bgcolor="#333333"
text="#CC3300">
      <h1>The Soothsayer Says:</h1>

      <p>Hello, $name. The answer to your question is YES!</p>

    </body>
  </html>
```

Figure 4.4 shows the output results.

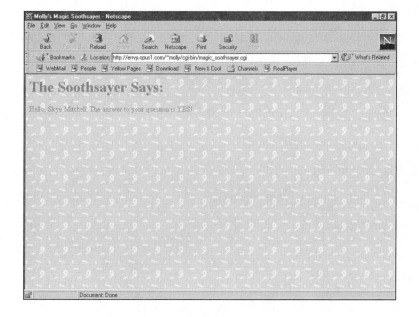

Figure 4.4

The fully customized output.

Forms (Only) a Programmer Could Love

In the last example, we used the CGI.pm module to read and manipulate the input from the form. but CGI.pm can do a lot more than that. Some of the most useful functions it includes are HTML shortcuts, which you can use to generate your CGI output without

CGI.pm also allows you to use its functions in different ways. If you're comfortable with object-oriented programming, you can use the object interface, as we do in most of the examples in this book. If you're just starting out, the functional interface may be easier to get along with. Just bear in mind that although it's less flexible, there's also less that you have to remember.

hand-coding any HTML at all. This is particularly advantageous in that it streamlines code and makes the coding process quicker and more efficient.

In the following example, we demonstrate how to use HTML shortcuts with the functional interface.

How to Use

1. Copy the script into your text editor.

2. Save the script as second.cgi.

3. Place the script in your cgi-bin directory.

4. Change the permissions to make executable by all users:

   ```
   chmod a+x second.cgi
   ```

Using the object interface, the code would look like this:

second.cgi

```perl
#!/usr/bin/perl -w

use CGI;

$q = new CGI;

# If we got some input, display the result page

# Otherwise, display the form
if ($q->param) {

    # Here we use CGI.pm's HTML shortcuts to build the
    # page, instead of coding the HTML by hand.

    print $q->header,                    # the standard HTTP header
          $q->start_html('My First CGI'),  # start the page and
                                         # set the title

          $q->h1('My First CGI'),        # "<h1>My First CGI</h1>"
          $q->p, 'Hello, ',              # "<p>Hello"
          ucfirst($q->param('name')),
          '! This is my first CGI!',
          $q->end_html;                  # end the page ("</html>")

} else {

    print $q->header,
          $q->start_html("What's your name?"),
          $q->h1("What's your name?"),
```

second.cgi (continued)

```
    $q->start_form,              # create a form that
                                 # points back at us
    $q->p, "Your name: ",
    $q->textfield('name'),       # "<input type='text' ...
    $q->p, submit,
    $q->end_form,
    $q->end_html;

}
```

This script creates the HTML for you, and you don't need any additional HTML files when you use it.

A Better Form Script

This script is similar to the first two, but it advances on their concepts by adding error checking and security using Perl's *taint* mechanism.

Perl's taint mechanism marks any information that comes from outside of the actual script as being tainted data. The mechanism then won't let that data be used in any sensitive operation. For example, you can't use tainted data as the name of a file to open. This adds the ability for you to control errors and ensure that scripts are as secure as possible.

The Better Form script includes this security and error checking. We'll point out where this is occurring in the script by bolding the relevant code and explanatory comments.

Can you untaint data? You can indeed, by using Perl's regular expression matching. Doing this allows a script author to pass through anything that doesn't look suspicious, but stop processing if the input seems weird, contains shell meta-characters, pathnames, or commands that weren't expected.

How to Use

1. Copy form into your text editor.

2. Save form as better.cgi.

3. Place the form in your cgi-bin directory.

4. Change the permissions to make executable by all users:

   ```
   chmod a+x better.cgi
   ```

better.cgi

```perl
#!/usr/bin/perl -wT

# We've turned on taint checks (the -T switch in the first line),
# so we need to explicitly set these environment variables.
# This is a security feature.

# PATH must not include any directory we're allowed to write to
$ENV{'PATH'}  = '/bin:/usr/bin:/usr/local/bin';
$ENV{'SHELL'} = '/bin/sh';          # set a standard shell
$ENV{'ENV'}   = '';                 # clear ENV
$ENV{'IFS'}   = '';                 # and IFS, just to be safe

use CGI;

# strict forces you to use good programming practices such as
# declaring all of your variables -
# it makes debugging MUCH easier.
use strict;
use vars qw($ START   $CGI);        # These are the only global
                                    # variables we use

$CGI = "better.cgi";             # The name of the script


# We use eval to catch any errors that might occur
# and set $ START   to the real start of the code
eval { main() }; $ START   =  LINE  ;


# If eval { main() } has produced an error,
# the special $@ variable will
# hold the error message.
if ($@) {
  chomp($@);                        # Cut extraneous returns from $@

  # Use $ START   to determine the real
  # line where the error occurred
  # These are regular expressions -- one of perl's most powerful,
  # and most unreadable, features.
  $@ =~ s/\(eval\) line (\d+)/${CGI} . " line " .
     ($ START  -$1-1)/e;
  $@ =~ s/( at ).*( line )/$1${CGI}$2/;

  my $error_message = $@;

  print <<ERR;
Content-type: text/html

  <html>
    <head><title>Error</title></head>
    <body>
      <h1>Error</h1>
      <code>$error_message</code>
    </body>
```

better.cgi (continued)

```
</html>
ERR

}

exit(0);

# main

sub main {
  my ($q, $self, $html, $name);

  # create the CGI object and start the page
  # notice that we can use all of CGI.pm's HTML shortcuts
  # in object-oriented mode, as well, but we have to
  # do so through our CGI object.
  $q    = new CGI;
  $self = $q->url;
  $html = $q->header .
  $q->start_html("CGI: It's not just for breakfast anymore!");


  # If we've gotten some input, display the result page.
  # Otherwise, display the input form.
  if ($q->param){

    # Make sure that the input we get doesn't look weird
    $name = untaint( ucfirst($q->param('name')) );

    $html .= <<HTML;
<h1>My Second CGI</h1>
<p>Hello $name! This is my secure CGI!</p>
HTML

  } else {

    $html .= <<FORM;
<h1>What is your name?</h1>

<form action="$self" method="post">
  <p>Your name: <input type="text" name="name"/></p>
  <p><input type="submit"/></p>
</form>
FORM

  }

  $html .= $q->end_html;
  print $html;
}

# other subroutines

# untaint
# in:  untrusted scalar
```

better.cgi (continued)

```
# out: trusted scalar, or dies if in is suspicious
# description:
#  untaint uses perl's regular expressions to check for sucpicious-
#  looking input values (things that look like shell macros, etc),
#  and to remove the 'taint' from any input that doesn't look
#  suspicious, so that we can use it in dangerous operations like
#  opening files. Processing input through a regular expression
#  like this is the ONLY way to remove its taintedness.
sub untaint {
  my $val = shift;

  # very strict: allow only letters, numbers, and white space
  my $ok_chars = '[\w\s]';

  die "Illegal character(s) in input ($val)" unless
    ($val =~ /^($ok_chars+)$/);

  return $1;

}
```

Modifying the Script

This script is a medley of the first two, using both hand-built HTML
and CGI.pm functions. You modify this script in the exact way you
modified the first.cgi script. Look for the input and output sections
of the script, and customize the HTML and content to meet your
needs.

In Greater Detail: About Regular Expressions

In better.cgi, we've used regular expressions twice, in two different ways.
The first pair of expressions

```
$@ =~ s/\(eval\) line (\d+)/${CGI} . " line " .
    ($  START  -$1-1)/e;$@ =~ s/( at ).*( line )/$1${CGI}$2/;
```

uses Perl's s/// operator to substitute everything between the second
pair of slashes for whatever part of the subject string ($@) matches the
regular expression (usually called a pattern) in the first pair of slashes.

In this case, we're looking in an error message, which is likely to look
something like this:

Something went wrong at (eval) line 60.

Our first substitution removes the word (eval), replacing it with the
name of the script, as set in the $CGI variable, uses the $ START

variable to calculate the real line number where the error occurred, and substitutes that for the line number in the error message.

The second line in the pair is a fallback, making sure that whatever is between at and line in the error message is the name that we want our users to see. One pitfall to beware: the special =~ operator. If you write

```
$holiday_card =~ s/Easter/Passover/g;
```

then you'll replace all the instances of Easter in $holiday_card with Passover. But if you write

```
$holiday_card = s/Easter/Passover/g;
```

$holiday_card will now contain the number of times Easter was replaced with Passover in the special variable $_.

We also use a regular expression in the untaint function:

```
my $ok_chars = '[\w\s]'; die "Illegal character(s) in input
($val)" unless  ($val =~ /^($ok_chars+)$/);

return $1;
```

In this case, we use the // operator: we're just matching, not substituting. Notice that you can use a variable to make a regular expression more readable: the value of the variable will be interpolated into the pattern, just like it would be into a string.

The ^ and $ characters at the beginning and end of the pattern mean that the expression must match from the beginning to the end of the script.

The + after $ok_chars means that we want to match at least one character, with no maximum number to match.

Finally, but most importantly in this case, by putting our pattern in parentheses, we set the special variable $1 to whatever matched our pattern. We then return that match, instead of the original input to the function: that's how untainting works in Perl.

It's assumed that if you've processed the variable through a regular expression, and found it to be acceptable, you know what you're doing with it, and should be allowed to do what you want.

Creating a Guestbook

Now that you've got some basic scripting concepts down, including a familiarity of how CGI and Perl code looks, how to use CGI.pm, and what taint checking is all about, let's move on to a much more complex—and useful—script. In this case, you're going to create the classic guestbook used on so many Web sites.

How to Use

1. Copy the script into your text editor.

2. Save the script as guestbook.cgi.

3. Place the script in your cgi-bin directory.

4. Change the permissions to make executable by all users:

   chmod a+x guestbook.cgi

5. Edit the script, setting the $GUESTBOOK variable to the correct path to your guestbook file.

guestbook.cgi

```perl
#!/usr/bin/perl -wT

$ENV{'PATH'}  = '/bin:/usr/bin:/usr/local/bin';
$ENV{'SHELL'} = '/bin/sh';
$ENV{'ENV'}   = '';
$ENV{'IFS'}   = '';

use CGI;

use strict;
use vars qw($  START   $CGI $GUESTBOOK);

# change this to the real path to your guestbook file
$GUESTBOOK = "/home/molly/public_html/guestbook";
$CGI       = "guestbook.cgi";

eval { main() }; $  START   =   LINE  ;

if ($@) {
  chomp($@);

  $@ =~ s/\(eval\) line (\d+)/${CGI} . " line " .
    ($  START   -$1-1)/e;
  $@ =~ s/( at ).*( line )/$1${CGI}$2/;

  my $error_message = $@;

  print <<ERR;
Content-type: text/html

<html>
  <head><title>Error</title></head>
  <body>
```

guestbook.cgi (continued)

```
    <h1>Error</h1>
    <code>$error_message</code>
  </body>
</html>
ERR

}

exit(0);

# main

sub main {
  my $q = new CGI;

  # If we got some input, add a guestbook entry with that input
  # Otherwise, show the guestbook.

  if ($q->param()) {
    add_entry($q);
  } else {
    display_guestbook($q);
  }
}

# subroutines

# in:  CGI object
# out:
# description:
#  Reads the guestbook file & prints it as html
sub display_guestbook {
  my $q = shift;
  my ($html,$e,$num_entries,$entries);

  $html = $q->header . $q->start_html("My Guestbook");

  # The '.=' operator appends the right side of the
  # expression to the left side; this line is functionally
  # equivalent to saying '$html = $html . $q->h1("My Guestbook");
  $html .= $q->h1("My Guestbook");

  open (GB, "<$GUESTBOOK") ||
    die "Unable to read guestbook file '$GUESTBOOK' (error: $!). " .
        "Please try again later, or contact the webmaster of this " .
    "site for assistance";

  # Get a read lock on the guestbook
  # The '\*GB' is a reference to the filehandle
  # we just created when we opened the guestbook.
  # We need to lock it so that nobody tries to write
  # to it while we're reading it, which could produce
  # 'unpredictable' results.
  lock_filehandle(\*GB, 'R');
```

guestbook.cgi (continued)

```perl
  while (!eof(GB)) {
    my $e = new CGI(\*GB);              # read the 'frozen' CGI input
    $num_entries++;                     # increment the entry counter
    $entries .= draw_guestbook_entry($e); # and draw the entry
  }

  close (GB);

  # Insert the count of entries, and the entries themselves, into
  # the html page
  if ($num_entries) {
    $html .= "<p>Signed $num_entries time" . (($num_entries > 1) && ("s"));
    $html .= $entries . "</p>";
  } else {
    $html .= "<h3>No entries!</h3><hr/>";
  }

  $html .= entry_form($q);             # add the form to the page
  $html .= $q->end_html;               # and end the page

  print $html;
}

# in:  CGI object
# out:
# description:
#  Adds entry to guestbook file, then prints guestbook html
sub add_entry {
  my $q = shift;
  my ($name,$email,$homepage,$msg,$entry,$url);

  $url = $q->url;

  untaint_params($q); # check & clean up the input

  # Open the guestbook for appending
  open (GB, ">>$GUESTBOOK") ||
    die "Unable to write to guestbook (error: $!). " .
        "Please try again later, or contact the webmaster " .
        "of this site for assistance";

  # get a write lock on the guestbook,
  # so that nobody else tries to read or write
  # to it while we're writing to it
  lock_filehandle(\*GB, 'W');

  $q->save(\*GB); # 'freeze' the CGI input into the file

  # closing automatically removes the file lock
  close GB;
```

guestbook.cgi (continued)

```perl
   # say thanks, with a link back to the questbook
   print    $q->header,
     $q->start_html("Thanks"),
     $q->h1("Thanks!"),
     $q->h3("Your message has been added to my guestbook."),
     $q->p,
     $q->a({href=>$q->url}, "Go back to the guestbook"),
     $q->end_html;
}

# in:  guestbook entry
# out: guestbook entry in html format
# description:
#  Format a guestbook entry as html
sub draw_guestbook_entry {
  my $entry = shift;
  my $author;

  # import the CGI input  into a namespace, for easy
  # interpolation below.
  $entry->import_names('E');

  # include email & homepage links, if present
  $author = $E::name;
  if ($E::email =~ /(.*?)@((.*?)\.)+.*/) {
    $author = qq|<a href="mailto:$E::email">$E::name</a>|;
  }

  if ($E::homepage) {

    # make sure the homepage url begins with http://
    $E::homepage =~ s|^(http://)?|http://|;

    # qq means 'double quote' -- it works the same as putting
    # "quotes" around something. We use it here because the
    # something we're quoting has quotes in it already.
    $author .= qq| (<a href="$E::homepage">$E::homepage</a>)|;
  }

  # 'here documents' aren't just for printing -- you can assign
  # them to a variable or, as here, return them directly from
  # a function
  return <<ENTRY;
<p><b>$author</b>
<br/>$E::message</p>
<hr/>
ENTRY

}

sub entry_form {
  my $q    = shift;
  my $url = $q->url;
```

guestbook.cgi (continued)

```perl
  my $form = <<E_FORM;
<h3>Sign my guestbook:</h3>
<form action="$url" method="post">
<p><b>Name</b>: <input type="text" name="name"/></p>
<p><b>E-mail</b>: <input type="text" name="email"/></p>
<p><b>Homepage</b>: <input type="text" name="homepage"/></p>
<p><b>Message</b>:</p>
<p><textarea cols="30" rows="6" wrap="virtual" name="message">Type your message here.</textarea>
<p><input type="submit"/></p>
</form>
E_FORM

  # You don't have to use 'return' to return a value; the value
  # of the last expression in a function will automatically be
  # returned. In this case the expression is just a variable,
  # so the value of the variable is returned.
  $form;
}


# untaint_params
# in:  CGI object
# out: trusted (scalar) params, or dies if suspicious input seen
# NOTE: this function will NOT work properly with multi-value params!
# If you submit a <select> field with multiple selections, you'll get
# an odd result: the number of selections made, not the selections
# themselves. Later in the book we'll show you how to deal with
# multiple-value fields in a function like this.
sub untaint_params {
  my $q = shift;
  my (@k, $k, $p);

  @k = $q->keywords;

  foreach $k(@k) {
    $q->param(-name=>$k, -value=>untaint($q->param($k)));
  }
}

sub untaint {
  my $val = shift;

  # allow alphanumeric characters, whitespace, and punctuation
  my $ok_chars = q|[\w\s.,:/?!\-@'"]|;

  die "Illegal character(s) in input ($val)" unless
    ($val =~ /^($ok_chars*)$/);

  return $1;

}

# lock_filehandle
# in:  filehandle
```

guestbook.cgi (continued)

```
# out: -
# description: flock()s a filehandle, for concurrency-safe access
#   This won't work on operating systems (like MacOS) that don't
#   support flock().
sub lock_filehandle {
  my $fh   = shift;
  my $lock = shift;
  use Fcntl qw(:flock);

  my $lock_code;

  if ($lock =~ /^r/i) {
    $lock_code = LOCK_SH;
  } elsif ($lock =~ /^w/i) {
    $lock_code = LOCK_EX;
  } else {
    $lock_code = LOCK_UN;
  }

  # give it two tries
  unless (flock ($fh, $lock_code | LOCK_NB)) {
    unless (flock($fh, $lock_code)) {
      die "flock: could not get $lock lock on $GUESTBOOK";
    }
  }

  return 1;
}
```

Other Files Needed

You will need a guestbook file, which is a plain text file that must be given world-write-able permissions. To create the guestbook file, from the Unix command line, type

```
touch /path/to/guestbook; chmod a+w /path/to/guestbook
```

Of course, you'll replace the /path/to/guestbook line with the path to your guestbook location.

You'll also want to create an HTML file that links to your guestbook. In this case, we've designed a home page with a link to the guestbook (see Figure 4.5).

Click on the link, and you'll get to the guestbook, where you can read other entries, and add and submit one yourself (see Figure 4.6).

Although you can put the guestbook file anywhere you like, it is best to put it somewhere outside the Apache htdocs tree. Keeping anything that you don't want to show up in someone's browser outside this tree will aid in keeping your data secure. It's a good habit to get into.

Figure 4.5

A home page with guestbook link.

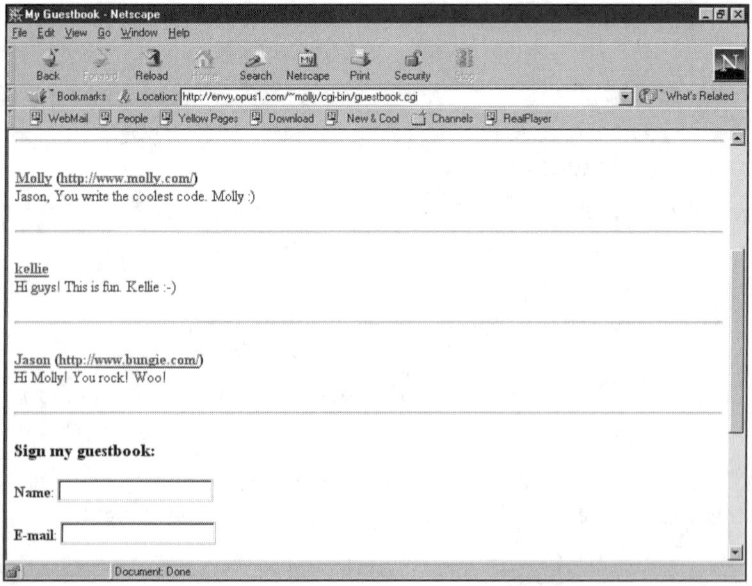

Figure 4.6

The guestbook.

guestbook.html

```
<html>
<head>
    <title>Sign Our Guestbook!</title>
</head>

<body bgcolor="#FFFFCC" text="#000000" link="#CC6600" vlink="#0099CC"
alink="#FFCC66">

<blockquote>

<font face="arial,helvetica,sans-serif" size="5" color="#0099CC"><b>Designing
with Perl</b></font>

<font face="arial,helvetica,sans-serif">
Welcome to the home page. We wrote this book to
help you use Perl to empower your Web site design and development.
</p>
<p>
Jason Pellerin is the programmer who developed the code within the book, and
Molly E. Holzschlag helps readers understand how to use the code
and apply it to daily designs.
</p>
<p>
Come say hello!  <a href="cgi-bin/guestbook.cgi">Read and sign</a> the guestbook,
created with scripts provided in the book (naturally)!
</p>

</font>

</blockquote>

</body>
</html>
```

Modifying the Script

Modify the HTML within the script to your tastes. For example, if you'd like to change the form to include a field for a nickname, you can do so by adding the field to the form section of the script.

In our example, we've placed the file in /usr/local/data/guestbook.

Modifying the Guestbook Form

```
<h3>Sign my guestbook:</h3>
<form action="$url" method="post">
<p><b>Name</b>: <INPUT type="text" name="name"/></p>
<p><b>E-mail</b>: <INPUT type="text" name="email"/></p>
<p><b>Homepage</b>: <INPUT type="text" name="homepage"/></p>
```

Modifying the Guestbook Form (continued)

```
<p><b>Nickname</b>: <INPUT type="text" name="nickname"/></p>
<p><b>Message</b>:</p>
<p><textarea cols="30" rows="6" wrap="virtual" name="message">Type your message
here.</textarea></p>
<p><input type="submit"/></p>
</form>
```

The Classic Mailto Form

Perhaps the most popular type of form in use, the Mailto form allows you to create a page with standard form input fields for the collection of information from your site visitors. This information might include their name and e-mail address, and an area where they can write feedback.

Upon submitting the form, the information is sent to the server, where it is processed by the script, organized, and output to a file that is then sent on to the e-mail address of your choice. Because this script is a bit long, we'll split it up into a few chunks.

How to Use

This script uses Net::SMTP to send its mail. If you aren't running sendmail locally, or want to use another server, you'll also have to edit the script, changing the $SMTP_SERVER variable to the name or IP address of the server you want to use.

1. Copy the script into your text editor.

2. Save the script as mail_form.cgi.

3. Place the script in your cgi-bin directory.

4. Change the permissions to make executable by all users:

   ```
   chmod a+x mail_form.cgi
   ```

5. Install the Net tools package from CPAN. You can find the tools at http://www.perl.com/CPAN-local/modules/by-module/Net/.

mail_form.cgi

```
#!/usr/bin/perl -wT
$ENV{'PATH'}  = '/bin:/usr/bin:/usr/local/bin';
$ENV{'SHELL'} = '/bin/sh';
```

mail_form.cgi (continued)

```
$ENV{'ENV'}   = '';
$ENV{'IFS'}   = '';

use CGI;

# import the Net::SMTP module, an easy interface to
# email servers.
use Net::SMTP;

use strict;
use vars qw($ START   $CGI $SMTP_SERVER);

$CGI          = "mail_form.cgi";
$SMTP_SERVER = "localhost";

eval { main() }; $ START   =   LINE  ;

if ($@) {
  error_page($@);
}

exit(0);

# main
```

The main function (shown later) does three things: checks the input to make sure it looks accurate, builds an e-mail message, and then sends that message.

Other Files Needed

To access the mail script, you'll need a standard HTML form, complete with text fields and submit buttons. You can customize this page any way you like. We've included a simple example here. In this case, we've provided for the success or failure of the form (shown in bold). If the form succeeds, the site visitor will receive a page that announces success should the form submission fail, the visitor will receive notice of the failure with directions on how to resubmit the form.

Mailto HTML Form

```
<html>
<head>
<title>Mail Us!</title>
</head>
```

Mailto HTML Form (continued)

```
<body bgcolor="#FFFFCC" text="#000000" link="#CC6600" vlink="#0099CC"
alink="#FFCC66">
<font face="arial, helvetica, sans-serif" size="5" color="#0099CC">
<b>Mail Us!</b></font>
<p>

<form action="cgi-bin/mail_form.cgi" method="post">

<!--Uncomment these (and change the URLs to something that makes
    sense for your site) to use custom success or failure pages
<input type=hidden name="_success_url"
value="http://localhost/perlbook/chap_04/good.html"/>
<input type=hidden name="_fail_url"
value="http://localhost/perlbook/chap_04/bad.html"/>
-->

<font face="arial, helvetica, sans-serif" size="2">
To: <input name="_to" size="25"/></p>
<p>
From: <input name="_from" size="23"/></p>
<p>
Interest: </p>
<p>
<select multiple size=4 name="interest">
<option>HTML</option>
<option>Perl</option>
<option>CGI</option>
<option>Web Design</option>
</select></p>
<p>
Message:</p>
<p>
<textarea wrap="virtual" cols="50" rows="5" name="text"></textarea></p>
<p>
<input type="submit" value="Send It!"/></p>
</font>
</form>

</body>
</html>
```

In Figure 4.7, you can see the input e-mail form that we've created.

Once the mail form input is submitted, it will be sent to the e-mail recipient.

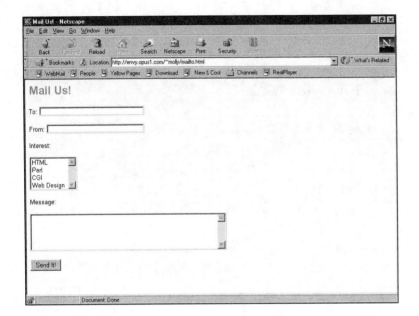

Figure 4.7
The classic mailto form.

In Greater Detail: Accuracy Checking in the Mailto Script

We check the accuracy of the input with **untaint_params()**, which calls **untaint()** on each of the form fields submitted to the script. The accuracy of the input is assured by checking for the presence of required fields via the %required variable. %required is a "hash," also called an "associative array." Hashes are very handy for storing a group of named values. Hash variables in Perl always start with a %, except when used to access an item in the hash. In that case, because you're accessing a single item, the variable begins with a $. See below, where we set the entire %required hash using the variable %required, but access a single member of that hash with the expression $required{'_to'}. Here we use it to keep a list of the fields our e-mail form just can't do without: the To:, From:, and Subject: message headers.

```
sub main {
  my ($q, $self, $good, $err, $r, %message, @missing);

  # The fields every email message needs
  my %required = ( '_to'      => 'To:',
                   '_from'    => 'From:',
                   '_subject' => 'Subject:');
  $q = new CGI;
```

```
# untaint everything
untaint_params($q);

# assume the best
$good = 1;

# make sure required fields are present (To:, From:, Subject:)
foreach $r(keys %required) {
  unless (defined $q->param($r)) {
    $good = 0;                    # we can't send the message
    push @missing, $required{$r};  # tell the user why
  }
}

die "The following required fields are missing: " .
      join (', ', @missing) . ". " .
      "Please contact the maintainer of this web site for help." unless $good;

# build body of message from other fields
# (fields whose names don't start with '_')
build_message(\%message,$q);

# send the mail (we submit $q to this routine so that it
# can set $q->param('err_msg') if it  encounters an error)
$good = send_message(\%message,$q);

# if mail has been a success, go to success url (if any given),
#  or output default success page
# or if mail has failed, go to failure url, or output default
#  failure page
result_page($good,\%message,$q);
}
```

We build the message by stepping through the CGI input, and adding fields to the header, or the body, of the message, as appropriate. There are a couple of interesting things in this function.

First is the qw() operator, which turns a list of words into an array. The code

```
@amphibians =qw(frog newt toad salamander);
```

does the same thing as these two pieces of code:

```
@amphibians = split(/ /, "frog newt toad salamander ");
@amphibians = ('frog', 'newt', 'toad', 'salamander');
```

but is easier to write, and to read, than both.

Next is a new use of the arrow operator (->), which we've seen quite a bit before in an object context. But in this case, we use it with a hash reference, not with an object. How? The arrow operator (->) is a form of "syntactic sugar" that makes it easy to access the values stored in a reference variable of any kind. Here we use it like this:

```
$m_ref->{$f} = $q->param("_$f");
```

Once we've built the header, we build the rest of the message by listing all of the other fields, in a format like:

```
Field name: field value
# build message
# in:  reference to message hash, CGI object
# out: -
# description:
#    Builds the test of the message from the input submitted to
#    the CGI
sub build_message {
  my $m_ref     = shift;
  my $q         = shift;
  my @hed_flds = qw(to from subject);
  my ($f, $k, $val, $body, @tmp);

  # first the header
  foreach $f(@hed_flds) {
    $m_ref->{$f} = $q->param("_$f");
  }

  # now the body of the message, with
  # a helpful title.
  $body = "Output of $CGI follows\n";

  # the x operator concatenates a number of copies
  # of a string into one big string. For example,
  # 'frog x 5' would produce 'frogfrogfrogfrogfrog'.
  # Here we're using it to make a nice dividing line
  # under the message title.
  $body .= '-' x (length($body)-1) . "\n\n";

  # output fields in alphabetical (actually lexical) order
  # (a field name 'Apples' will come before one named 'aardvarks')
  foreach $k(sort $q->param) {

    # skip all of the header fields
    next if $k =~ /^_/;
    @tmp = ();

    push @tmp,  $q->param($k);
    $val = join ', ', @tmp;
    $body .= "$k: $val\n";

  }
  $m_ref->{'body'} = $body;
}
```

We could also write this as ${$mref}{$f} = $q->param("_$f") — which is a lot harder to read. The arrow operator is also used to access the data and methods of Perl objects, because Perl objects are really references. More on that later.

Next, we'll try to actually send the message. We create a new Net::SMTP object, which initiates a connection with the server set in the $SMTP_SERVER variable. We go step-by-step through the process of sending a message, making sure that the mail server will accept the sender, the addressee, and the message data.

All our dealings with the mail server are enclosed in an eval{} block, so that we can easily end our attempt at any time by die'ing with an error message. We want to be able to send a custom failure page, so we don't want to die all the way out to the main eval{} block, and catch any mail server errors right here. If something has gone wrong, we save the error message in a CGI parameter, and return a false value. Otherwise, we return true.

```
# send_message
# in:  reference to message hash, CGI object
# out: success or failure
# description:
#   Tries to send the email message. If it fails, it
#   sets a CGI param('err_str') and returns FALSE
sub send_message {
  my $m_ref = shift;
  my $q     = shift;
  my $smtp;

  # catch any errors here, so that the user's failure page
  # will be displayed, instead of the default error message,
  # if anything goes wrong.
  eval {
    $smtp = Net::SMTP->new($SMTP_SERVER);

    # make sure we connected
    die "SMTP server not responding" unless ref $smtp;

    # tell the server who we're sending from
    $smtp->mail($m_ref->{'from'}) ||
      die "Server did not accept sender's address";

    # ... and who were sending to
    $smtp->to($m_ref->{'to'}) ||
      die "Server did not accept recipient address";

    # and finally send the message itself
    unless ($smtp->data( "To: " . $m_ref->{'to'} . "\n" .
            "Subject: " . $m_ref->{'subject'} . "\n" .
            "\n" .
            $m_ref->{'body'} ))
    {
    $smtp->quit;
```

```
    die "Failed to send mail";
      }

  $smtp->quit; # close the connection to the mail server

};

  # If we catch an error, save the error message
  # and return 0 (FALSE)
  if ($@) {
    $q->param('err_str', $@);
    return 0;
  }

  # otherwise return 1 (TRUE)
  return 1;
}
```

When this function is called, the message has been built, and sent (or not). All we need to do here is inform the user of the result: If it's good, we send it to the success_page defined in the calling HTML form, or just echo back their input, if no success page is set.

If we couldn't build or send the message, we send the user to a custom fail_page, if one is defined in the form, or just output the standard error page, if no fail page is defined.

```
# result_page
# in:  success or failure
# out: -
# description:
#   Sends feedback to the user about whether their form submission
#   succeeded or not.
sub result_page {
  my $good  = shift;
  my $m_ref = shift;
  my $q     = shift;

  if ($good) {

    # if the form included a '_success_url' field,
    # send the user to that url. Otherwise, output
    # the default success page
    if ($q->param('_success_url')) {
      # CGI.pm makes a lot of things easy, including
      # redirection.
      print $q->redirect($q->param('_success_url'));
    } else {

      # the default success page: echo back the submitted form
      print $q->header,
```

Here's a life-lesson for the budding programmers out there: The end, from the user's perspective, is often just the beginning of the work for *you*. In this case, there are a few functions left, functions that do some important work behind the scenes.

```perl
        $q->start_html('Form submitted'),
        $q->h3('Your information has been submitted successfully'),
        $q->dump,
        $q->end_html;

    }
  } else {

    # If there was a '_fail_url' field, send the user there.
    # Otherwise, send the default failure page
    if ($q->param('_fail_url')) {

      print $q->redirect($q->param('_fail_url'));
    } else {

      # the default failure page: the main error page
      error_page($q->param('err_str'));
    }

  }
}
```

We've taken the standard error page output from our previous scripts, and encapsulated it into a function of its own. This enables us to output the error page at any time, from any place in the script, without repeating a lot of code.

```perl
# error_page
# in:  error message
# out: -
# description: outputs error message to browser in simple HTML page
sub error_page {
  my $msg = shift;

  chomp($msg);


  # use $  START  to determine the real line where the error
occurred
  $msg =~ s/\(eval\) line (\d+)/${CGI} . " line " . ($ START  -$1-
1)/e;
  $msg =~ s/( at ).*( line )/$1${CGI}$2/;

  print <<ERR;
Content-type: text/html

<html>
  <head><title>Error</title></head>
  <body>
    <h1>Error</h1>
    <code>$msg</code>
  </body>
```

```
</html>
ERR

  exit(0);

}
```

Next, and last, come a revision of the untaint_params() and
untaint() functions used in better.cgi and guestbook.cgi. There are
couple of important differences between these functions and the
ones in the previous script. First, untaint() allows a broader range
of punctuation to be submitted, in keeping with the more generalized
mail_form.cgi, which may be called from any number of different
forms.

Second, untaint_params() is revised to work with form fields that
submit multiple values. To do this, we take advantage of a quirk in
Perl's handling of arrays: They can't be nested by inserting one array
into another (although you can embed one array in another by using
references). In other words, this code:

```
@array = ('one', 'two', ('three', 'four', 'five'));
```

is exactly equivalent, in function, to this code:

```
@array = ('one', 'two', 'three', 'four', 'five');
```

They both produce the array ('one', 'two', 'three', 'four', 'five'). We
take advantage of this by using a temporary array, and pushing each
form field's value into that array; this way, we can deal with every
field the same way, as if it were an array. Most of them will just be
arrays with only one value.

```
# security routines

# untaint_params
# in:  CGI object
# out: trusted  params, or dies if suspicious input seen
sub untaint_params {
  my $q = shift;
  my (@k, $k, $p, @tmp, $t, @safe);

  @k = $q->param;

  foreach $k(@k) {
    @tmp = ();
    push @tmp, $q->param($k);
```

```perl
    foreach $t(@tmp) {
      push @safe, untaint($t);
    }

    $q->param($k, @safe);
  }
}

# untaint
# in:  untrusted scalar
# out: trusted scalar, or dies if in is suspicious
# description:
sub untaint {
  my $val = shift;

  # allow alphanumeric characters, whitespace, and most punctuation
  my $ok_chars = q|[\w\s.,:/?!\-@'"#$%\^&()+=_\\<>]|;

  die "Illegal character(s) in input ($val)" unless
    ($val =~ /^($ok_chars*)$/);

  return $1;

}
```

What's Up Next

You've got some basic scripting skills under your belt now, so it's time to move on to something a bit more challenging. In Chapter 5, "Features and Functions," we'll share a variety of powerful scripts that will allow you to manage your Web sites from behind the scenes, as well as introduce you to a few more useful Perl modules.

Features and Functions

One of the powers of Perl is not only its ability to help deliver Web pages with organized information, but the way in which it works behind the scenes to assist developers in getting their job done. Instead of being displayed or outputted to HTML pages, most of the scripts that fall into this category are run exclusively on the server side.

In this chapter, we're going to introduce you to several modules, scripts, and utilities that you can use to enhance and manage your Web site with finesse.

Examples include scripts that help you manage other scripts on your site as well as utilities to rename files behind the scenes, detect browsers, check links, squash bugs, and validate code.

Adding Taint Checking

Taint checking was introduced in Chapter 4, "Working with Forms," where we used it to ensure that forms would be secure, and no *tainted* data would be allowed to enter the scripting process.

Because this level of security is important for most scripts, this module makes the basic taint check routine available to every script, so you don't have to type it in to scripts individually.

How to Use

1. Copy the code into your text editor.

2. Save the code as Taintcheck.pm.

3. Place the Taintcheck.pm file into the site_perl directory in /usr/lib/perl, or wherever your site keeps Perl modules that are not part of the standard distribution. If you don't have access to the site_perl directory, create a private Perl library folder somewhere outside of your htdocs tree, and place Taintcheck.pm there. Make sure that your Perl library folder is readable (but *not* writable) for all users.

4. If you put Taintcheck.pm into a private library folder, you will
   have to include the line use lib /path/to/library; (replacing
   /path/to/library with the actual path to your library folder) in
   each script where you use Taintcheck.pm.

Taintcheck.pm

```
package Taintcheck;

use Exporter;

$ENV{'PATH'}  = '/bin:/usr/bin:/usr/local/bin';
$ENV{'SHELL'} = '/bin/sh';
$ENV{'IFS'}   = '';

@ISA    = qw(Exporter);
@EXPORT = qw(untaint_params untaint);

use CGI;
use strict;

# untaint_params
# in:  CGI object
# out: trusted  params, or dies if suspicious input seen
#
# This version of untaint_params supports multi-valued parameters.
# It calls untaint() on each of the values.
sub untaint_params {
  my $q = shift;
  my (@k, $k, @tmp, $t, @safe);

  @k = $q->keywords;

  foreach $k(@k) {
    @tmp = ();
    push @tmp, $q->param($k);

    foreach $t(@tmp) {
      push @safe, untaint($t);
    }

    $q->param($k, @safe);
  }
}

# untaint
# in:  untrusted scalar
```

Taintcheck.pm (continued)

```
# out: trusted scalar, or dies if in is suspicious
# description:
sub untaint {
  my $val = shift;
  return unless $val;

  # allow alphanumeric characters, whitespace, and most punctuation
  my $ok_chars = q|[\w\s.,:/?!\-@'"#$%\^&()+=_\\<>]|;

  die "Illegal character(s) in input ($val)" unless
    ($val =~ /^($ok_chars*)$/);

  return $1;

}
```

Once you have the taint check module installed, you'll now add the following line into any script you want to have run the taint check on.

```
use Taintcheck;
```

For instance, here's the start of a script that uses Taintcheck.

```
#!/usr/bin/perl -wT

use lib '/home/molly/perl_lib';

use strict;
use Taintcheck;
```

Be sure to point to the library where the appropriate module resides. We've pointed to the perl_lib on our server, where the taint check, as well as other modules, have been placed.

You can add the use `Taintcheck` line in any script where taint-checking is required, and you will then be able to use the functions it exports, untaint_params() and untaint(), in that script.

Keeping Time

As we've mentioned before, modules are a powerful way of adding entire processes to a given script by simply pointing to the module in the script. In this case, we're going to introduce another Perl module, which exports useful time and date functions. These include getting any given file's size and date last modified, getting a file's age in days, and outputting a Unix time stamp that is easy to read.

How to Use

1. Copy the code into your text editor.

2. Save the code as Timefuncs.pm.

3. Place Timfuncs.pm into the Perl library on your server.

Timefuncs.pm

```perl
package Timefuncs;

use Exporter;

$ENV{'PATH'}  = '/bin:/usr/bin:/usr/local/bin';
$ENV{'SHELL'} = '/bin/sh';
$ENV{'IFS'}   = '';

@ISA    = qw(Exporter);
@EXPORT = qw(file_stats file_age date_string);

use strict;

# file_stats
# in:  file name
# out: modifcation date and size of file
sub file_stats {
  my $file = shift;
  my ($size, $mtime);

  # The -s operator returns the file size
  $size = (-s $file);

  # The stat function returns a large array of file
  # information. We're only interest in the 9th element,
  # the time that the file was last modified.
  $mtime = (stat $file)[9];

  # functions in perl aren't limited to returning
  # a single value - unlike in C, for example.
  # Here we're returning two values, in an array.
  # If you need to return a large array, it's better
  # (most of the time) to return an array reference instead.
  return ($mtime, $size);
}

# file_age
# in:  file name
# out: age of file in days
sub file_age {
  my $file  = shift;
  # The -M function returns the age of the file in days
```

Timefuncs.pm (continued)

```
  # relative to the time that the program started.  Since
  # CGI programs tend to run only for a short time, this
  # is a good-enough figure on how old a file is.
  return int(-M $file);
}

# date_string
# in:  unix timestamp
# out: nice, human-readable date string
sub date_string {
  my $ts = shift;

  # The POSIX module comes standard with Perl and
  # includes the strftime function which can be used
  # to produce nicely-formatted date strings.
  use POSIX;

  # The format string below returns the time as:
  #      mm/dd/yyyy hh:mm am
  return
    POSIX::strftime("%D %I:%M %P", localtime($ts));

}
```

As with the taint check module, you'll add a line of code to any file you'd like to be able to run the time functions on. Here's the code:

```
use Timefuncs;
```

And here's a code snippet with the code in place:

Time Function Example

```
#!/usr/bin/perl -wT

use lib '/usr/home/molly/perl_lib';

use strict;
use Timefuncs;
```

Other Files Needed

To be able to access the time information produced by the time functions module from the command line, you'll need to add a script. The following Perl script is a simply utility that will allow you to access the output of the time functions module from the Unix command line.

How to Use

1. Copy the code into your text editor.

2. Save the code as get_all_stats.pl.

3. Place the file onto the server somewhere in your executable path. If you don't have root access, try ~/bin (the bin directory in your home directory).

4. Make the file exectuable with chmod a+x get_all_stats.pl.

get_all_stats.pl

```perl
#!/usr/bin/perl -w

use lib '/path/to/library';  # replace with the real path

use Timefuncs;

$f = $ARGV[0];

die "usage: get_all_stats.pl file_name" unless $f;

($m, $s) = &file_stats($f);

print "File $f is size $s KB, " .
      "last modified $m seconds since the epoch.\n";

print "Age " . &file_age($f) . " days\n";

print "Modifcation date ($m) in human-readable form:
" . &date_string($m) . "\n";
```

Once installed, you can get the information you require by typing ./get_all_stats.pl [filename] from the Unix command line (see Figure 5.1).

Figure 5.1

Getting file stats.

```
TelStar: envy.opus1.com                                              _ 8 X
File  Edit  Connection  Window  Help
       or need to $$$ MAKE MONEY FAST $$$!, send e-mail to:
         - hostmaster@dispatch.net

Make yourself at home.
You have new mail.
molly@envy:/usr/home/molly$ cd public_html/
molly@envy:/usr/home/molly/public_html$ ls
bad.html                  first_cgi.html           index.html
cgi-bin/                  first_func.html          mailtest.html
chap_05/                  good.html                mailtest.html~
chap_06/                  guestbook                mailtest2.html
chapter_6/                guestbook.html           mailto.html
date.shtml                images/                  win2u*
molly@envy:/usr/home/molly/public_html$ cd chap_05/
molly@envy:/usr/home/molly/public_html/chap_05$ ls
Taintcheck.pm             contest.html             roll_pages.pl*
Timefuncs.pm              dbm_example.pl*          signup.cgi*
buggy_nocarp.cgi*         get_all_stats.pl*
buggy_oo.cgi*             link_check.pl*
molly@envy:/usr/home/molly/public_html/chap_05$ ./get_all_stats.pl Timefuncs.pm
size 1157, mod 925150791
age 8
modifcation date (925150791) in human-readable form: 4/26/1999 11:19 am
molly@envy:/usr/home/molly/public_html/chap_05$
```

You can modify the script to your server's preferences. For example, if your server uses default.htm instead of index.html as the default, you can change the script variables to make this work properly on your server.

Automating Pages by Day

This Perl script is a very handy tool for Web designers who want to design and upload pages in advance, and then have them roll over to the index page (or any other page) when the command is invoked.

This is a clever way to keep entry pages fresh and timely without having to actually create the entry HTML pages for each of your directories, uploading them one at a time day in and day out. Instead, you can create a full batch of pages and they will update upon your command. You can also set up a "cron" or "at" job on your system to make the script run at a particular time every day (see "Modifying the Script," later in this section).

How to Use

1. Copy the script into your text editor.

2. Save the script as roll_pages.pl.

3. Place the script in your executable path.

4. Customize the @DIRs variable to match the directories where you'd like to use the script.

5. Customize the $DEFAULT variable to match the name of the default file for your server.

roll_pages.pl
___

```perl
#!/usr/bin/perl -wT

use lib '/path/to/library'; # replace with the real path

use strict;
use Taintcheck;

use vars qw($DEFAULT @DIRS $TODAY);

#
# GLOBALS
#

# The name of the default file, as set in your
# web server configuration
$DEFAULT = 'index.html';

# The directory or directories to look in for files to roll over
@DIRS    = ( '/home/httpd/html' );

# If a day of the week is explicitly passed to the script
# (eg by typing "./roll_pages.pl Monday", then roll over the
# page for that day. Otherwise, roll over the page for today.
$TODAY   = untaint( $ARGV[0] ) || today();

roll_pages();

#
# SUBROUTINES
#

# roll_pages
#
# step through list of active directories (@DIRS),
# copying $TODAY.html to $DEFAULT
sub roll_pages {
  my ($d, $f, $tmp);

  foreach $d(@DIRS) {
    $tmp = '';
    $f   = "$d/$TODAY.html";

    unless (-r $f) {
      warn "Cannot roll $f: file is not readable, " .
```

roll_pages.pl (continued)

```
            "or does not exist!";
      next;
    }

    # It's unlikely that you want to activate last week's page,
    # so issue a warning if it looks like that's what's happening
    warn "$f is more than 6 days old" if (&age($f) > 6);

    # read and write the file
    unless (open (SRC, "<$f")) {
      warn "Cannot roll $f: file could not be opened: $!";
      next;
    }

    unless (open (TRG, ">$d/$DEFAULT")) {
      warn "Cannot roll $f: could not write to $d/$DEFAULT: $!";
      close SRC;
      next;
    }

    while (<SRC>) {
      print TRG $_;
    }

    close SRC;
    close TRG;

    print "$d/$DEFAULT updated with contents of $f\n";
  }

}

#
# today
#
# return the name of the day of the week
sub today {

  my ($now, @days);

  @days = qw(sunday monday tuesday wednesday
             thursday friday saturday);

  $now = time;

  # The 6th element of the localtime array is the day of the week
  # Convert that number to a name, using the @days array
  return $days[ (localtime(time))[6] ];

}

#
# age
#
```

roll_pages.pl (continued)

```
# return the age of the file in days
sub age {
  my $file  = shift;
  return int(-M $file);
}
```

To run the script, simply type `./roll_pages.pl` from the command prompt. The script will look through your directories for any pages named by the current day, and rename them as the default HTML page. If it's Tuesday, all tuesday.html files will be rolled over to index.html files.

Modifying the Script

You can modify this script to make it run automatically at a pre-determined time each day. You can do this with a scheduling application known as *cron*. The file used to tell the application what to run and when is known as a *crontab*.

On a Unix system you could enter a line like the following into your crontab, by typing `crontab -e`, then entering the information:

```
2 0 * * * /path/to/roll_pages.pl
```

(replacing `/path/to/roll_pages/pl` with the actual path to the script). This will run the script every night at two minutes past midnight. To check your crontab, you can type `crontab -l` at the command line.

You can also pass a specific day name to the script. So, if it's Tuesday, but you want all the Wednesday files to roll over, simply type `./roll_pages.pl` wednesday and any wednesday.html files will roll over to the default index file.

On a Windows NT system, you'll have to use the `at` command to do this. Type `at /help` for instructions.

Checking Links

Tired of click, click, clicking your way through all the links on a site to make sure they work? Or, have you gotten lazy and ignored your links because it's simply too time consuming and dull to go through the process? This script is the answer to your link prayers. It will check all the links within your site, as well as external links if you so desire.

How to Use

1. Get the LWP::UserAgent bundle from CPAN and install it.

2. Install HTML::Parse and HTML::LinkExtor from CPAN.

3. Copy the script into your text editor.

4. Save the script as link_check.pl.

5. Place the script in your executable path.

link_check.pl

```perl
#!/usr/bin/perl
#
# link_check.pl
#
# a web robot that checks all links on a submitted site,
# to the submitted depth, optionally checking external
# links as well.
#

use lib '/usr/home/molly/perl_lib';
use Taintcheck;

use LWP::RobotUA;         # a polite mini web client
use HTML::LinkExtor;      # used to extract links from page
use Getopt::Std;          # eases processing of command-line
                          # arguments

use strict;
use vars qw($opt_e $opt_v $USAGE $ROOT
            $DEPTH $REPORT $OWNER @CHECKED $PAGES @BAD);

$USAGE = "usage: link_checker.pl [-ev] url [depth]\n";

getopt();

die $USAGE unless @ARGV;

# replace with your real email address
$OWNER = "you\@your.email.adr";
$ROOT  = $ARGV[0];                    # where to start checking
$DEPTH = $ARGV[1] || 2;               # how deep to check

# The -v option traditionally means 'verbose'; ie, spit out a
# ton of information as you run
($opt_v) && (print(('-' x 60) . "\nlink_check.pl started at " .
  localtime(time) . "\n\n"));
```

link_check.pl (continued)

```perl
check_links($ROOT,0);

$REPORT .= (scalar @BAD) . " bad link(s) were found in
    $PAGES page(s).\n";

(@BAD) && ($REPORT .= join ("\n ", @BAD) . "\n");

print $REPORT;

($opt_v) && (print("\n\nlink_check.pl finished at " .
  localtime(time) . "\n" . ('-' x 60) . "\n\n"));


exit;

# subroutines

sub check_links {
  my $cur_page_url = shift;
  my $cur_depth    = shift;
  my $parent_url   = shift;

  my ($bot, $req, $res, $links, $a_links, $link);

  # stop now if we've already visited this page
  if (in_array( $cur_page_url, \@CHECKED)) {
    return;
  }

  ($opt_v) && (print(('  ' x $cur_depth) .
    "-- CHECK $cur_page_url\n"));

  # start up the robot
  $bot = new LWP::RobotUA( 'dwp_linkbot/0.1', $OWNER );

  # Wait between requests so that we don't slam the web server.
  # RobotUA does some sleeping for us, but we
  # want to be extra nice.
  sleep(2);

  if ($cur_depth < $DEPTH) {

    $PAGES++;
    push @CHECKED, $cur_page_url;

    # find the current page, or add err to report and return
    $req = new HTTP::Request( 'GET', $cur_page_url );
    $res = $bot->request($req);

    unless ($res->is_success) {
      ($opt_v) && (print(('  ' x $cur_depth) . "** FAILED:
```

link_check.pl (continued)

```perl
            $cur_page_url: " . $res->status_line . "\n"));
        push @BAD, "$parent_url: $cur_page_url (" .
          $res->status_line . ")";
        return;
    }

    # get links on current page
    ($links, $a_links) = get_links($res);

    # Just check HEAD for non-page links - we don't want to
    # download whole images, etc.
    foreach $link(@$links) {
      if (($opt_e) || (local($link))) {
          $req = new HTTP::Request( "HEAD", $link);
          $res = $bot->request($req);

          unless ($res->is_success) {
            ($opt_v) && (print((' ' x ($cur_depth+1)) .
              "** FAILED: $link: " . $res->status_line . "\n"));
            push @BAD, "$cur_page_url: $link (" .
             $res->status_line .")";
          }
      }
    }

    # recurse on each of the <a href> links
    foreach $link(@$a_links) {

      # if we're checking all links, or the link is local,
      # open the page and check it's links. Increment the
      # depth counter, so that we don't check deeper into
      # the site than we're supposed to.
      if (($opt_e) || (&local($link))) {
        &check_links($link, $cur_depth+1,$cur_page_url);
      }
    }
  }
}

sub get_links {
  my $res   = shift;
  my $base  = $res->base;
  my $p     = new HTML::LinkExtor( undef, $base);

  my (@links, @a_links, $l, $tag, %attr);
  $p->parse($res->content);

  foreach $l($p->links) {
    ($tag, %attr) = @$l;
```

link_check.pl (continued)

```perl
    if ($tag eq 'a') {
      push @a_links, values %attr;
    } else {
      push @links, values %attr;
    }
  }

  # Can't just return (@links, @a_links) - the arrays would be
  # squished together into one big array; we need to keep them
  # separate, so we return two array references.
  return (\@links, \@a_links);
}

sub local {
  my $link = shift;

  return $link =~ /^$ROOT/;
}

sub in_array {
  my $item    = shift;
  my $arr_ref = shift;
  my $a;

  foreach $a(@$arr_ref) {
    ($item eq $a) && (return 1);
  }

  return 0;
}
```

Running the script is easy. You can use several options, depending upon the type of output you'd like to get, type

```
./link_check.pl [-ev] site [depth]
```

The –e option searches external links as well as local links. The –v option gives you detailed feedback as to the link status (see Figure 5.2). The depth option can be used to determine how deeply into a site the script will plumb. For example, if the depth option is left at its default value of 2, it will check links in the URL you submit to the script, and on each page successfully loaded from a link found in that URL. To load the pages linked to on *those* pages, and check their links, you would set the depth to 3.

This is a server-friendly script, so it waits several seconds between requests to the server. If you have a very large site to check, do it overnight.

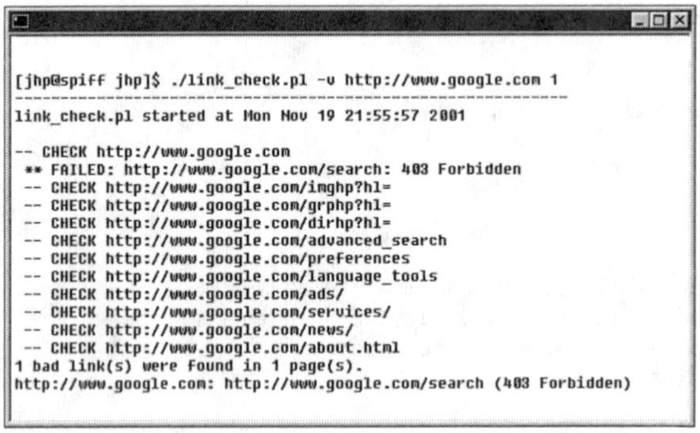

Figure 5.2

Checking links using link_check.pl.

```
[jhp@spiff jhp]$ ./link_check.pl -v http://www.google.com 1
-----------------------------------------------------------------
link_check.pl started at Mon Nov 19 21:55:57 2001

-- CHECK http://www.google.com
 ** FAILED: http://www.google.com/search: 403 Forbidden
 -- CHECK http://www.google.com/imghp?hl=
 -- CHECK http://www.google.com/grphp?hl=
 -- CHECK http://www.google.com/dirhp?hl=
 -- CHECK http://www.google.com/advanced_search
 -- CHECK http://www.google.com/preferences
 -- CHECK http://www.google.com/language_tools
 -- CHECK http://www.google.com/ads/
 -- CHECK http://www.google.com/services/
 -- CHECK http://www.google.com/news/
 -- CHECK http://www.google.com/about.html
1 bad link(s) were found in 1 page(s).
http://www.google.com: http://www.google.com/search (403 Forbidden)
```

Bug Checking

This script demonstrates how to employ the useful CGI Carp module from CPAN to check your scripts for errors. The information that Carp provides you with is much more user-friendly, particularly for the non-programmer. If you don't have it in your scripts, you'll have to search for the displayed error (see Figure 5.3) on your server's documentation. In many cases, this information isn't available to you. Rather, your ISP's system administrator has it, and may not be able to get the information to you.

Adding bug checking will give you real information, right into the server. This script is a revisit of the first_oo.cgi form you worked with in Chapter 4. However, we've stuck an error in there to walk you through the experience of debugging your scripts.

How to Use

1. Copy the script into your text editor.

2. Save the script as buggy_oo.cgi.

3. Place the form in your cgi-bin directory on your server.

4. Change the permissions to make executable by all users:

   chmod a+x buggy_oo.cgi

5. Visit the page in your browser to see the error results

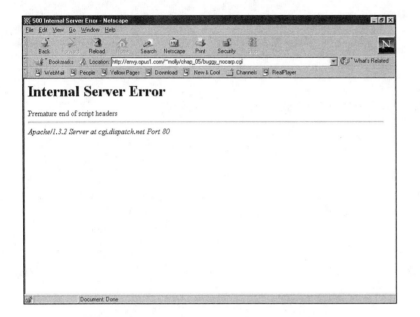

Figure 5.3

The error page displayed by the browser.

---

buggy_oo.cgi

```perl
#!/usr/bin/perl -w
#

use CGI;
use CGI::Carp qw(fatalsToBrowser);

$q    = new CGI;
$self = $q->url;

print $q->header;

#
# If we've gotten some input, display the result page.
# Otherwise, display the input form.
```

buggy_oo.cgi (continued)

```
#
if ($q->param()){

  $name = ucfirst( $q->param('name') );

  print <<HTML;
  <html>
    <head>
      <title>My First CGI</title>
    </head>

    <body>
      <h1>My First CGI</h1>

      <p>Hello, $name! This is my first CGI!</p>

    </body>
  </html>

HTML

} else {

  # The end-tag for this print is intentionally
  # misspelled.
  print <<FORM;
  <html>
    <head>
    <title>What's your name?</title>
  </head>

  <body>
    <h1>What is your name?</h1>

    <form action="$self" method="post">
      <p>Your name: <input type="text" name="name"/></p>
      <p><input type="submit"/></p>
    </form>

  </body>
</html>

FRM

}
```

Pay close attention to the way in which they are quite different from the example that does *not* have the Carp module in the script (see Figure 5.4).

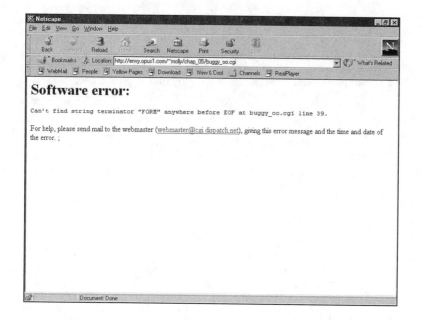

Figure 5.4
The error information that is displayed when the Carp module is used.

Validating Forms

This is another example of a helpful module used to validate forms. Validation is helpful for a number of reasons, including

- Making sure form security is at a maximum

- Checking to see that the information retrieved from the form is the information for which you are asking

- Ensuring that no key elements are missing

This script is an easy and elegant way to ensure that the information inputted into your form is complete. Use this module in your script for any form on your Web sites. The script shown here provides an example of a form script with the module in effect.

How to Use

1. Copy the script into your text editor.

2. Save the script as signup.cgi.

The CGI::Validate module should be resident on Apache servers. If it is not available, check for it at CPAN (see Chapter 3, "Scripting Basics").

3. Change the form action in the HTML page to point to signup.cgi in your cgi-bin directory, and save the page on your Web server as contest.html.

4. Change the permissions to make executable by all users:

```
chmod a+x signup.cgi
```

contest.html

```
<html>
<head><title>Sign up to win!</title>
</head>

<body>
<h1>Win win win!!</h1>

<p>Please fill out the contest entry form below. Fields marked
with a <font color="red" size=7>*</font> are required.

<form action="signup.cgi" method="post">

<p>First name: <input type="text" name="first_name">
<font color="red" size=7>*</font>
<p>Last name: <input type="text" name="last_name">
<font color="red" size=7>*</font>
<p>Phone: <input type="text" name="phone">
<font color="red" size=7>*</font>
<p>E-mail:  <input type="text" name="email">
<font color="red" size=7>*</font>
<p>How much you hate beanie babies on a scale of one to ten:
<input type="text" name="beanies" size="2">
<p><input type="submit" value="Enter and WIN!">

</form>

</body>
</html>
```

Signup.cgi

```
#!/usr/bin/perl -wT

$ENV{'PATH'}  = '/bin:/usr/bin:/usr/local/bin';
$ENV{'SHELL'} = '/bin/sh';
$ENV{'ENV'}   = '';
$ENV{'IFS'}   = '';

use lib '/path/to/library';
use Taintcheck;

use CGI;
```

Signup.cgi (continued)

```perl
# This tells the module what functions and variables we want
use CGI::Validate qw(CheckFormData    # check the data
                     addExtensions    # add custom data types
                     %Missing         # find missing fields
                     %Invalid         # ... invalid fields
                     %Blank           # ... blank fields
                     %InvalidType);   # ... and fields with bad info

use strict;
use vars qw($_START  $CGI);

$CGI = "signup.cgi";

eval { main() }; $_START_ = __LINE__;

if ($@) {
  chomp($@);


  $@ =~ s/\(eval\) line (\d+)/${CGI} .
    " line " . ($_START_ -$1-1)/e;
  $@ =~ s/( at ).*( line )/$1${CGI}$2/;

  my $error_message = $@;

  print <<ERR;
Content-type: text/html

<html>
  <head><title>Error</title></head>
  <body>
    <h1>Error</h1>
    <pre>
    $error_message
    </pre>
  </body>
</html>
ERR

}

exit(0);

# main

sub main {
  my $err;

  #
  # Add our custom 'phone number' type to the validator
  # (This ugly regular expression looks for (123) 456-7890 ,
  # with the () and - being optional
```

Signup.cgi (continued)

```perl
&addExtensions ( Phone => sub {
            $_[0] =~ /^\(?\d{3}\)?[\-\s]?\d{3}[\-\s]?\d{4}/
                    } );

my $q = &CheckFormData( 'first_name=s',
                        'last_name=s',
                        'phone=xPhone',
                        'email=e',
                        'beanies:i'
) or do {
  if (%Missing) {
    $err .= "<li>Missing form elements: " .
            join(', ', keys %Missing) . "</li>";
  }
  if (%Invalid) {
   $err .= "<li>Invalid form elements: " .
            join(', ', keys %Invalid) . "</li>";
  }
  if (%Blank) {
    $err .= "<li>Blank form elements: " .
            join(', ', keys %Blank) . "</li>";
  }
  if (%InvalidType) {
    $err .= "<li>Form elements with bad data: " .
            join(', ', keys %InvalidType) . "</li>";
  }

};

if ($err) {
  die "<p>Your contest entry could not be processed. " .
      "Please correct the following errors:\n</p>" .
      "<ul>\n $err \n</ul>\n";
}

print $q->header,
      $q->start_html("Thanks!"),
      $q->h1("Thank you for playing!"),
      $q->p("We'll notify you if you're the lucky winner!"),
      $q->end_html;
}
```

Now, visit the page in your browser to see the error results that this example will flash back at the individual who attempts to input form data that is incomplete or inaccurate (see Figure 5.5).

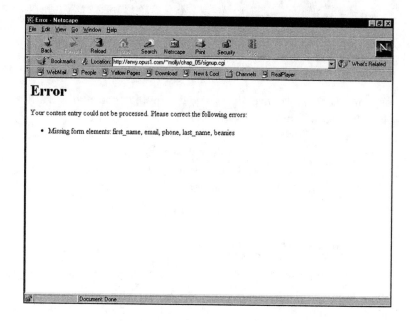

Figure 5.5

An invalid form entry results in an error when using the CGI:Validate module.

What's Up Next

In this chapter, you learned how to refine your scripts using modules, run useful utility scripts from the command line, check scripts for bugs, and validate forms effectively. In Chapter 6, "Customizing Pages," you'll add browser detection and routing to your toolbox, as well as work with cookies to track visitors to your guestbook. We'll also cover some related methods of customizing pages, such as using Server Side Includes (SSIs), and an inline form of Perl to enhance your pages with time and date and random events.

Customizing Pages

Now you're ready for more sophisticated scripting applications that will add custom features to your pages. Scripts featured in this chapter include browser and operating system detection and routing, and a method to track users who visit your guestbook. We've also stepped aside from strict Perl and CGI to show you some similar, helpful customization features that you can do with server-side includes (SSIs).

Detecting and Routing Browsers

Browser detection is helpful when you want deliver customized information to a given browser type, version, and specific operating system. In Figure 6.1, you can see the results the script provides when visited with Microsoft Internet Explorer, Version 5.0, on the Windows 98 platform.

Figure 6.1

Detecting the browser type, version, and platform.

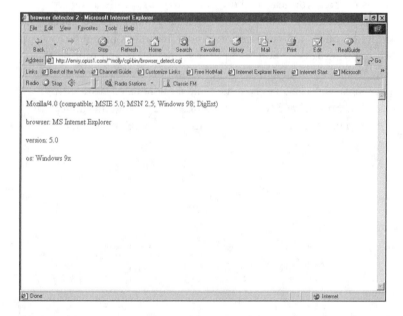

Detecting and Routing Browsers

The script in this section will detect browsers by determining the
identification of that browser. Then, the script returns that information to the server. At that point, the information is tied in with the
upcoming script. Once the browser is effectively detected, you can
then route it to pages appropriate for the browser type and version.

How to Use

1. Copy the code into your text editor.

2. Save the code as browser_detect.cgi.

3. Place the form in your cgi-bin directory on your server.

4. Change the permissions to make executable by all users:

   ```
   chmod a+x browser_detect.cgi
   ```

browser_detect.cgi

```
#!/usr/bin/perl -wT

$ENV{'PATH'}  = '/bin:/usr/bin:/usr/local/bin';
$ENV{'SHELL'} = '/bin/sh';
$ENV{'ENV'}   = '';
$ENV{'IFS'}   = '';

use lib '/path/to/library';
use Taintcheck;

use CGI;
use strict;
use vars qw($  START    $CGI);

$CGI = "browser_detect.cgi";

eval { main() }; $  START   =    LINE  ;

if ($@) {
  chomp($@);
```

browser_detect.cgi (continued)

```perl
  $@ =~ s/\(eval\) line (\d+)/${CGI} . " line " .
    ($  START  -$1-1)/e;
  $@ =~ s/( at ).*( line )/$1${CGI}$2/;

  my $error_message = $@;

  print <<ERR;
Content-type: text/html

<html>
  <head><title>Error</title></head>
  <body>
    <h1>Error</h1>
    <code>$error_message</code>
  </body>
</html>
ERR

}

exit(0);

# main

sub main {
  my ($q, $ua, $br, $vr, $os);

  $q = new CGI;

  # The web server will set $ENV{'HTTP_USER_AGENT'} with
  # the value reported by the browser
  ($br, $vr, $os) = browser_version($ENV{'HTTP_USER_AGENT'});

  print     $q->header,
    $q->start_html('browser detector'),
    $q->p,
    $ENV{'HTTP_USER_AGENT'},              # echo back the $ENV var.
    $q->p,
    "browser: $br",                       # then print our guesses
    $q->p,
    "version: $vr",
    $q->p,
    "os: $os",
    $q->end_html;

}

# browser_version
# in:  HTTP_USER_AGENT environment variable
# out: browser name, version, and os
# description:
#    uses perl's pattern matching to guess the browser name and
#    version, and the operating system it's running on.
```

browser_detect.cgi (continued)

```perl
sub browser_version {
  my $ua = shift;

  my ($browser, $version, $os, $b, $o);

  # the browser pattern is a hash of arrays.
  # each array in the hash has two values:
  #  1. the pattern that identifies the browser
  #  2. the pattern that identifies the browser version
  my %browser_pat = ( 'Netscape Navigator' =>
                        [ 'mozilla(?!.*?(msie|opera))',
                          'mozilla/([\d.]+)' ],
                      'MS Internet Explorer' =>
                        [ 'compat.*?msie',
                          'mozilla/([\d.]+)' ],
                      'Opera' =>
                        [ 'opera',
                          '(\d+)' ],
                      'Lynx' =>
                        [ 'lynx',
                          'lynx/([\d.\w]+)'] );

  # the OS pattern is a straight forward hash
  my %os_pat     = ( 'Macintosh'    => 'mac',
                     'Windows 9x'   => 'windows.*?9\d',
                     'Windows NT'   => 'windows.*?nt',
                     'Windows 2000' => 'windows.*?2000',
                     'Linux'             => 'linux',

                          # a reasonable guess
                     'Unix'              => 'x11(?!.*linux)' );

  # step through the hash, looking for a match
  foreach $b(keys %browser_pat) {
    if ($ua =~ /$browser_pat{$b}->[0]/i) {
      $browser = $b;
      last;
    }
  }

  # do the same for OS
  foreach $o(keys %os_pat) {
    if ($ua =~ /$os_pat{$o}/i) {
      $os = $o;
      last;
    }
  }

  # then use the matched browser type to
  # determine how to guess the browser version
  if ($ua =~ /$browser_pat{$browser}->[1]/i) {
    $version = $1;
  }

  return ($browser, $version, $os);
}
```

Other Files Needed

To test the script, you can create a simple HTML file that links to it:

1. Open your text editor.

2. Create a standard HTML document.

3. Add a link to the browser_detect.cgi script.

4. Upload the HTML to the appropriate directory on your server.

HTML Document for Browser Detection

```
<html>
<head>
<title>Simple CGI Script</title>
</head>

<body>
<p>
<br/>
<br/>

<div align="center">
<a href="/cgi-bin/browser_detect.cgi">Testing Browser Detect</a>
</div>
</p>
</body>
</html>
```

Once you've got the HTML file loaded onto the server, test the file using your browser. In Figure 6.2, you can see the browser detect information displayed within the browser, this time showing Netscape Navigator, version 4.07, running on Windows 98.

Routing Browsers

Once you've determined the make and model of browser a surfer is using, redirecting her to a page set up for her browser is very easy. Just add the following function to the browser_detect.cgi script.

```
sub route_browser {
  my $q  = shift;
  my $ua = shift;
  my ($br, $vr, $os) = browser_version($ua);

  # default to the page readable by anyone
  my $page = 'text_only.html';

  # this is the most straightforward way to
  # pick the page. You could also set up a hash of hashes
```

```
# organized like browser => version => page, which would
# make this function much shorter.

if ($br eq 'Netscape Navigator') {
  if ($vr >= 4) {
     $page = 'fancy.ns.html';
  } else {
     $page = 'basic.ns.html';
  }
} elsif ($br eq 'MS Internet Explorer') {
  if($vr >= 4) {
     $page = 'fancy.msie.html';
  } else {
     $page = 'basic.msie.html';
  }
} elsif ($br eq 'Opera') {
  $page = 'standard.html';
}

$q->redirect($page);
}
```

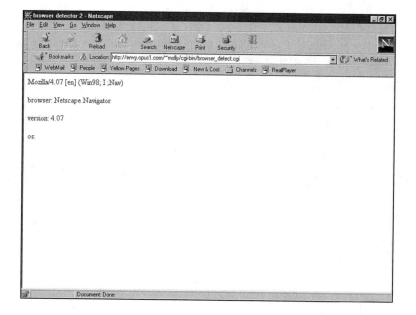

Figure 6.2

The script effectively detects the visiting browser.

How to Use

1. Copy the code into the browser_detect file.

2. Customize the elsif statements to go to the pages of your choice. For example, where we have stated "fancy.ns.html," you'll want to replace with your HTML filename.

3. Save the file.

4. Place the file in your cgi-bin directory on your server.

5. Change the permissions to make executable by all users:

```
chmod a+x browser_detect.cgi
```

At this point, the browser will effectively re-route the browser to the appropriate pages that you've defined.

Cookies

Want a cookie? We prefer chocolate Milanos, and we can assure you that numerous cookies were eaten during the writing of this book!

Cookies have gotten a bad rap. Unschooled individuals think that cookies can steal personal information from them, and then this information can be used for marketing or other purposes by the host site. This isn't entirely true. Cookies retrieve the information, true, but they *save* it to the visitor's computer, not the server. This is why they are generally safe to use.

However, advertisers at several different Web sites *can* use cookies to track your progress from one site to another.

Cookies, in Web development terms, are small scripts that save information to a site visitor's hard drive. This can help the designer customize the way a site behaves during future visits. For example, with cookies, you can create a site that welcomes visitors back by name, tracks purchases, or saves the visitor's place from where they were during the last visit (see Figure 6.2).

For a Perl programmer using CGI.pm, using Netscape's "magic cookies" to keep a bit of information on a user's computer is very easy. Hand-coding your HTTP headers to produce cookies that work can be very difficult, but CGI.pm takes care of all the heavy lifting for you. The same is true for reading cookies. A script to read a cookie from the user's browser can be as short and simple as this:

```perl
#!/usr/bin/perl

use CGI;

my $q = new CGI;

my $cookie = $q->cookie('dwp_test_cookie')
  || "Cookie has not been set";

print  $q->header,
       $q->start_html("Cookie Reader"),
       $q->p, "Cookie: $cookie",
       $q->end_html;
```

Actually, most of that script is dedicated to printing out the Web page that echoes the cookie value, not reading the cookie itself.

Setting a cookie is just as easy. Here's another short example:

```perl
#!/usr/bin/perl

use CGI;

my $q = new CGI;
my $cookie_val = 'Rhododendron Festival';
my $cookie = $q->cookie(-name=>'dwp_test_cookie',
          -value=>$cookie_val);

print $q->header(-cookie=>$cookie),
     $q->start_html("Cookie Writer"),
     $q->p, "Your cookie has been set to $cookie_val",
     $q->p, "Visit the ",
     $q->a({-href=>'read_cookie.cgi'}, "Cookie Reader"),
     " to read your cookie.",
     $q->end_html;
```

Try using these two examples together, to see the cookie in action. If you want to see what you're actually storing in a user's cookie file, take a look at your own after running write_cookie.cgi.

Your cookie file may be in one of many different places, depending on your browser and operating system. Try searching your hard drive for a file named "cookie" and you'll probably find it.

Advanced Guestbook with Cookies

In this example, we show you how to add a cookie to the guestbook you created in Chapter 4, "Working with Forms." What this script does is save the user information so upon next visit, he or she is greeted by name. We fondly call it the "spooky" guestbook, because to the untrained eye, it knows exactly who a return visitor is!

How to Use

1. Copy the code into your text editor.

2. Save the code as guestbook_2.cgi.

3. Transfer the file to your server.

4. Change the permissions as follows:

   ```
   Chmod a+x guestbook_2.cgi
   ```

guestbook_2.cgi

```perl
#!/usr/bin/perl -wT

$ENV{'PATH'}  = '/bin:/usr/bin:/usr/local/bin';
$ENV{'SHELL'} = '/bin/sh';
```

guestbook_2.cgi (continued)

```perl
$ENV{'ENV'}  = '';
$ENV{'IFS'}  = '';

use lib '/usr/local/htdocs/perlbook/chap_05';
use Taintcheck;
use Timefuncs;

use CGI;

use strict;
use vars qw($  START   $CGI $GUESTBOOK);

$CGI       = "guestbook_2.cgi";
$GUESTBOOK = "/path/to/guestbook"; # replace with real path

eval { main() }; $  START   =   LINE  ;

if ($@) {
  chomp($@);

  $@ =~ s/\(eval\) line (\d+)/${CGI} . " line " .
    ($  START   -$1-1)/e;
  $@ =~ s/( at ).*( line )/$1${CGI}$2/;


  my $error_message = $@;

  print <<ERR;
Content-type: text/html

<html>
  <head><title>Error</title></head>
  <body>
    <h1>Error</h1>
    <code>$error_message</code>
  </body>
</html>
ERR

}

exit(0);

# main

sub main {
  my $q = new CGI;

  if ($q->param()) {
    add_entry($q);
  } else {
    display_guestbook($q);
```

guestbook_2.cgi (continued)

```perl
  }
}

# subroutines

# in:  CGI object
# out:
# description:
#  Reads the guestbook file & prints it as html
#
sub display_guestbook {
  my $q = shift;
  my ($html,$e,$num_entries,$entries,$cookie,$thanks);

  $html = $q->header . $q->start_html("My Spooky Guestbook");

  $html .= $q->h1("My Spooky Guestbook");

  open (GB, "<$GUESTBOOK") ||
    die "Unable to read guestbook file " .
        "'$GUESTBOOK' (error: $!). " .
        "Please try again later, or contact " .
        "the webmaster of this site for assistance";

  # get a read lock on the guestbook
  lock_filehandle(\*GB, 'R');

  # read and process the entries
  while (!eof(GB)) {
    my $e = new CGI(\*GB);
    $num_entries++;
    $entries .= draw_guestbook_entry($e);

    # Here's where things get 'spooky': If the user has signed
    # the guestbook, she'll have a cookie set that will tell us
    # when she signed it.
    if ($e->param('cookie') == $q->cookie('sg_signed_at')) {
      $thanks = "<p>Hello, <b>" . $e->param('name') .
          "</b>! Thanks for signing my guestbook on " .
          date_string($e->param('cookie')) . "</p>\n";
    }
  }

  close (GB);

  # Insert the count of entries, and the entries themselves, into
  # the html page

  if ($num_entries) {
    $html .= "<p>Signed $num_entries time" .
          (($num_entries > 1) && ("s"));
    $html .= " &#183; Last signed " .
```

guestbook_2.cgi (continued)

```perl
                 date_string( (file_stats( $GUESTBOOK ))[0] );
    $html .= $thanks if $thanks;
    $html .= $entries . "</p>";
  } else {
    $html .= "<h3>No entries!</h3><hr>";
  }

  $html .= &entry_form($q);
  $html .= $q->end_html;

  print $html;
}

# in:  CGI object
# out:
# description:
#  Adds entry to guestbook file, then prints guestbook html
#  Also sets a cookie with the current time
sub add_entry {
  my $q = shift;
  my ($name,$email,$homepage,$msg,$entry,$url,$cookie);

  $url = $q->url;

  # it's often easier to access parameters than cookies,
  # so save the value here first
  $q->param('cookie', time);

  # then create a cookie, which we'll put in the outgoing
  # http header
  $cookie = $q->cookie(  -name=>'sg_signed_at',
                    -value=>$q->param('cookie') );
  untaint_params($q);

  # write the submission to the guestbook
  open (GB, ">>$GUESTBOOK") ||
    die "Unable to write to guestbook (error: $!). " .
       "Please try again later, or contact the webmaster " .
       "of this site for assistance";

  # get a write lock on the guestbook
  lock_filehandle(\*GB, 'W');

  $q->save(\*GB);

# closing automatically removes the file lock
  close GB;

  # say thanks, with a link back to the questbook
  # here's where the cookie actually gets set on the
  # user's computer
```

guestbook_2.cgi (continued)

```
  print    $q->header( -cookie=>$cookie ),
    $q->start_html("Thanks"),
    $q->h1("Thanks!"),
    $q->h3("Your message has been added to my guestbook."),
    $q->p,
    $q->a({href=>$q->url}, "Go back to the guestbook"),
    $q->end_html;
}
```

The rest of the code is exactly the same as that in the original guestbook.cgi, except that we are also getting the untaint functions from Taintcheck.pm (see Chapter 5, "Features and Functions").

```
# in:  guestbook entry
# out: guestbook entry in html format
# description:
#  Format a guestbook entry as html
#
sub draw_guestbook_entry {
  my $entry = shift;
  my $author;
  # import the params into a namespace, for easy
  # interpolation below.
  $entry->import_names('E');

  # include email & homepage links, if present
  $author = $E::name;
  if ($E::email =~ /(.*?)@((.*?)\.)+.*/) {
    $author = qq|<a href="mailto:$E::email">$E::name</a>|;
  }

  if ($E::homepage) {

    # make sure the homepage url begins with http://
    $E::homepage =~ s|^(http://)*(.*)$|http://$2|;
    $author .= qq| (<a href="$E::homepage">$E::homepage</a>)|;
  }
  return <<ENTRY;
<p><b>$author</b>
<br/>$E::message</p>
<hr/>
ENTRY

}

sub entry_form {
  my $q   = shift;
  my $url = $q->url;
```

Perl Web Site Workshop

```perl
  my $form = <<E_FORM;
<h3>Sign my guestbook:</h3>
<form action="$url" method="post">
<p><b>Name</b>: <input type="text" name="name"/></p>
<p><b>E-mail</b>: <input type="text" name="email"/></p>
<p><b>Homepage</b>: <input type="text" name="homepage"/></p>
<p><b>Message</b>:</p>
<p><textarea cols="30" rows="6" wrap="virtual" name="message"></p>
<p>Type your message here.
</textarea>
<input type="submit"></p>
</form>
E_FORM

  $form;
}

# lock_filehandle
# in: filehandle
# out:
# description: flock()s a filehandle, for concurrency-safe access
sub lock_filehandle {
  my $fh   = shift;
  my $lock = shift;

  use Fcntl qw(:flock);

  my $lock_code;

  if ($lock =~ /^r/i) {
    $lock_code = LOCK_SH;
  } elsif ($lock =~ /^w/i) {
    $lock_code = LOCK_EX;
  } else {
    $lock_code = LOCK_UN;
  }

  # give it two tries
  unless (flock ($fh, $lock_code | LOCK_NB)) {
    unless (flock($fh, $lock_code)) {
      die "flock: could not get $lock lock on $GUESTBOOK";
    }
  }

  return 1;
}
```

Figure 6.3 shows the personalized greeting upon return, courtesy of the cookie saved to Molly's hard drive.

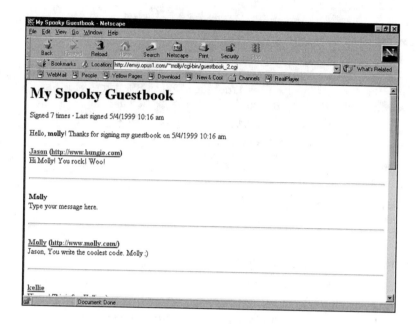

Figure 6.3
The personalized results.

Using Perl with SSI

Up to this point, we've covered CGIs that produce whole HTML pages. But this isn't the only thing CGI can do. Alhough the output of a CGI must comprise a complete HTTP conversation—so you can't, for the most part, stick a CGI in the middle of an otherwise static page—you can play some "stupid Web server tricks" to get dynamic content into an otherwise static page.

A very easy way to do this is to enable server-side includes (SSIs) in your Apache setup. Usually, this is set up by your system administrator. Check with your ISP to see if you can use server-side includes. We've included some simple information to help you set up an Apache server to handle SSIs.

SSI is most often used to include pieces of static HTML within other static HTML pages—for example, to put a standard navigation bar on all the pages of a site, without having to code that bar on each individual page.

You can also use SSI to run CGI scripts. This section will teach you how to set up Apache to enable SSI, and a selection of short examples of what SSI will let you do.

Apache isn't the only server that can handle SSIs. You'll need to check with your server documentation or your systems administrator for more information if you're working with a server other than Apache and would like to use SSIs.

Setting Up Apache to Enable SSIs

Here's what you need in your Apache httpd.conf to enable SSI. First, in each <Directory> section in which you'd like SSI to be active, make sure the Options line includes +Includes. To use SSI across your site, you can edit your main site root <Directory> section like this:

```
<Directory "/path/to/site/root">     Options Indexes
FollowSymLinks ExecCGI +Includes
```

Then you'll have to tell the server which files to process through the SSI systems:

```
AddType text/html .shtml
AddHandler server-parsed .shtml
```

Including Time and Date

Many sites want to include the current date and time on a page. Using SSI, this is very easy. First, you'll create the echo_date.cgi script, upload it, and set the appropriate permissions on the file, just as you would any other CGI file.

echo_date.cgi

```
#!/usr/bin/perl -w

use lib '/path/to/library';
use Timefuncs;
print "Content-type: text/html\n\n", &date_string(time);
```

The backward single quotes around /usr/games/fortune are called "backticks," they're a shorthand way of running another program on the system and reading the output from that program. You can do this with just about anything, from games like fortune, to system utilities like netstat and ps. Ain't Unix great?

To include this script in a page, you'd add this to your HTML:

```
<!--#include virtual="/path/to/echo_date.cgi" -->
```

Now, rename the page with an .shtml extension. When a visitor pulls up this page, it will echo the time and date.

Randomizing a Quote

If you'd like to liven up your home page with a random quote or two, and you're using a Unix server with the fortune command (a just-for-fun command that will respond to the command with a quotation) available, just add an SSI for this little script:

fortune.cgi

```perl
#!/usr/bin/perl

print "Content-type: text/html\n\n";

$f = `/usr/games/fortune`;        # run fortune & get the output
$f =~ s/\n/<br\/>\n/g;            # replace newlines with <br/>

print $f;
```

Last Modification of Page

A more useful date and time, for your Web site users, than the current time, is often the last modification time of the page they're browsing. Luckily, the Web server sets an environment variable with just that information.

last_mod.cgi

```perl
#!/usr/bin/perl
print "Content-type: text/html\n\n", $ENV{'LAST_MODIFIED'};
```

The native formatting of the modification date might not be the format you want your users to see. So, to get a different format, you could either get the stats on the file yourself and use the date_string() function, or you could use the Date::Manip module from CPAN, which can interpret and output all kinds of date and time formatting, to rewrite the environment variable into a format you like.

Playing with Random Images

Everything we've done so far in Perl has dealt with reading and writing text; but Perl isn't limited to working with text. Here's an example of how to work with images. We used JPEGs in this example, but you can use other Web graphics such as GIFs for your random process.

You can use this script in a page by setting the source (src) attribute of an image tag, like this:

```
<img src="/path/to/random_img.cgi">
```

This is a simple example; it just picks a random image from a pre-defined directory. But you could easily extend it to serve rotating banner ads, or, as we'll see later on, to draw the images itself, instead of reading pre-built images from disk.

If your Web server doesn't support SSI, or your Webmaster or site administrator won't let you activate it, you can still do some cool stuff. The only proviso is that you have to do it with images or JavaScript. Why? Because images and JavaScripts are the only standard ways to insert the contents of one HTTP conversation into the results of another; or, in less geeky terms, to put a piece of one page into another.

random_img.cgi

```perl
#!/usr/bin/perl

# print the http header -- for an image in this case
print "Content-type: image/jpeg\n\n";

$IMAGE_DIR = 'images';   # the directory where our images are, often
#a subdirectory of the root directory

# open the image dir, or output an error, which will wind up
# in apache's error log. The $! variable contains the system
# error message.
opendir (IMGD, $IMAGE_DIR) || die "Could not open image dir: $!";

# select only the .jpeg images in the directory,
# and only the ones we're allowed to read
@images = grep { /\.jpeg$/ && (-r "$IMAGE_DIR/$_") } readdir IMGD;
closedir IMGD;

# pick a random image
$img_num = int(rand(scalar @images));
$img_file = "$IMAGE_DIR/" . $images[$img_num];

# open the image file
open (IMG, "mg_file") || die "Could not open image file: $!";
```

random_img.cgi (continued)

```
# set the image filehandle to binary mode, since we're
# reading a binary file
binmode(IMG);

# clear the end of line marker, so that we
# can load the image file in one slurp, only do it
# for the duration of this block though.
{
   local $/=undef;
   print <IMG>; # read and output the image file
}

# clean up after ourselves
close IMG;
```

Of course, if you want to, you can use SSI instead of loading the image yourself. SSI is more convenient and less complicated than CGI, but it can also be less secure without a skilled administrator who can set up the server to avoid security problems.

To use the SSI version of random image, you'll need to insert an HTML image tag like this into your page:

```
<img src="<!--#include virtual="rand_img_name.cgi" -->">
```

rand_img_name.cgi

```
#!/usr/bin/perl

# print the http header -- for an image in this case
print "Content-type: text/plain\n\n";

$IMAGE_DIR = 'images';    # the directory where our images are

# open the image dir, or output an error, which will wind up
# in apache's error log. The $! variable contains the system
# error message.
opendir (IMGD, $IMAGE_DIR) || die "Could not open image dir: $!";
@images = grep { /\.jpeg$/ && (-r "$IMAGE_DIR/$_") } readdir IMGD;
closedir IMGD;

$img_num = int(rand(scalar @images));
$img_file = "$IMAGE_DIR/" . $images[$img_num];

print $img_file;
```

The Whole Kit 'n' Kaboodle

Here's an example Web page that uses all the earlier scripts. We've provided a shot of the randomized results in Figure 6.4.

ssi_test.shtml

```
<html>
<head><title>SSI Test page</title></head>
<body>

<h1>SSI Test pages</h1>
<p>
Echo date: <!--#include virtual="echo_date.cgi" -->
</p>
<p>
Last modified: <!--#include virtual="last_mod.cgi" -->
</p>
<p>
Random quote: <br/>
 <!--#include virtual="fortune.cgi" -->
</p>
<p>
<img src="<!--#include virtual="rand_img_name.cgi"-->">
</p>
<p>
A Random image, with the source from SSI.
<p>
<p>
<img src="random_img.cgi">
</p>
<p>
A random image, image data from CGI.
</p>
<p>
Perl ENV values: <!--#include virtual="print_env.cgi" -->
</p>
</body>
</html>
```

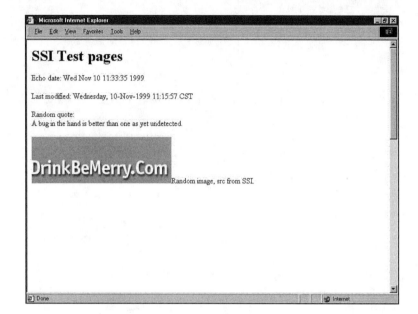

Figure 6.4

In this image, we show the top portion results of the Whole Kit 'n' Kaboodle example: date, modification date, a random quote, and a random image.

What's Up Next

It's time for some entertainment! Chapter 7, "Fun and Games," will provide a relaxing and enjoyable journey through scripts that allow you to use Perl for fun and games. Of course, there's a method to our madness: We're giving you this entertainment break before we really put you through your paces with more aggressive Perl scripts.

Fun and Games

Everyone needs a break now and then, and this chapter will show you how to give your site visitors some much-needed R&R. Of course, although you can use all these scripts for fun, most can be applied for serious reasons, too.

We'll look at a couple of scripts that allow you to display time and page hits using GD, a Perl interface that lets you draw pictures and use lines, shapes, and text.

Then, we'll move on to an interactive script for fun and function: a user poll. This script allows you to give a site visitor a multiple-choice list of options based on your own content. The script records the votes, and then displays the results in a nice bar graph. Whether a *Cosmopolitan*-style love vote or a serious political poll, this script is very good whenever you'd like to add interactivity to your site.

Finally, we'll show you how to create the much-loved game of Hangman. A bit more complex than the other scripts in this chapter, you'll see how Perl can be used not only to create an interactive interface for a user, but store information intelligently, behind the scenes.

Displaying Time

If you'd like to add a digital clock to your page, you can do so using this CGI program. It taps into the power of GD, a Perl interface for graphics. GD should already be in existence on your server, but if it's not, a visit to CPAN will help you get the module.

Unisys, the company that owns the patent on LZW compression used in GIFs and other file formats, sued the author of GD. Now only .png or .jpg files can be generated by GD. Because many browsers cannot render .png files, we're going to use .jpg files.

How to Use

1. Copy the clock.cgi code into your text editor.

2. Set the path to the library where GD resides.

3. Save the code as clock.cgi and upload it to your cgi-bin. Once there, set permissions: **chmod a+x clock.cgi**.

clock.cgi

```perl
#!/usr/bin/perl

use lib '/path/to/library';
use GD;
use POSIX;   # For the date pretty-printing

$img = new GD::Image(71,16);

$black = $img->colorAllocate(0,0,0);
$green = $img->colorAllocate(0,200,10);

$img->fill(0,0,$black);

$readout=POSIX::strftime("%I:%M %P", localtime time);

$img->string(gdSmallFont,3,1,$readout,$green);

# send the image to the browser
# the Expires: header will keep browser's from caching it,
# ensuring that users always see an accurate clock (or at least
# a recently updated one)
binmode STDOUT;
print "Expires: now\n","Content-type: image/jpeg\n\n",$img->jpeg;
```

Other Files Needed

You'll want to create a simple HTML file so you can see the script in
action. To do so:

1. Open your text editor.

2. Create a standard HTML document.

3. Add an image link to the script, such as `<img src="/cgi-bin/clock.cgi">`.

4. Upload the HTML to the appropriate directory on your server.

HTML Document Example for clock.cgi

```
<html>
<head>
<title>What Time is It?</title>
</head>

<body>
<p>
<br/>
<br/>

<div align="center">

<img src="/cgi-bin/clock.cgi">
</p>
</body>
</html>
```

Once you've got the HTML file loaded onto the server, test the file using your browser to make sure everything is working properly (Figure 7.1).

Figure 7.1

The time clock in action.

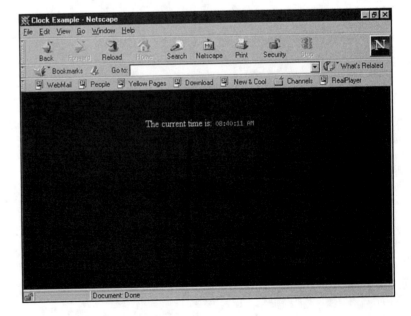

Hit Counter

Everyone is familiar with the ubiquitous hit counter. Hit counters say to the world "Look at my page! I've had this many visitors."

Appropriate mostly for home pages, hit counters are a lot of fun, especially for HTML newcomers. This hit counter is a bit more sophisticated than many of those out there on the Web. It automatically figures out which page it's on, using the HTTP_REFERER environment variable.

Global Variables Used in counter.cgi

This script includes some global variables we'd like to introduce you to at this point. These variables are used in any scripts that require them.

- `# referring pages must come from one of these hosts @HOSTS_ALLOW = ('localhost');` This variable is an array of host-names that you want to allow the CGI script to reside on. It works with `@DIRS_ALLOW` to make sure that the counter is only incremented when it's actually used on a page *on your server*, not just when someone types the URL or includes your counter on a page in their server.

- `# referring pages must be under one of these dirs # DO NOT begin paths with / @DIRS_ALLOW = ('perlbook/ chap_games');` This code works with the HOSTS_ALLOW variable to achieve the restricted increment described above.

- `$FIGURES = 6;` This variable sets how many numbers you want the counter to be. For example, if the variable is set to 6, your results would look like this: `000026`. If you set this variable to 4, your results would be: `0026`.

- `$FONT = gdGiantFont;` This variable is specific to GD, and sets the font that the counter will use to display the numbers.

- `$STATS = 'stats'; @BG = (0, 0, 0); @FG =(50, 200, 255);` This is the name of the DBM database that will store your page statistics. `@BG` is the background color of the counter (in red, green, and blue) and `@FG` is the foreground color.

How to Use

1. Copy the counter.cgi code into your text editor.

2. Set the path to the library where GD resides.

This script uses Perl's built-in SDBM database to store the hit counts for each page. SDBM is a simple database that comes with Perl and most Unix and related operating systems. SDBM allows you to quickly store and retrieve items in key->value pairs. For example, if you had a database of cartoon character last names, the key would be "Fred" and the corresponding value would be "Flintstone." For faster performance, use the **GDBM_File** or **DB_File** modules from CPAN. If you decide to use one of those, you'll have to update the **tie** statements in the script to use the module you choose, according to its perldoc documentation.

Save the code as counter.cgi and upload it to your cgi-bin.
Once there, set permissions on the file, **chmod a+x
counter.cgi.**

counter.cgi
_____

```perl
#!/usr/bin/perl

$| = 1;    # don't buffer script output

use lib '/path/to/library';
use GD;
use SDBM_File;
use Fcntl;

use strict;
use vars qw(@HOSTS_ALLOW @DIRS_ALLOW
            $FIGURES $FONT $STATS @BG @FG);

# referring pages must come from one of these hosts
@HOSTS_ALLOW = ('www.yourhost.com');   # set to your host

# referring pages must be under one of these dirs
# DO NOT begin paths with /
@DIRS_ALLOW  = ('');                    # leave blank for all

$FIGURES     = 6;                       # size of counter
$FONT        = gdGiantFont;
$STATS       = '/path/to/stats';        # path to stats SDBM file
@BG          = (0, 0, 0);               # background color
@FG          = (50, 200, 255);          # digit color

&main();

sub main {
  my ($img, $x_size,$y_size,$string,
      $ref, %stats, $count,$bg,$fg);

  # calculate the image size, based on size of chosen font
  $x_size = ($FONT->width * $FIGURES) + 4;
  $y_size = $FONT->height +2;
  $img    = new GD::Image($x_size,$y_size);

  $bg = $img->colorAllocate(@BG);
  $fg = $img->colorAllocate(@FG);

  $img->fill(0,0,$bg);

  # who's calling?
  $ref = $ENV{'HTTP_REFERER'};

  if (allowed_page($ref)) {
    tie(%stats, 'SDBM_File', $STATS, O_CREAT|O_RDWR, 0666)
      || die "no tie: $!";
```

```
      $stats{$ref}++;
      $count = $stats{$ref};
      untie %stats;

      # make the string, padded with 0's on the front
      $string = '0' x ($FIGURES - length("$count")) . $count;

      # add string to image
      $img->string($FONT,2,1,$string,$fg);

      # output to browser
      binmode STDOUT;
      print "Expires: now\n",
            "Content-type: image/gif\n\n", $img->gif;

   }
}

sub allowed_page {
  my $ref = shift;

  my ($host, $path, $h_ok, $p_ok);

  if ($ref =~ m|http://([^/]+)/(.*)|i) {
    $host = $1;
    $path = $2;
  }

  $h_ok = $p_ok = 0;

  foreach my $h(@HOSTS_ALLOW) {
    if ($h =~ /^$host$/i) {
      $h_ok = 1;
      last;
    }
  }

  foreach my $p(@DIRS_ALLOW) {
    if ($path =~ m|^$p|) {
      $p_ok = 1;
      last;
    }
  }

  return ($h_ok && $p_ok);
}
```

Other Files Needed

As with clock.cgi, you'll need an HTML document into which to add
the call to the counter. You can use any document within your Web
site, or even more than one! We recommend sticking with one—usually

You'll want to configure the counter itself to prevent someone from swiping it. Set the allowed hosts to include *at least* the name of your Web server, and the allowed directories to include only the directories whose pages you'll put the counter on.

your entry page—unless you have a special reason to want to use the script on another page within your site.

1. Open your text or HTML editor.

2. Open or create an HTML document into which you'll be placing the counter.

3. Add a link to the script, using the image tag, `<img src="/cgi-bin/counter.cgi">`

4. Upload the HTML page (or pages) to the directory on your server.

5. Test your page! Your results should be similar to ours (see Figure 7.2).

Figure 7.2

The hit counter will tally how many hits your page receives

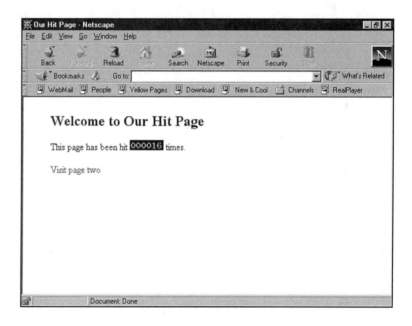

HTML Document Example for clock.cgi

```
<html>
<head>
<title>Molly's Way Cool Web Page</title>
</head>

<body bgcolor="#000000" text="#FFCC99" link="#FF9933" vlink="#CC6633"
alink="#FF9933">
```

HTML Document Example for clock.cgi (continued)

```
<blockquote>

<font face="arial, helvetica, sans-serif">
<p>
Hey, everyone!
<br/>
</p><p>
Welcome to my Way Cool Web Page. Be sure to look around, I'm adding
stuff all the time. Also, don't hesitate to <a
href="mailto:molly@molly.com">drop
me a line</a> if you have any suggestions for the site.
</p>
<p>
<a href="index2.html">Go to the next page . . . </a>
</p>

<div align="center">

<img src="/cgi-bin/counter.cgi">
</div>
</font>
</blockquote>
</body>
</html>
```

Use counters sparingly and only when necessary. They're fun, but many veteran Web surfers find them tiresome. Besides, the best statistics come directly from your server or statistic software, which gives you a lot of accurate information about not only how many people are visiting your site, but from where, using what browser, and so forth.

User Poll

Most folks love taking polls. All kinds of sites can benefit from a poll of this nature, whether it's for pure entertainment (see Figure 7.3), or the results are attempting to express some specific viewpoint.

How to Use

To set up your user poll, you'll need to first install quickpoll.cgi in your cgi-bin directory. You'll then create a couple of polls, and the templates the CGI uses.

Essentially, the relationship is pretty straightforward. The site visitor inputs his or her answers into the poll page, and submits the answers. The poll script then filters the input, deciding what to do with it. Any information that should be collated and presented back to the site visitor with results is done so, and the results will be sent to the browser in a bar graph or other layout.

Figure 7.3

The Cookie Crazy poll.

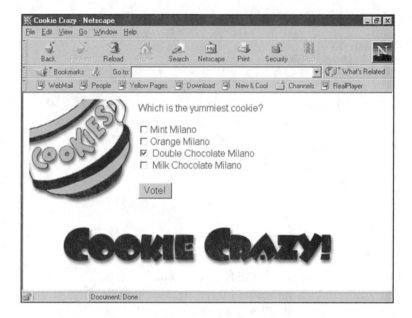

To set up your polls, first create a poll directory somewhere outside of your htdocs tree. Then, for each poll, you'll create a subdirectory in your poll directory with the name of the poll. In our example, the poll directory is /usr/home/molly/polls, and our first poll is in /usr/home/molly/polls/cookie. Make each poll directory world-writable (see Chapter 3, "Scripting Basics"), and put a custom file, which you'll call poll.conf, in each one.

Your directory structure will look something like this:

```
polls/
    pollone/
        poll.conf
        votes
    polltwo/
        poll.conf
        votes
```

The poll.conf is your text file, and the votes is the DBM (database file) that manages your votes. The format of the poll.conf file is simple.

poll.conf

```
Q: Which is the yummiest cookie?
A: Mint Milano
A: Orange Milano
A: Double Chocolate Milano
A: Milk Chocolate Milano

# description
Who loves cookies?
```

Of course, you can (and should!) modify the poll.conf file to contain as many questions and answers as you like.

The CGI script is a bit long, so we'll take it piece by piece. Let's start with the standard security settings, and the eval{} block to catch any script errors.

quickpoll.cgi

```perl
#!/usr/bin/perl -wT

$ENV{'PATH'} = '/bin:/usr/bin:/usr/local/bin';
$ENV{'SHELL'} = '/bin/sh';
$ENV{'ENV'} = '';
$ENV{'IFS'} = '';

use lib '/path/to/library';
use Taintcheck;

use CGI;
use CGI::FastTemplate;
use SDBM_File;
use Fcntl;

use strict;
use vars qw( $CGI $_START  $POLL_DIR $TMPL_DIR);

# GLOBALS

$CGI      = 'quickpoll.cgi';
$POLL_DIR = '/path/to/polls';       # path to polls dir
$TMPL_DIR = '/path/to/templates';   # path to templates dir

# MAIN
```

quickpoll.cgi (continued)

```perl
eval { main(); };

# ERRORS

if ($@) {

  print "Content-type: text/html\n\n",
        "uh-oh: $@";

}
```

Let's take a look at the main subroutine. This is basically a dispatcher, determining from the script input whether to display the poll ballot, record a vote, or show the poll results.

```perl
sub main {
  my $q = new CGI;
  my ($do, $poll, %polls, $page);

  die "No input to $CGI" unless $q->param;

  # check input
  &untaint_params($q);

  # build list of polls in $POLL_DIR
  %polls = get_polls($POLL_DIR);

  # for convenience
  $do = $q->param('do');
  $poll = $q->param('poll');

  # make sure the poll exists
  die "Unknown poll ($poll)" unless exists($polls{$poll});

  # handle different actions

  if ($do eq 'vote') {

    record_vote($q,$poll);
    $page = show_results($q,$polls{$poll});

  } elsif ($do eq 'results') {

    $page = show_results($q,$polls{$poll});

  } else {

    $page = show_ballot($q,$polls{$poll});

  }

  print $q->header, $page;
}
```

Recording the actual votes is the simplest part of the script. tie
makes it easy: We just increment the DBM record keyed by the value
of the vote.

```perl
sub record_vote {
  my $q        = shift;
  my $poll_name = shift;
  my %votes;

  # connect to DBM file storing votes
  tie (%votes, 'SDBM_File',
      "$POLL_DIR/$poll_name/votes", O_CREAT|O_RDWR, 0666)
        || die "Could not write to $POLL_DIR/$poll_name/votes";

  # increment my vote
  $votes{$q->param('vote')}++;

  # save to disk
  untie %votes;
}
```

Of course, you don't want to keep your poll results a secret, so you'll
want to display them on a nice page, with a lovely bar graph. To
make the output customizable, we make use of CGI::FastTemplate.
Templates will be covered more in depth in Chapter 8.

```perl
sub show_results {
  my $q    = shift;
  my $poll = shift;

  my ($poll_name, $tpl, %votes, $total,
      $answer, $num, $pct, $block, $p);

  # how many pixels each pct point counts for
  # in the bar graph
  $block = 2;
  $poll_name = $q->param('poll');

  $tpl = new CGI::FastTemplate;
  $tpl->set_root($TMPL_DIR);

  # get the results template
  $tpl->define( 'results', 'quickpoll_results.html' );

  # and the result row
  $tpl->define( 'rows', 'quickpoll_row.html' );

  # connect to votes data
  tie (%votes, 'SDBM_File',
      "$POLL_DIR/$poll_name/votes", O_RDONLY, 0666)
        || die "Could not read votes for $poll_name";
```

```perl
# get vote totals
for my $a(0..$#{$poll->{'ANSWERS'}}) {
  $total += $votes{$a};
}

# construct the rows, one for each answer
for my $a(0..$#{$poll->{'ANSWERS'}}) {

  $answer = $poll->{'ANSWERS'}->[$a];
  $num    = $votes{$a} || 0;
  $pct    = 0;

  # watch for the old divide by 0!
  ($total)  && ($pct = int(($num/$total) * 100));

  $tpl->assign( 'ANSWER' => $answer,
        'NUM'    => $num,
        'PCT'    => $pct,
        'WIDTH'  => ($pct * $block)+1 );

  $tpl->parse( 'ROWS' => '.rows' );

}

# and the main page
$tpl->assign($poll);
$tpl->parse('MAIN'=>'results');

$p = $tpl->fetch('MAIN');

if (($p) && (($$p)) {
  return $$p;
}
}
```

To get any votes, you need to show a ballot. Again, we use CGI::FastTemplate to allow easy customization of the ballot page.

```perl
sub show_ballot {
  my $q    = shift;
  my $poll = shift;

  my ($tpl, $answers, $p);
  $tpl = new CGI::FastTemplate;
  $tpl->set_root($TMPL_DIR);

  $tpl->define( 'ballot', 'quickpoll_ballot.html' );

  for my $a(0..$#{$poll->{'ANSWERS'}}) {
    $answers .= "<input type=\"radio\" " .
                "name=\"vote\" value=\"$a\"/>" .
                  $poll->{'ANSWERS'}->[$a] . "<br>\n";
  }
```

```
# save the HTML code into the variable
# that will appear in the template
$poll->{'ANSWERS'} = $answers;
$poll->{'POLL'}    = $q->param('poll');

$tpl->assign( $poll );

$tpl->parse( 'MAIN' => 'ballot' );

$p = $tpl->fetch('MAIN');

if (($p) && ($$p)) {
  return $$p;
}
}
```

We also need to take care of some "bookkeeping"—reading the various poll.conf files from the directories in the polls directory, so that we know what questions to ask for each poll.

```
# The $POLL_DIR contains other directories, each one
# corresponding to a poll. Within those directories are two
# files, one a regular text file, poll.conf, the other
# a DBM file, votes.
#
sub get_polls {
  my $dir = shift;

  my (@dirs, %polls);

  # get dirs in poll dir
  opendir (PLDR, $dir) || die "Could not open poll dir $dir";

  # use grep to pick out directories, except those that begin
  # with a dot (.), from the contents of $dir; and from those,
  # only include the directories that contain a poll.conf file
  @dirs = grep { (-d "$dir/$_") &&
                 !(/^\./)        &&
                 (-r "$dir/$_/poll.conf") } readdir PLDR;

  closedir PLDR;

  # build a hash of poll name => poll configuration
  foreach my $d (@dirs) {
    $polls{$d} =  read_poll_conf("$dir/$d");
  }

  return %polls;
}

sub read_poll_conf {
  my $dir = shift;
```

```perl
  my (%conf,$fld,$val,$tmp);

  open (CONF, "$dir/poll.conf")
    || die "Could not read $dir/poll.conf";

  while (<CONF>) {
    chomp;
    next if /^#/;      # skip comments
    next if /^\s*$/;   # and blank lines

    # the question starts with Q:, and there can only be one
    if (/^Q.*?:\s+(.*)$/) {
      $conf{'QUESTION'} = $1;

    # answers start with A:, and there can be a bunch
    } elsif (/^A.*?:\s+(.*)$/) {
      $tmp = $conf{'ANSWERS'};
      $tmp ||= [];
      push @$tmp, $1;
      $conf{'ANSWERS'} = [ @$tmp ];

    # anything else is part of the optional description
    } else {
      $conf{'DESCRIPTION'} .= $_;
    }
  }

  die "Bad poll conf"
    unless ($conf{'QUESTION'} && ($conf{'ANSWERS'}));

  return \%conf;
}
```

Wshew! Got all that? Great! Now you'll want to create some HTML templates for the poll's interface.

First, let's create the ballot template form.

quickpoll_ballot.html

```html
<html>
<head><title>The Great Cookie Vote</title></head>
<body>

<p>$QUESTION<br/></p>
<p>
<form action="/cgi-bin/quickpoll.cgi" method="post">
<input type="hidden" name="do" value="vote"/>
<input type="hidden" name="poll" value="$POLL"/>
$ANSWERS
</p><p><input type="submit" value="Vote!"/></p>
</form>

</body>
</html>
```

Modify this file to match your design needs, using backgrounds, colors, and any other form fields necessary.

Now, let's create the results template. This template will hold all the information from the final results.

quickpoll_results.html

```
<html>
<head><title>Poll Results</title></head>
<body>

<p>$QUESTION</p>

<table>

$ROWS

</table>

</body>
</html>
```

This subtemplate will be repeated once for each answer in the poll, and sent to the quickpoll_results.html page.

quickpoll_row.html

```
<tr>
  <td><b>$ANSWER</b></td>
  <td><img src="blue.gif" height="12" width="$WIDTH" align="left"/>
      ( $NUM / ${PCT}% )
  </td>
</tr>
```

Figure 7.3 (shown at the beginning of this script segment) shows the poll within the context of a Web page.

Hang That Man!

Our meatiest script in this chapter is the classic Hangman game (see Figure 7.4). This script illustrates a very important technique in CGI programming: saving state. The saving state concept is very important to learn and understand in general, and it's easy to envision it through the demonstration of this game.

A cool way to use the poll is in an SSI include—that way you can include the ballot, or the results, inside of another page very easily. See Chapter 6, "Customizing Pages," for more information on SSIs.

Figure 7.4

Playing Hangman.

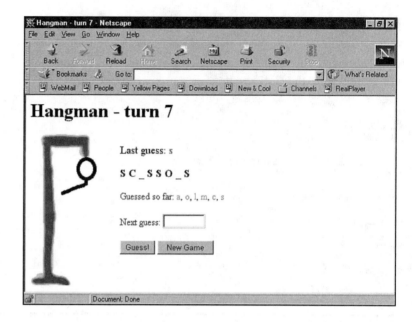

Because HTTP is a stateless protocol, you don't have a built-in way of knowing whether the person accessing this CGI is starting a new game or continuing an old one, or where he left off in that old game.

To deal with that, some kind of session tracking is required. This helps the program remember who is playing what game, and how he's doing. Tracking allows the game to send the user back the correct information when he makes his next move.

There are several ways to accomplish a save state. Some are easy, but offer less security; others are very secure, but quite difficult.

In this example, we use the most straightforward means of achieving the tracking goal that also prevents the most obvious means of cheating. We use a client-side cookie, and a server-side session record keyed to the value of that cookie. This game session ID tells us the sequence of moves that a specific player is playing now. As a result, the client's browser remembers what game is being played, and the server remembers what is happening—which moves are being made (and have already be made) in that specific game.

How to Use

1. Download the script. Note that we've broken it up into descriptive chunks here to make it easier to follow along.

2. Put the script in an appropriate directory on your server. Set permissions for the script, **a+x hangman.cgi.**

3. Create a word list file. Place one word per line, and watch your spelling!

4. Create the individual gallows images necessary to build the hangman.

hang_words.txt

```
chihuahua
ostrich
chimp
cookie
perl
weasel
plastic
bonus
scissors
dynamite
```

hangman.cgi

```perl
#!/usr/bin/perl -wT

$| = 1;  # don't buffer output

$ENV{'PATH'}  = '/bin:/usr/bin:/usr/local/bin:';
$ENV{'SHELL'} = '/bin/sh';
$ENV{'ENV'}   = '';
$ENV{'IFS'}   = '';

use lib '/path/to/library';
use Taintcheck;

use CGI;
use SDBM_File;
use Fcntl;
use FreezeThaw qw(freeze thaw); # to store game state in DBM file

use strict;
use vars qw($CGI $ START   $WORDS
            $SESSIONS $GALLOWS $BODY_PARTS);
```

hangman.cgi (continued)

```
# GLOBALS
$CGI        = 'hangman.cgi';
$WORDS      = '/path/to/words';            # your words file
$SESSIONS   = '/path/to/games';            # game sessions dbm
$GALLOWS    = '/path/to/gallows/images';   # gallows images
$BODY_PARTS = 7;                           # number of images

# MAIN
eval{ main(); }; $ START  =  LINE ;

# ERRORS
if ($@) {
  chomp($@);

  $@ =~ s/\(eval\) line (\d+)/${CGI} .
      " line " . ($ START  -$1-1)/e;
  $@ =~ s/( at ).*( line )/$1${CGI}$2/;

  my $error_message = $@;

  print <<ERR;
Content-type: text/html

<hmtl>
  <head><title>Error</title></head>
  <body>
    <h1>Error</h1>
    <code>$error_message</code>
  </body>
</html>
ERR

}
```

At this point, the script has to try to restore the state of the player's game before figuring out what to do next.

To restore the state, the script must deal with four different possibilities:

- There's no input

- The player has chosen to start a new game

- The game session ID submitted is invalid

- The game session ID submitted is valid

In all but the last case, we'll start a new game. For the last, we'll load the game state from the stats DBM file and try to restore that state. The following code handles starting a new game.

```
# SUBROUTINES
sub main {
  my $q = new CGI;

  untaint_params($q);

  my $game;

  # No input? must be a new game
  unless ($q->param) {
    new_game($q);
    return;
  }

  # we also want to provide a way to start a new game
  # explicitly
  if ($q->param('submit') =~ /new game/i) {

    $q->delete_all();    # clear all params
    &new_game($q);

  } elsif ($q->param('session_id')) {

    # try to restore the past game state
    die "Game id out of date or incorrect (" .
      ($q->param('session_id')) .
      "). Please start a new game."
        unless ($game = restore_game($q->param('session_id')));

    continue_game($game,$q);
  } else {

    # something has gone wrong -- probably bad input
    die "No game id submitted. Please start a new game.";
  }
}
```

Restoring a game is fairly straightforward. The game state is stored
as a record in a DBM file, which makes it easy to quickly retrieve the
full record. Of course, we must know the record key (which in this
case we've set as the game session ID).

The formatting of the game record is left to another useful module
called FreezeThaw. We need FreezeThaw because we can't store the
hash we use as a game record in a DBM database directly. Only
scalar values (strings or numbers) can be used as DBM keys and
records. FreezeThaw translates complex Perl data types into strings,
and then back again, so it makes it easy to use the data format we
want, without having to worry about the minutiae of storing it in
string format and reading back out again.

FreezeThaw is not part of the standard Perl distribution, so you will have to download it from CPAN and install it.

```perl
# restore_game
#
# given a session id, load the session record
# from the DBM file, and restore the game state
sub restore_game {
  my $id = shift;
  my (%sessions, %game);

  return unless $id;

  tie(%sessions, 'SDBM_File', $SESSIONS, O_RDONLY, 0666)
    || die "Could not open game session data";

  return unless $sessions{$id};

  %game = thaw($sessions{$id});

  return unless ($game{'word'} && $game{'status'});

  return \%game;
}
```

Once the game state is restored, we have to change it to reflect the player's next move, and then save it again. FreezeThaw makes saving the state of the move quite easy, but calculating the new state from the old is somewhat complex.

If the player has made a new guess, we need to figure out whether she has guessed right or wrong, and whether she's won or lost. If she hasn't guessed, or if she's continuing a game that has just begun, we only need to send her a screen showing the current state of things.

```perl
# continue_game
#
# append the new guess to the guess list,
# save the new game state, and produce
# the correct output page
sub continue_game {
  my $game = shift;
  my $q    = shift;

  my ($id,$tmp,$g);

  eval {

    if ((ref $q) && ($q->param)) {

      if ($q->param('guess')) {

        $g = $q->param('guess');
```

```
      # here's another way of finding out if
      # a value is a member of an array
      $tmp = ':' . join(':', @{$game->{'guesses'}}) . ':';
      die "You already guessed $g!" if ($tmp =~ /:$g:/i);
        push @{$game->{'guesses'}}, $g;

      # now the fun part -- did we win, lose,
      # match, or mismatch?
      $game->{'status'} = take_turn($game);

      # save state for next time
      save_game_state($q->param('session_id'),$game);

      # and output results
      draw_game_page($q,$game);

    } else {

      # nothing was guessed, just echo back the last page
      draw_game_page($q,$game);

    }

  } else {
    $id = save_game_state(undef, $game);
    draw_game_page($q, $game, $id);
  }

};

if ($@) {
  chomp($@);
  gameplay_error($q,$@);
}
}
```

Saving the game is the flip side of restoring, and just as simple—not
quite as simple as starting a whole new game, though.

```
sub save_game_state {
  my $session_id = shift;
  my $game_state = shift;;

  my (%sessions);

  tie(%sessions, 'SDBM_File', $SESSIONS, O_CREAT|O_RDWR, 0666)
    || die "Failed to open game sessions data";

  unless ($session_id) {
    $session_id = time;

    while ($sessions{$session_id}) {
      $session_id++;
    }
  }
```

```
    $sessions{$session_id}   = freeze(%$game_state);

    untie %sessions;

    return $session_id;
}
# new_game
#
# pick a random word from the words file,
# and generate a new session id and a new
# record in the sessions DBM file
sub new_game {
  my $q = shift;
  my (%game);

  $game{'word'}    = pick_word();
  $game{'status'}  = 'new';
  $game{'guesses'} = [];

  &continue_game(\%game, $q);
}
```

The function `take_turn` is the real heart of the game: It is where the
game state is updated to reflect the player's last guess.

We have to jump through some hoops to make the game behave the
way we expect Hangman to behave. We want to be able to guess a
single letter, or the whole word, but not a substring (for example, we
can't guess "cat" in "catamaran" and have it recorded as a hit). And,
of course, we want to win when we've matched the whole word,
whether letter-by-letter or all at once, and to lose when we've had
more bad guesses than the hanging man has body parts.

We do this by using Perl's pattern matching to try to remove each
legal guess from the word, determining that we've won if the word
ends up blank at the end, and that we've lost if we've accumulated
too many bad guesses.

```
sub take_turn {
  my $game  = shift;

  # remove good guesses from word
  # and from $game->{'guesses'}
  my ($word, @guesses, $bad_guesses);
  @guesses = @{$game->{'guesses'}};
  $word    = $game->{'word'};

  foreach my $g (@guesses) {

    if (length($g) == 1) {
```

```
    # if the guess matches, remove each instance
    # from the word. Otherwise, add 1 to bad guesses
    unless($word =~ s/$g//gi) {
        $bad_guesses++;
    }

  } else {

    # if a guess is longer than one character,
    # if must match the whole word to count
    # we compare it with the original copy of the
    # word, in case other letters have been removed

    if ($game->{'word'} =~ /^$g$/i) {
        $word = '';
    } else {
        $bad_guesses++;
    }

  }
}

if (! $word ) {

  # if word is empty, you win!
  return 'won';

} elsif ($bad_guesses >= $BODY_PARTS) {

  # if count of bad guesses >= number of body parts,
  # you lose.
  return 'lost';

}

return 'playing';
}
```

Once we know what the new game state is, and we've saved it, we need to show it to the player. For this, we have three simple pages: one if you win, one if you lose, and one for every other turn in the game.

In this example, we've included the HTML code for the pages in the documents. More advanced users can try using templates!

Drawing the win and loss screens is easy enough, but for the some-other-turn screen, we need to display the gallows and the word, with correctly guessed letters filled in and blanks for unknown letters. We also need to display the last guess, and the player's history of guesses, with some distinction between good and bad guesses.

For the last guess and the guess history, we go through the list of guesses, checking each against the word, coloring the good ones green and the bad red.

To display the word, we rely on some more pattern matching tricks. First, we convert the array of guesses into a big string, which we can easily match against to find which are in the word and which aren't. Then we go through the word character-by-character, replacing those that haven't been guessed with an underscore (_) character.

Of course, if it's the player's first turn in a new game, we don't have to do any of that, so if the array of guesses is empty, we skip all that processing, and convert the whole word to underscores.

To display the gallows, we just add up the number of bad guesses, and append that number to the name of the gallows image. For this to work, of course, you'll need to create the gallows images, and put them all together in the $GALLOWS directory named at the top of the script, and give them names like gallows_0.gif, gallows_1.gif, and so forth.

```perl
sub draw_game_page {
  my $q    = shift;
  my $game = shift;
  my $id   = shift || $q->param('session_id');

  my ($title, $word, $url, $guesses, $g, $msg,
      $gallows, @tmp, $turns, $parts, $length,
      $tmp, $char);

  if ($game->{'status'} eq 'won') {

    # we have a winnah!
    draw_win_page($q,$game);

  } elsif ($game->{'status'} eq 'lost') {

    # oh well...
    draw_loss_page($q,$game);

  } else {

    # some turn in the middle

    $url     = $q->url;
    $turns   = 1;
    $length  = length($game->{'word'});
    $parts   = 0;

    if (@{$game->{'guesses'}}) {
      $turns = scalar @{$game->{'guesses'}} + 1;
      $title = "Hangman - turn $turns";

      # make the guesses line look nice
      # with green for good, red for bad
      foreach $g (@{$game->{'guesses'}}) {
```

```
      if (((length($g) == 1) && ($game->{'word'} =~ /$g/i))
          || ($game->{'word'} =~ /^$g$/i)) {
        push @tmp, "<font color=\"darkgreen\">$g</font>";
      } else {
        push @tmp, "<font color=\"red\">$g</font>";
        $parts++;
      }
    }

    $guesses = join(', ', @tmp);

    # tell the player whether their last guess
    # was right or wrong
    $g = $game->{'guesses'}->[ $#{$game->{'guesses'}} ];
    $msg = "Last guess: ";

    if (((length($g) == 1) && ($game->{'word'} =~ /$g/i))
       || ($game->{'word'} =~ /^$g$/i)) {
      $msg .= "<b><font color=\"darkgreen\">$g</font></b>";
    } else {
      $msg .= "<b><font color=\"red\">$g</font></b>";
    }

    # draw the word, with " _ " in place of
    # unguessed letters

    $tmp = ':' . join(':', @{$game->{'guesses'}}) . ':';

    # see if the whole word has been guessed
    if ($tmp =~ /:$game->{'word'}:/i) {
      $word = join(" ", split(//,$game->{'word'}));
    } else {

      # go through the word character by character,
      # seeing if each has been guessed

      my @word = split(//, $game->{'word'});
      foreach $char (@word) {
        $char = uc($char);

        if ($tmp =~ /:$char:/i) {
          $word .= " $char ";
        } else {
          $word .= " _ ";
        }
      }
    }
  }

} else {

    # this is their first turn

    $title   = "Welcome to Hangman!";
    $guesses = "<i>none</i>";
    $length  = length($game->{'word'});
    $word    = " _ " x $length;
    $turns   = 0;
```

```perl
        $msg     = '';
        $parts   = 0;    # the gallows itself
    }

    print $q->header;
    print <<GAME;
<html>
<head><title>$title</title></head>
<body bgcolor="white">

<h1>$title</h1>

<img src="$GALLOWS/gallows_$parts.gif" align="left"/>
<br/>
<p><font size=+1>$msg</font></p>
<p><font size=+1><b>$word</b></font></p>
<p>Guessed so far: $guesses</p>
<form action="$url" method="post">
<input type="hidden" name="session_id" value="$id"/>
<p>Next guess: <input type="text" name="guess" size="$length"
maxchars="$length"/></p>
<p><input type="submit" name="submit" value="Guess!" default/>
   <input type="submit" name="submit" value="New Game"/></p>
</form>
</body>
</html>
GAME

  }
}

sub draw_win_page {
  my $q    = shift;
  my $game = shift;

  my ($word, $turns, $url, $min);

  $word  = $game->{'word'};
  $turns = scalar @{$game->{'guesses'}};
  $url   = $q->url;
  $min   = (time - $q->param('session_id')) / 60;

  print $q->header;
  print <<VICTORY;
<html>
<head><title>You win!</title></head>
<body bgcolor="white">
  <h1>Congratulations!</h1>

  <p> You correctly guessed the word <b>$word</b>
      in <b>$turns</b> tries,
      and it only took you <b>$min</b> minutes!</p>

  <p> <a href="$url">Click here</a> to play again.</p>
```

```perl
</body>
</html>
VICTORY

}

sub draw_loss_page {
  my $q    = shift;
  my $game = shift;

  my $word = $game->{'word'};
  my $url  = $q->url;

  print $q->header;
  print <<DEFEAT;
<html>
<head><title>You lose!</title></head>
<body bgcolor="white">
  <h1>Too bad!</h1>

  <img src="$GALLOWS/dead.gif" align="left"/>
  <p> You're dead. The word was: <b>$word</b><p>

  <p> <a href="$url">Click here</a> to play again.</p>

</body>
</html>
DEFEAT

}
```

Finally, we have two "bookkeeping" functions. One function picks a word for each new game from a text file in a simple format (see the following example), and the other lets us display a different error message for mistakes such as guessing the same letter twice. Note that these error messages are distinct from program error messages.

```perl
sub pick_word {

  my (@words, $word);

  open (WRDS, "<$WORDS")
    || die "Could not open words file $WORDS";
  @words = <WRDS>;
  close WRDS;

  $word = $words[ rand @words ];
  chomp($word);

  return $word;
}

sub gameplay_error {
  my $q   = shift;
  my $err = shift;
```

```
  my $url = $q->url;
  my $id  = $q->param('session_id');

  # chop off the line number
  $err =~ s/at .*line.*$//;

  print $q->header;
  print <<GAME_ERR;
<html>
<head><title>Uh oh...</title></head>
<body bgcolor="white">

<h1>Uh oh!</h1>

<p> $err </p>

<p><b><a href="$url?session_id=$id">Back to the game!</b></a></p>

</body>
</html>

GAME_ERR

}
```

What's Up Next

We hope you had fun learning to work with graphics, polls, and a classic Perl game. Now it's time to get very serious and look into how to design pages with templates.

Using templates enables you, as the designer, to automate many portions of your Web site. In Chapter 8, "Designing with Templates," you'll learn to create Web templates, and, using the intelligence of Perl, you're only required to add text to automatically update pages.

Designing with Templates

Now that you've relaxed with some fun and games, it's time to dig deep into the power of Perl in the context of Web publishing. In this chapter, we're going to show you how to begin making your Web site do updates and changes without you! You only need to set things up, add fuel from time to time, and let the publishing system you're going to create here do all the hard work.

Let's say you currently publish, or want to publish, a Web site that has a standard design and layout in place. For a site of that nature, it makes sense to use this publishing system instead of hand-coding the various components. It saves time and can actually reduce error because the Perl code does the thinking for you.

It's important to understand that you're working with some essential pieces that work together to create the system. These components include:

- Raw text, formatted in a standard way

- HTML templates that call fields from the text files

- Perl modules—you've already worked with these and know that they are essentially scripts that call other scripts

- Perl scripts that pull together the aforementioned components and assemble the resulting page

Think of the publishing module as a group of individual stories that can be modified in a variety of ways. Even though the basic structure of the system will require careful and appropriate setup, you can get as creative as you want with the system.

Ultimately, the type of site that we create from the site that you create is going to be very different in appearance and content, but the way it works will be very similar.

Setting Up Directories

Before we get into the nitty-gritty of scripts, we want to make sure you're able to set up your system appropriately. Begin first by creating a directory hierarchy on your system. Figure 8.1 shows a chart that demonstrates the way the directory is set up.

With a clear idea in mind as to the geography of the system, here's a step-by-step to help you in getting the structure in place.

1. FTP to your root directory, using your FTP client.

2. Create a new directory within the root directory and call it images. This will be where all of your site images pulled from the templates will go.

3. Create another directory, and name it Publisher.

4. The third directory you make should be called stories.

5. A directory called "Story" should now be created. Inside this directory, create *another* directory and name it Text.

6. Finally, create a directory called tmpl. Your templates will go in this directory.

When this is set up, you'll want to begin thinking about the content of your site and how it is arranged. This is handled by the creation and placement of raw text and HTML templates into the system.

Figure 8.1

The directory structure and icons depicting where the various file types will go within the system.

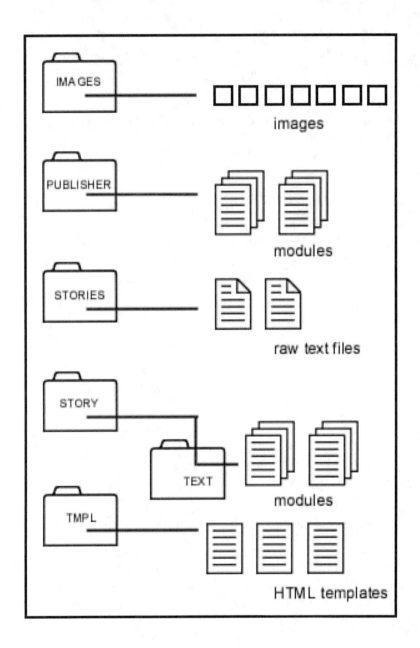

Setting Up Text Files and Templates

The first step is to select some content—a story or text-based page item that you'd like to have published.

To create the story file:

1. Open your text editor.

2. Create a standard text file including the text and variables you'll want to have reflected in the final published page.

3. Upload the file to an appropriate directory on your server.

Example Story File

```
HEADLINE: Missing Lion Found!
SUBHEAD: Students at YBI High find missing lion near school
AUTHOR: YBI Media
TEXT:
An escaped lion, who goes by the name of Linus, was found by a group of students
from YBI High in the foothills close to their school yesterday. "It was scary at
first" said Patty Plane, a junior from YBI High, "but then we realized he was
very weak and unable to move. We called the zoo, because we'd heard he was
missing."

Linus was removed from the woods by zoo personnel. He was treated for dehydration
and minor cuts and is now back in his habitat. No one was injured during the
incident.
```

You'll also need to create at least one or several templates that will help you lay out and modify the script. These templates are written in HTML.

1. Open your text editor.

2. Create an HTML document including a form and several template style options.

3. Upload the HTML to the appropriate directory on your server.

HTML Template Example

```
<html>
<head>
    <title>School Safari: News</title>
    <style>
    BODY {
        margin-top: 0px;
        margin-left: 0px;
    }
    </style>
</head>
```

HTML Template Example (continued)

```
<body bgcolor="#FFFFFF" text="#000000" link="#CC6666" vlink="#993333"
alink="#003300" >

<img src="images/pub_hed.gif" width=585 height=19 border=0 alt="header map"/>

<table border="0" width="585" cellpadding="5" cellspacing="0">
<tr>

<td valign="top" align="left" width="450">
<p>
<br/>
<img src="images/pub_sub.gif" width=104 height=19 border=0 alt="news &
views"/></p>

<p>
<font size="4">$HEADLINE</font>
<br/>
<font size="3"><i>$SUBHEAD</i></font>
<br/>
<font size="2"><b>by $AUTHOR</b></font>
</p><p>

$TEXT


</td>

<td valign="top" align="left" width="135" bgcolor="#993333">
<img src="images/lion.jpg" width=121 height=125 border=0 alt="image of lion"/>

<font size="2" face="arial, helvetica, sans-serif" color="#FFFFFF">
Missing lion found! Read <i>news</i> to find out more.
</font>

</td>

</tr>
</table>
</body>
</html>
```

In Figure 8.2, you see the template file *before* it's published. The reason the images aren't available is because the story file must be published to the proper directory in order to pick the images up. Currently, you're looking at the raw template file, which exists on its own in the template (tmpl) directory.

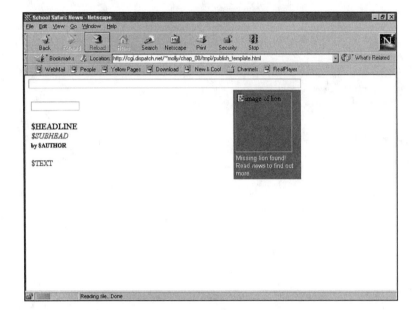

Figure 8.2
The raw template file.

You'll see we've included variables such as $HEADLINE and $TEXT. When the template scripts are run, the layout of this page will incorporate the story information based on these variables. This means you can upload a new story any time you want, run the correct scripts, and the fresh story will replace the old one.

Creating the Template CGI

The foundation of our automation example lies in the ability to create templates. This script encapsulates, in a simplified form, the way the modules in this chapter work.

How to Use

1. Install the CGI::FastTemplate module from CPAN.

2. Copy template.cgi into your text editor.

3. Save the script as template.cgi.

4. Place the file in the root directory on your server.

5. Change the permissions to make executable by all users:

   ```
   chmod a+x template.cgi
   ```

template.cgi

```perl
#!/usr/bin/perl -wT
#

#
# We've turned on taint checks (the -T switch in the bang line),
# so we need to explicitly set these environment variables.
# This is a security feature.
#
$ENV{'PATH'}  = '/bin:/usr/bin:/usr/local/bin';
$ENV{'SHELL'} = '/bin/sh';
$ENV{'ENV'}   = '';
$ENV{'IFS'}   = '';

use lib '/usr/home/molly/perl_lib';
use Taintcheck;

use CGI;
use CGI::FastTemplate;

#
# strict forces you to use good programming practices such as
# declaring all of your variables -- it makes debugging MUCH easier.
#
use strict;
use vars qw($__START__ $CGI $TMPL_DIR $STORY_DIR);

$CGI       = 'template.cgi';
$TMPL_DIR  = '/usr/home/molly/chap_06/templates';
$STORY_DIR = '/usr/home/molly/chap_06/stories';

#
# We use eval to catch any errors that might occur
#
eval { main() }; $__START__ = __LINE__;

#
# If eval { main() } has produced an error, the special $@ variable will
# hold the error message.
#
if ($@) {
  chomp($@);

  #
  # use $__START__ to determine the real line where the error occurred
  #
  $@ =~ s/\(eval\) line (\d+)/${CGI} . " line " . ($__START__-$1-1)/e;
  $@ =~ s/( at ).*( line )/$1${CGI}$2/;

  my $error_message = $@;

  print <<ERR;
Content-type: text/html
```

template.cgi (continued)

```
<html>
  <head><title>Error</title></head>
  <body>
    <h1>Error</h1>
    <code>$error_message</code>
  </body>
</html>
ERR

}

exit(0);

# main

sub main {
  my ($q, $story_ref, $s);

  $q    = new CGI;

  untaint_params($q);

  $story_ref = read_story($q);

  print $q->header,
        ${draw_story($q,$story_ref)};

}

# draw_story
# in:  CGI object, story ref
# out: html page, containing story,
#      with layout $q->param('template')
sub draw_story {
  my $q         = shift;
  my $story_ref = shift;

  my ($tpl, $tmpl, $page);

  $tmpl =  $q->param('template');

  die "No template submitted!" unless $tmpl;

  # Look in $TMPL_DIR for $tmpl, $tmpl.tpl, and $tmpl.html
  # If we can't find any of those, give up.

  if (-r "$TMPL_DIR/$tmpl") {

    # we don't have to do anything special

  } elsif (-r "$TMPL_DIR/$tmpl.tpl") {
    $tmpl .= '.tpl';
```

template.cgi (continued)

```perl
  } elsif  (-r "$TMPL_DIR/$tmpl.html") {
    $tmpl .= '.html';
  } else {
    die "Could not locate template file '$tmpl' in $TMPL_DIR";
  }

  $tpl = new CGI::FastTemplate;
  $tpl->strict();
  $tpl->set_root($TMPL_DIR);
  $tpl->define(tmpl=>$tmpl) || die "Could not define template $tmpl: $!";
  $tpl->assign($story_ref) || die "Could not assign template values: $!";
  $tpl->parse(PAGE => "tmpl");

  $page = $tpl->fetch("PAGE");

  # FastTemplate doesn't return error values,
  # so we have to do our own test here to make
  # sure we got some kind of result
  die "Could not parse template $tmpl: $!" unless $$page;

  return $page;
}

# read_story
# in:  CGI obect
# out: ref to hashof story values, eg
#        HEADLINE => "Man Bites Dog",
#        AUTHOR   => "Mike Royko"
#        TEXT     => "A man bit a dog today [...] "
sub read_story {
  my $q         = shift;

  my ($story_file,$field,$line,%story);

  die "No story submitted!" unless $q->param('story');

  $story_file = "$STORY_DIR/" . $q->param('story');

  # look in $STORY_DIR for $story and $story.txt
  unless (open (STORY, "<$story_file")) {
    unless (open (STORY, "<$story_file.txt")) {
      die "Could not read story $story_file";
    }
  }

  $story{'STORY'} = $q->param('story');

  $field = '';

  while ($line = <STORY>) {
```

template.cgi (continued)

```
  if ($line =~ /^([a-zA-Z0-9_\-]+):\s+(.*?)$/) {
    chomp($line);
    $story{$1} = $2;
    $field = $1;
  } elsif ($line eq ".\n") {
    $field = '';
  } else  {

    if ($field) {
  $story{$field} .= $line;
    } else {
  $story{'TEXT'} .= $line;
    }

  }

}

close STORY;

# do some basic html conversion: make plain text 'paragraphs' into <p> tags
foreach $field(keys %story) {
  $story{$field} =~ s/\n\n/<p>/g;
}

return \%story;
}
```

Publishing Pages Using Modules

Now we're going to look at the modules you will need within the
publishing system to perform various functions.

The Story::Text Module

This module will open and read the story file, and set things up for
the publishing portion of the automation system.

How to Use

1. Copy the module into your text editor.

2. Save the module as Text.pm.

3. Place the module in your Perl library directory. Since the name
   of the module is Story::Text, the module must be saved in the
   Story directory of your Perl library. So if your Perl library is
   /home/htdocs/lib/perl, save the module as /home/htdocs/lib/
   perl/Story/Text.pm.

Story::Text.pm

```perl
package Story::Text;

# for security
$ENV{'PATH'}  = '/bin:/usr/bin:/usr/local/bin';
$ENV{'SHELL'} = '/bin/sh';
$ENV{'ENV'}   = '';
$ENV{'IFS'}   = '';

use strict;
use vars qw($AUTOLOAD);

my %fields = ( 'story_file' => undef,
               'story'      => undef,
               'target'     => undef,
               'template'   => undef,
               'title'      => undef,
               'author'     => undef,
               'summary'    => undef,
               'error'      => undef, );

sub new {
  my $proto = shift;
  my $file  = shift;
  my $class = ref($proto) || $proto;
  my $self  = { %fields };

  bless $self, $class;

  # quit now if we can't read the story
  return unless $self->_initialize($file);

  return $self;
}

sub _initialize {
  my $self = shift;
  my $file = shift;

  $self->story_file( $file );
  $self->read_story();
}

# read_story
# in:  CGI obect
# out: ref to hashof story values, eg
#      HEADLINE => "Man Bites Dog",
#      AUTHOR   => "Mike Royko"
#      TEXT     => "A man bit a dog today [...] "
sub read_story {
  my $self = shift;
  my ($story_file,$field,$val,$line,%story);

  $story_file = $self->story_file;
```

```perl
unless ($story_file) {
  $self->error("No story file set");
  return;
}

# look for $story and $story.txt
unless (open (STORY, "<$story_file")) {
  unless (open (STORY, "<$story_file.txt")) {
    $self->error("Could not read story $story_file");
    return;
  }
}

$story{'STORY'} = $story_file;

$field = '';
$val   = '';

while ($line = <STORY>) {

  if ($line =~ /^([A-Z][A-Z0-9_\-]+):\s+(.*?)$/) {
    chomp($line);

    # first store any long field we've already built
    $story{$field} = $val if (($field) && ($val));

    # now set the working field to the new field
    # and the working val to the new val
    $field = uc($1);
    $val   = $2;

  } elsif ($line eq ".\n") {

    # store the old working field
    $story{$field} = $val if (($field) && ($val));

    # clear the working field & val
    $field = '';
    $val   = '';
  } else  {

    if ($field) {
  $val .= $line;
    } else {
  $story{'TEXT'} .= $line;
    }

  }

}

# finally, get the last field
$story{$field} = $val if (($field) && ($val));
```

```perl
  close STORY;

  # do some basic html conversion: make plain text 'paragraphs' into <p> tags
  foreach $field(keys %story) {
    $story{$field} =~ s/\n\n/\n<p>/g;
  }

  $self->story(\%story);

  # assign other fields
  $self->target( $story{'TARGET'} ) if ($story{'TARGET'});
  $self->template( $story{'TEMPLATE'} ) if ($story{'TEMPLATE'});

  return 1;
}

sub title {
  my $self = shift;

  if (@_) {
    $self->{'title'} = shift;
    return @_;
  }

  return $self->{'title'} if ($self->{'title'});

  if ($self->story->{'TITLE'}) {
    $self->title( $self->story->{'TITLE'} );
    return $self->story->{'TITLE'};
  }

  if ($self->story->{'HEADLINE'}) {
    $self->title( $self->story->{'HEADLINE'} );
    return $self->story->{'HEADLINE'};
  }
}

sub author {
  my $self = shift;

  if (@_) {
    $self->{'author'} = shift;
    return @_;
  }

  if ($self->story->{'AUTHOR'}) {
    $self->author( $self->story->{'AUTHOR'} );
    return $self->story->{'AUTHOR'};
  }
}

sub summary {
  my $self = shift;
```

```perl
  if (@_) {
    $self->{'summary'} = shift;
    return @_;
  }

  if ($self->story->{'SUMMARY'}) {
    $self->summary( $self->story->{'SUMMARY'} );
    return $self->story->{'SUMMARY'};
  } elsif ($self->story->{'TEXT'}) {
    # grab the first 20 words of the text,
    # or until the first paragraph, whichever
    # is shorter.

    my ($tmp, $tmp2, $tmp3);
    $tmp = $self->story->{'TEXT'};
    $tmp2 = '';
    $tmp3 = '';

    if ($tmp =~ /((\S+\s){0,20})/s) {
      $tmp2 = $1;

      # cut any trailing spaces or punctuation,
      # add an elipsis
      $tmp2 =~ s|<p>|\n|g;
      $tmp2 =~ s|[\W]+$||;
      $tmp2 .= "...";
    }

    if ($tmp =~ /^(?:\s*<p>\s*)?(.+?)<p>/s) {
      $tmp3 = $1;
     }

    # if we only got one, return that one
    return $tmp2 if (($tmp2) && (!$tmp3));
    return $tmp3 if (($tmp3) && (!$tmp2));

    # otherwise, return the shorter of the two
    if (length($tmp2) < length($tmp3)) {
      $self->summary( $tmp2 );
      return $tmp2;
    } else {
      $self->summary( $tmp3 );
      return $tmp3;
    }
  }
}

sub AUTOLOAD {
  my $self = shift;
  my $type = ref($self) || (die "$self is not an object" );
  my $name = $AUTOLOAD;

  $name =~ s/.*:://;
  unless (exists $self->{$name}){
```

Story::Text.pm (continued)

```
      die "Can't access '$name' field in object of class $type";
  }

  if (@_) {
    return $self->{$name} = shift;
  } else {
    return $self->{$name};
  }
}

sub DESTROY {
  my $self = shift;

  warn "wrong type" unless ref $self;
}
```

You can (and should!) test that your story was found and read successfully. To do this, add the following line *after* the my $story line you added earlier:

```
die $story->error if $story->error;
```

Publisher.pm

This is the publishing module. Its responsibility is to build the HTML page originally described in the template.cgi script. Publisher.pm takes the data from the story, such as the headline or author variables, and adds them into the predefined spots within the HTML template. After Publisher.pm builds the HTML file, it saves the file, too.

You can easily publish static pages from dynamic data, which will improve the responsiveness of your site, and also reduce the load on the Web server.

How to Use

1. Copy the module into your text editor.

2. Save the module as Publisher.pm.

3. Place the module in your Perl library directory.

4. Now, open a script that you want to have be influenced by this module.

5. At the top of the script, add the line:

```
use Publisher
```

Within the script, add the line:

```
my $p = new Publisher( $story );
```

Publisher.pm

```
package Publisher;

# for security
$ENV{'PATH'}  = '/bin:/usr/bin:/usr/local/bin';
$ENV{'SHELL'} = '/bin/sh';
$ENV{'ENV'}   = '';
$ENV{'IFS'}   = '';

use CGI::FastTemplate;
use strict;
use vars qw($AUTOLOAD);

my %fields = ( 'tpl'      => undef,
               'tmpl_dir' => undef,
               'tmpl'     => undef,
               'story'    => undef,
               'page'     => undef,
               'target'   => undef,
               'error'    => undef, );

sub new {
  my $proto = shift;
  my $story = shift;
  my $class = ref($proto) || $proto;
  my $self  = { %fields };

  bless $self, $class;
  $self->_initialize($story);
  return $self;
}

sub _initialize {
  my $self  = shift;
  my $story = shift;
  my $tpl   = new CGI::FastTemplate;

  $self->story($story);
  $self->tpl($tpl);
}

sub template_dir {
  my $self = shift;
```

Publisher.pm (continued)

```perl
  my $dir  = shift;
  my $tpl  = $self->tpl;

  $tpl->set_root($dir);
  $self->tmpl_dir($dir);
}

sub use_template {
  my $self      = shift;
  my $tmpl_name = shift;
  my $tmpl_file = shift;

  my $tpl       = $self->tpl;
  my $td        = $self->tmpl_dir;

  if ($self->story) {
    $tmpl_file ||= $self->story->template;
  }

  unless ($tmpl_file) {
    $self->error( "Publisher: no template specified" );
    return;
  }

  if (-r "$td/$tmpl_file") {

    # we don't have to do anything special

  } elsif (-r "$td/$tmpl_file.tpl") {
    $tmpl_file .= '.tpl';
  } elsif  (-r "$td/$tmpl_file.html") {
    $tmpl_file .= '.html';
  } else {
    $self->error("Publisher: could not locate template file '$tmpl_file' in
$td");
    return;
  }

  $tpl->define( $tmpl_name=>$tmpl_file );
  $self->tmpl( $tmpl_name );
}

sub publish {
  my $self      = shift;
  my $story     = shift;
  my $tmpl      = shift;
  my $target_fl = shift;

  $story     ||= $self->story;
  $target_fl ||= $self->target;
  $tmpl      ||= $self->tmpl;

  unless (ref $story) {
    $self->error("Publisher: no story specified");
```

```
    return;
  }

  unless ($target_fl) {
    $self->error("Publisher: no target file specified");
    return;
  }

  unless ($self->build_page($story,$tmpl)) {
    $self->error("Publisher: unable to build page with template $tmpl");
    return;
  }

  unless ($self->write_file($target_fl)) {
    $self->error("Publisher: unable to write file $target_fl");
    return;
  }

  return 1;
}
sub build_page {
  my $self  = shift;
  my $story = shift;
  my $tmpl  = shift;

  my $tpl   = $self->tpl;

  my ($p,$t);

  $t = $tmpl || $self->tmpl;

  $tpl->clear_href();
  $tpl->assign( $story->story );
  $tpl->parse( 'MAIN'=>$t );

  $self->page( $tpl->fetch('MAIN') );

  $p = $self->page;

  if (($p) && ($$p)) {
    return 1;
  } else {
    $self->error("Publisher: could not build page");
    return;
  }
}

sub write_file {
  my $self = shift;
  my $file = shift;
  my $p    = $self->page;
  my ($wf);
```

Publisher.pm (continued)

```perl
  $file ||= $self->target;

  # if $file is a directory,
  # write to $file/[story_file_name].html
  if (-d $file) {
                $wf = $self->story->story_file;
                # remove the path from story_file
                $wf =~ s|^(.*)/||;
                # add extension, if it doesn't have one
                $wf =~ s|(\.html)*$|.html|;
                # remove trailing slash from $file
                $file =~ s|/*$||;
                $file = "$file/$wf";
              }

              $self->target($file);

  unless ($$p) {
    $self->error("Publisher: no page to write");
    return;
  }

  unless (open (PF, ">$file")) {
    $self->error("Publisher: could not write to $file: $!");
    return;
  }

  print PF $$p;
  close PF;

  return 1;
}

sub story {
  my $self  = shift;
  my $story = shift;

  if ($story) {
    $self->{'story'}  = $story;
    ($story->target) && ($self->{'target'} = $story->target);
    ($story->template) && ($self->use_template('page', $story->template));
  }

  return $self->{'story'};
}

sub AUTOLOAD {
  my $self = shift;
  my $type = ref($self) || (die "$self is not an object" );
  my $name = $AUTOLOAD;

  $name =~ s/.*:://;
  unless (exists $self->{$name}){
```

Publisher.pm (continued)

```
      die "Can't access '$name' field in object of class $type";
    }

    if (@_) {
      return $self->{$name} = shift;
    } else {
      return $self->{$name};
    }
}

sub DESTROY {
  my $self = shift;
  warn "wrong type" unless ref $self;
}
```

To actually publish a story you must first set the template directory, and the template to use. You can optionally overwrite the default target file, and create the page. Here's how:

```
$p->template_dir( $TEMPLATE_DIR ) | | die $p->error;
$p->use_template('MAIN'. $template ) || die $p->error;
($target) && ($p->target( $target ));
$p->publish90 | | die $p->error;
```

> If you want to assign another story to Publisher, or don't have the story set up before creating the Publisher, you can assign a story with $p->story($story);

Publisher::Index.pm

This module is a subclass of Publisher.pm. It enables you to take several stories, two template types, and combine them into a single index page. The templates here are a bit more restricted than those in Publisher.pm. This is because so much of the content is automated that each template must contain a specific field to handle it.

> As you might have noticed, Publisher uses the same error mechanism as Story (setting the $p->error value if anything has gone wrong). Both modules also return a true or false value from most methods if they have succeeded or failed respectively.

How to Use

1. Copy the module into your text editor.

2. Save the module as Index.pm.

3. Place the module in the Publisher directory of your Perl library. So if your Perl library is /home/htdocs/lib/perl, save the module as /home/htdocs/lib/perl/Publisher/Index.pm.

4. Now, open a script that you want to have influenced by this module.

5. At the top of the script, add the line

```
use Publisher::Index;
```

6. Create a Publisher::Index object by adding the following to the script code:

```
my $pi = new Publisher::Index;
```

7. Create a number of story objects, with Story::Text or any Story:: subclass

8. Add each story to the index with

```
$pi->add_story($story, [url for $story]);
```

9. Set the template dir, and page and item templates:

```
$pi->template_dir($TMPL_DIR);
die $pi->error unless $pi->use_template( 'page_template', $IDX_PAGE,
'page' );
die $pi->error unless $pi->use_template( 'item_template', $IDX_ITEM,
'item' );
```

10. Add the target file

```
$pi->target( "$PUB_DIR/index.html" );
```

11. Then you're ready to publish with

```
$pi->publish();
```

Index.pm

```
# Given a set of stories, a template dir, and
# templates for the whole page and each index item,
# builds an index with summaries of each story.
package Publisher::Index;

# for security
$ENV{'PATH'}  = '/bin:/usr/bin:/usr/local/bin';
$ENV{'SHELL'} = '/bin/sh';
$ENV{'ENV'}   = '';
$ENV{'IFS'}   = '';

# modules
use lib '/usr/local/htdocs/perlbook/chap_06';
use Publisher;

use CGI::FastTemplate;
use strict;
use vars qw(@ISA $AUTOLOAD);

@ISA = qw(Publisher);
```

Index.pm (continued)

```perl
my %fields = ( 'tpl'        => undef,
           'tmpl_dir'   => undef,
           'item_tmpl'  => undef,
           'page_tmpl'  => undef,
           'stories'    => undef,
           'page'       => undef,
           'target'     => undef,
           'error'      => undef, );

sub new {
  my $proto = shift;
  my $class = ref($proto) || $proto;
  my $self  = { %fields };

  bless $self, $class;
  $self->_initialize();

  return $self;
}

sub _initialize {
  my $self = shift;
  my $tpl  = new CGI::FastTemplate;
  $self->tpl($tpl);
}

sub publish {
  my $self      = shift;
  my $target_fl = shift;
  my $page_tmpl = shift;
  my $item_tmpl = shift;

  unless ($self->build_page($page_tmpl,$item_tmpl)) {
    $self->error("Publisher: unable to build page with templates $page_tmpl,
item_tmpl");
    return 0;
  }

  unless ($self->write_file($target_fl)) {
    $self->error("Publisher: unable to write file $target_fl");
    return 0;
  }

  return 1;
}

sub build_page {
  my $self  = shift;
  my $pt    = shift;
  my $it    = shift;
  my $tpl   = $self->tpl;
  my $st    = $self->stories;
```

Index.pm (continued)

```perl
  my ($s,$p);

  $pt ||= $self->page_tmpl;
  $it ||= $self->item_tmpl;

  # build the STORIES item for insertion into main page
  foreach $s(@$st) {

    $tpl->assign( 'ST_TITLE'   => $s->{'story'}->title,
          'ST_URL'     => $s->{'url'},
          'ST_AUTHOR'  => $s->{'story'}->author,
          'ST_SUMMARY' => $s->{'story'}->summary, );

    $tpl->parse( 'STORIES' => ".$it" );
  }

  # build main page
  $tpl->parse( 'MAIN' => $pt );
  $self->page( $tpl->fetch('MAIN') );

  $p = $self->page;

  return ($$p ne '');
}

sub use_template {
  my $self      = shift;
  my $tmpl_name = shift;
  my $tmpl_file = shift;
  my $which     = shift;

  my $tpl       = $self->tpl;
  my $td        = $self->tmpl_dir;

  if (-r "$td/$tmpl_file") {

    # we don't have to do anything special

  } elsif (-r "$td/$tmpl_file.tpl") {
    $tmpl_file .= '.tpl';
  } elsif  (-r "$td/$tmpl_file.html") {
    $tmpl_file .= '.html';
  } else {
    $self->error("Publisher: could not locate template file '$tmpl_file' in
$td");
    return;
  }

  $tpl->define( $tmpl_name=>$tmpl_file );
  $self->{"${which}_tmpl"} = $tmpl_name;
}
```

Index.pm (continued)

```perl
sub add_story {
  my $self  = shift;
  my $story = shift;
  my $url   = shift;

  my %val = ( 'story' => $story,
              'url'   => $url, );

  # stories is a ref to an array of story objects
  my $tmp = $self->stories;
  $tmp ||= [];
  $self->stories( [ @$tmp, { %val } ] );

  return scalar @{ $self->stories };
}

sub AUTOLOAD {
  my $self = shift;
  my $type = ref($self) || (die "$self is not an object" );
  my $name = $AUTOLOAD;

  $name =~ s/.*:://;
  unless (exists $self->{$name}){
    die "Can't access '$name' field in object of class $type";
  }

  if (@_) {
    return $self->{$name} = shift;
  } else {
    return $self->{$name};
  }
}
```

Other Files Needed

You'll need to ensure that the page template contains $STORIES variable, in the location where the list of stories should go.

The item template must contain:

```
$ST_TITLE (story title)
$ST_URL (story url, presumably within <a> tag)
$ST_AUTHOR (story author)
$ST_SUMMARY (story summary)
```

This module is particularly powerful. We show you how as we build upon it with other modules and scripts in Chapter 9, "Creating Your Own Portal."

Publishing Utilities

How the Publish and Story modules are used can be demonstrated
with the following utilities.

Publish.pl

This command-line script enables you to publish one or more stories
to HTML pages.

How to Use

1. Copy the script into your text editor.

2. Save the script as publish.pl

3. Place the script in a directory on your server.

4. Make the script executable by user:

   ```
   chmod u+x publish.pl
   ```

publish.pl

```perl
#!/usr/bin/perl -wT

use lib '/path/to/library';
use Publisher;
use Story::Text;
use Taintcheck;

use Getopt::Std;
use strict;
use vars qw($opt_f $opt_d $STORY $TEMPLATE $TARGET $TEMPLATE_DIR);

die usage() unless @ARGV;

getopts('fd');

$STORY         = untaint($ARGV[0]);
$TEMPLATE      = untaint($ARGV[1]);
$TARGET        = untaint($ARGV[2]);
$TEMPLATE_DIR = untaint($opt_d) || '/usr/home/molly/chap_06/templates';

if ($opt_f) {

  my $s;
  my @stories = read_opts_file( untaint($opt_f) );
```

publish.pl (continued)

```perl
  foreach $s(@stories) {
    publish_page(@$s);
  }

} else {

  die usage() unless $STORY;
  publish_page( $STORY, $TEMPLATE, $TARGET );

}

sub read_opts_file {
  my $file = shift;
  my ($story, $tmpl, $targ, @stories);

  # option file format is:
  # story [template] [target]
  open (OPTS, "<$file") || die "publish.pl: could not read options file
$file";

  while (<OPTS>) {
    chomp;
    push @stories, [ split(/[\s\t]+/, $_) ];
  }

  close OPTS;

  return @stories;
}

sub publish_page {
  my $story    = shift;
  my $template = shift;
  my $target   = shift;

  my ($s, $p);

  $s = new Story::Text($story);
  die "Could not read story $story" unless ref $s;

  $p = new Publisher($s);
  die "Could not create publisher for " . $story->story_file unless ref $p;

  $p->template_dir( $TEMPLATE_DIR ) || die $p->error;
  $p->use_template( 'MAIN', $template ) || die $p->error;
  ($target) && ($p->target( $target ));

  $p->publish() || die $p->error;
}

sub usage {
```

publish.pl (continued)

```
  return <<USAGE;
usage:
publish.pl [-d template_dir] story_file [template] [target_file] | -f file
Use -f file to read story/template/target triplets from a file
USAGE

}
```

To use this utility:

1. From the command line, type

    ```
    ./publish.pl /home/molly/stories/lion
    ```

This will publish the story file "lion" to the default target, using a default template. The results are shown in Figure 8.3.

Figure 8.3

The story is published to the template.

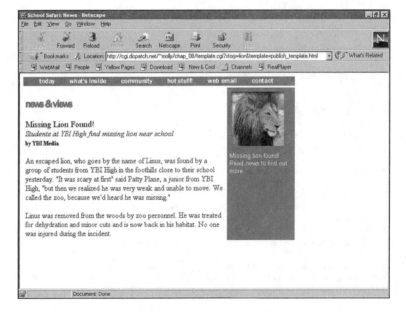

2. You can modify this by overriding the defaults by specifying them

    ```
    ./publish.pl lion yum.tpl /home/molly/html/index.html
    ```

This will now publish the milano cookie story using the yum.tpl template, overriding any settings for the original target.

3. You can also publish more than one story to a single file. To do so, type

```
publish.pl -f stories/a_bunch_of_stories.txt
```

Publishing Pages via E-mail

This Perl script gathers its input from e-mail, instead of reading the story off of the local disk. This allows you to add content from a remote location directly to your disk as well as from the local machine.

To set this up requires a new module, called Story::Text::Mail.pm. This module extends the Story::Text you worked with earlier by adding tools that authenticate the e-mail message against a list of authorized senders, acceptable publication directories, and a pass phrase. The e-mail headers will also be stripped from the message before parsing it as a story.

The first thing you'll want to do is set up the module, as follows:

1. Copy the module into your text editor.

2. Save the module as Mail.pm

3. Place the module in the Story/Text directory of your Perl library. So if your Perl library is /home/htdocs/lib/perl, save the module as /home/htdocs/lib/perl/Story/Text/Mail.pm.

Story::Text::Mail.pm

```
package Story::Text::Mail;

# inherit from Story::Text, adding:
#  - authenticate vs. allowed-addresses, allowed-relay, password
#  - strip mail headers, password line

# for security
$ENV{'PATH'}  = '/bin:/usr/bin:/usr/local/bin';
$ENV{'SHELL'} = '/bin/sh';
$ENV{'ENV'}   = '';
$ENV{'IFS'}   = '';
```

Story::Text::Mail.pm (continued)

```perl
use lib '/usr/local/htdocs/perlbook/chap_06';
use Story::Text;

use strict;
use vars qw(@ISA $AUTOLOAD);

@ISA = qw(Story::Text);

my %fields = ( 'story_msg'  => undef,
               'story_file' => undef,
               'target'     => undef,
               'story'      => undef,
               'template'   => undef,
               'title'      => undef,
               'author'     => undef,
               'summary'    => undef,
               'from'       => undef,
               'error'      => undef, );

sub new {
  my $proto     = shift;
  my $msg       = shift;
  my $auth_ip   = shift;
  my $auth_send = shift;
  my $auth_dir  = shift;
  my $pass_phr  = shift;

  my $class = ref($proto) || $proto;
  my $self  = { %fields };

  bless $self, $class;
  $self->_initialize($msg,$auth_ip,$auth_send,$auth_dir,$pass_phr);

  return $self;
}

sub _initialize {
  my $self      = shift;
  my $msg       = shift;
  my $auth_ip   = shift;
  my $auth_send = shift;
  my $auth_dir  = shift;
  my $pass_phr  = shift;

  $self->story_msg( $msg );
  $self->read_story();

  eval { $self->authenticate($auth_ip,$auth_send,$auth_dir,$pass_phr); };

  if ($@) {
    $self->{'error'} = "Authentication failed for message ($@):\n\n$msg";
```

```perl
    return;
  }

}

sub read_story {
  my $self = shift;
  my ($msg,$field,$val,$line,$hed,%story);

  $msg = $self->story_msg;

  unless ($msg) {
    $self->error("No content in submitted message:\n\n$msg");
    return;
  }

  $field = '';
  $val   = '';

  # chop the header off,
  # save the From: line
  $msg =~ s|^(.*?)\n\n||s;
  $hed = $1;

  if ($hed =~ m|^From: (.*?)$|m) {
    $story{'FROM'} = $1;
  }

  while ($msg =~ s|^(.*?\n)||s) {

    $line = $1;

    if ($line =~ /^([A-Z][A-Z0-9_\-]+):\s+(.*?)$/) {
      chomp($line);

      # first store any long field we've already built
      $story{$field} = $val if (($field) && ($val));

      # now set the working field to the new field
      # and the working val to the new val
      $field = $1;
      $val   = $2;

    } elsif ($line eq ".\n") {

      # store the old working field
      $story{$field} = $val if (($field) && ($val));

      # clear the working field & val
      $field = '';
      $val   = '';
    } else {

      if ($field) {
        $val .= $line;
```

Story::Text::Mail.pm (continued)

```perl
      } else {
    $story{'TEXT'} .= $line;
      }
    }
}

# finally, get the last field
$story{$field} = $val if (($field) && ($val));

# do some basic html conversion: make plain text 'paragraphs' into <p> tags
foreach $field(keys %story) {
   $story{$field} =~ s/\n\n/\n<p>/g;
}

$self->story(\%story);

# assign other fields
$self->target( $story{'TARGET'} ) if ($story{'TARGET'});
$self->template( $story{'TEMPLATE'} ) if ($story{'TEMPLATE'});
$self->from( $story{'FROM'} );

# in this module, the story_file is
# not the file we read the story from,
# but the file we want to save the
# story text in once we're done
# processsing it.
$self->story_file( $story{'FILE'} );
$story{'STORY'} = $story{'FILE'};

return 1;
}

sub authenticate {
  my $self      = shift;
  my $auth_ip   = shift;
  my $auth_send = shift;
  my $auth_dir  = shift;
  my $pass_phr  = shift;

  my $msg   = $self->story_msg;
  my $hed;
  my ($from, $sender_ip,$pass,$file);

  # remove & process the header
  $msg =~ s|^(.*?)\n\n||s;
  $hed = $1;
  return unless $hed;

  #
  # check from address vs. list of authorized submittors
  #
  if ($hed =~ /^From:\s+(.+)$/m) {
    $from = $1;
```

Story::Text::Mail.pm (continued)

```perl
  } else {
    return;
  }

  # this looks like we're testing
  # for html tags, but email addresses
  # have a similar structure -- sometimes
  if ($from =~ /<([^>]+)>/) {
    $from = $1;
  }

  # other email addresses may have
  # the non-address portion between
  # parentheses -- cut it
  $from =~ s|\(.*\)||g;

  # now that we have just the address, check
  # it vs. the auth list
  die "sender not authorized" unless in_list($auth_send,$from);

  #
  # check last 'received from' vs. list of authorized sending machines
  #
  if ($msg =~ /\nReceived: from
(?:[^\[]*?)\[(\d+\.\d+\.\d+\.\d+)\](?!.*?Received: from)/s) {
      $sender_ip = $1;
  } else {
      die "no received line found";
  }

  # check for passphrase in TEXT, remove if present
  die "passphrase not present in text" unless ($self->story->{'TEXT'} =~
s|\{$pass_phr\}||);

  #
  # check sender's ip vs. auth list
  #
  die "sender's ip not authorized" unless in_list($auth_ip,$sender_ip);

  #
  # check the target file
  #
  $file = $self->target;
  die "target file '$file' not in allowed directory" unless
in_dir_list($auth_dir,$file);

  if ($self->story_file) {
    die "story file " . ($self->story_file) . " not in authorized directory"
      unless in_dir_list($auth_dir,$self->story_file);
  }
```

Story::Text::Mail.pm (continued)

```perl
  return 1;
}


#
# write story fields to story_file
#
sub save {
  my $self = shift;
  my $file = $self->story_file;
  my $s    = $self->story;
  my ($f,$v);

  return unless $file;

  return unless open(SAVE, ">$file");

  foreach $f(keys %$s) {
    $v = $s->{$f};
    chomp($v);
    print SAVE "$f: $v\n";
  }

  return 1;
}

sub in_list {
  my $list = shift;
  my $item = shift;

  my ($i,$tmp);

  foreach $i(@$list) {
    return 1 if ($i eq $item);

    # make any wildcards into
    # a redular expressions
    if ($i =~ /\*/) {
      $tmp = $i;
      $tmp =~ s|\*|.*|g;

      return 1 if ($i =~ /^$tmp$/);
    }
  }
  return 0;
}

sub in_dir_list {
  my $dirs = shift;
  my $file = shift;

  my $d;
```

Story::Text::Mail.pm (continued)

```
foreach $d(@$dirs) {
  return 1 if ($file =~ m|^$d|);
}
return 0;
}
```

Here's the epublish.pl script that works with the module to create the
e-mail-based system. Using this module and the ePublish script
(found later in this section) is an excellent way of easily and quickly
updating content to a site via e-mail. Just have the updater or
author send an e-mail message in standard text format to an address
you've set up, and the script will automatically publish the story.

epublish.pl

```
#!/usr/bin/perl -wT

# Suggestions for improving security gladly accepted

use lib '/path/to/library';
use Story::Text::Mail;
use Publisher;
use Net::SMTP;

use strict;
use vars qw($IN $NOTIFY $OWNER $RESULT $TMPL_DIR $AUTHORIZED_IP
$AUTHORIZED_SENDER $AUTHORIZED_DIR $PASS $SMTP_SERVER);

# mail server to use for notification msg
$SMTP_SERVER = 'localhost';
# email address to notify of success or failure
$NOTIFY       = 'your@email'; #replace with your email address
# who should own created files?
$OWNER        = $NOTIFY;
# where to find templates
$TMPL_DIR     = '/path/to/templates'; #replace with path to your template directory

# who's allowed to publish, their publishing passphrases,
# the ip addresses they're allowed to send from, the
# templates they can use, and the dirs they're allowed
# to publish to

$AUTHORIZED_IP     = [ '127.*' ] ;
$AUTHORIZED_SENDER = [ 'wm@shakespeare.com' ]; #replace with addresses of story authors
$AUTHORIZED_DIR    = [ '/path/to/html/files' ]; #replace with path to save html files
$PASS              = 'cookie cookie cookie, good enough for me';
```

epublish.pl (continued)

```perl
while (<>) {
  $IN .= $_;
}

eval {
  $RESULT = publish($IN);
};

if($@) {

  # mail failure message & info to
  # notify address
  notify($@);

} else {

  # mail success message & info to
  # notify address
  notify($RESULT);
}

exit(0);

sub publish {
  my $text = shift;
  my ($s, $p);

  $s = new
Story::Text::Mail($text,$AUTHORIZED_IP,$AUTHORIZED_SENDER,$AUTHORIZED_DIR,$PASS);

  die $s->error if $s->error;

  $p = new Publisher($s);
  die $p->error unless $p->template_dir( $TMPL_DIR );
  die $p->error unless $p->use_template( 'MAIN', $s->template );
  die $p->error unless $p->publish();

  # write the story text to story_file
  $s->save();

  # set ownership/permissions on created files
  chown((getpwnam($OWNER))[2,3], $p->target,$s->story_file);


  return "Story '" . ($s->title) . "' published as " .
         ($p->target) . " by " . ($s->from) . " at " . scalar localtime(time);
}

sub notify {
  my $msg = shift;

  my $smtp = Net::SMTP->new($SMTP_SERVER);
```

epublish.pl (continued)

```
die "SMTP server not responding" unless ref $smtp;

die "Server did not accept sender's address" unless $smtp->mail('publisher');
die "Server did not accept recipient address" unless $smtp->to($NOTIFY);

unless ($smtp->data( "To: $NOTIFY\n" .
            "Subject: Publisher result\n" .
            "\n" .
            $msg .
            "\n--\nSubmitted story follows:\n\n" . $IN )) {
  $smtp->quit;
  die "Failed to send mail";

}

$smtp->quit;
}
```

You or your administrator will need to access and accomplish server-side concerns including:

- Ensure that sendmail is running on the machine.

- The sendmail aliases file must be edited appropriately.

- The administration must be willing to accept the security risk involved in running a root script as a method of receiving mail.

Although the concept of epublish is easy, the real challenge is in setting up the server properly.

Setting Up epublish.pl Carefully

To set up the sendmail portion, go to /etc/aliases, and add a line like

```
publisher: "|/path/to/epublish.pl"
```

Now, save the file, then run newaliases to make sendmail recognize the new alias. To set up epublish, make it SUID root (as root, type **chmod +sx epublish.pl**), and edit the variables at the top of the script to set up the authorization system to match your site. Set $AUTHORIZED_IP to a list of IP addresses from which you will accept messages.

This doesn't mean the epublish.pl script isn't secure. You just have to have an individual who knows what she is doing set up the system with care and precision. Sendmail is especially complex, and a variety of books have been written on the subject.

It is critical that you are very, very careful about what you put in this list. *Any* file in *any* directory in this list can be overwritten at *any* time by anyone smart enough to spoof an e-mail address, so we urge you to be careful.

This is compared to the last Received From: line in the mail header, so if you use POP mail from client machines, you'll need to add the IPs of all of the client machines, not the IP of the mail server. For $AUTHORIZED_SENDER, add the full e-mail addresses from which you will accept messages. For $AUTHORIZED_DIR, a list of those directories under which you'll allow files to be created.

Now, set the $PASS to some obscure (but relevant to you) phrase. This is the final line of defense—each submitted story must contain the $PASS, in angle brackets {}, somewhere in the TEXT field (it'll be stripped out during processing).

Finally, set the $NOTIFY address to the e-mail address of the Webmaster, or other person who should be notified of changes to the site. This address will be informed of all successful, and all failed, submissions to epublish.pl.

If you've done everything right, you should have a safe, powerful method of updating your site directly using e-mail.

Publishing a Full Directory

The publish_dir.pl script is another very useful script for managing updates. This script will publish an entire directory of stories to a target directory, as well as publishing a separate table of contents page. This page includes the title and author of each individual story, offers up a summary of the story, and automates a link from the contents page to each story.

How to Use

1. Copy the script into your text editor.

2. Save the script as publish_dir.pl

3. Place the script in the root directory on your server.

4. Make the script executable by user:

```
Chmod u+x publish_dir.pl
```

publish_dir.pl

```perl
#!/usr/bin/perl -w

use lib '/path/to/library';
use Story::Text;
use Publisher;
use Publisher::Index;

use Cwd;
use Getopt::Std;
use strict;
use vars qw($opt_p $opt_i $TMPL_DIR $DEFAULT_TMPL $STORY_DIR $PUB_DIR $IDX_PAGE
$IDX_ITEM $WWW_ROOT);

getopt('pi');

$WWW_ROOT      = '/usr/home/molly/public_html';
$TMPL_DIR      = '/usr/home/molly/chap_06/templates';
$DEFAULT_TMPL  = 'green';
$STORY_DIR     = full_path($ARGV[0]);
$PUB_DIR       = full_path($ARGV[1]);
$IDX_PAGE      = $opt_p || 'ix_page';
$IDX_ITEM      = $opt_i || 'ix_item';

die usage unless $STORY_DIR;

publish_dir($STORY_DIR);

sub publish_dir {
  my $dir = shift;
  my (@files,@stories,$p,$pi,$f,$s);

  # get list of text files in dir
  die "Could not open dir $dir" unless opendir (SDIR, $dir);

  # we only want text files whose names don't star with '.'
  @files = grep { (-T "$dir/$_") && (!/^\./) } readdir SDIR;
  closedir SDIR;

  die "No story (text) files in $dir" unless @files;

  # make a publisher & publisher::index
  $p  = new Publisher();
  $pi = new Publisher::Index();

  $p->template_dir($TMPL_DIR);
  $pi->template_dir($TMPL_DIR);

  # set pi story/page templates
  die $pi->error unless $pi->use_template( 'page_template', $IDX_PAGE, 'page' );
  die $pi->error unless $pi->use_template( 'item_template', $IDX_ITEM, 'item' );

  $pi->target( "$PUB_DIR/index.html" );
```

publish_dir.pl (continued)

```perl
  # for each file,
  foreach $f(@files) {

    # make a story object
    $s = new Story::Text("$dir/$f");

    # publish that story object
    # if successfully published, add story obj & url
    # to @stories
    $p->target($PUB_DIR);
    $p->use_template( 'page', $DEFAULT_TMPL );
    $p->story($s);

    if ($p->publish()) {
      # sdd the story, and a file path relative to the publication dir,
      # to the array of stories
      push @stories, [ $s, relative_path($PUB_DIR,$p->target) ];
      print "Published " . $s->story_file . " as " . $p->target . "\n";
    } else {
      warn "Could not publish story " . $s->story_file . " (" . $p->error . ")";
    }
  }

  die "Failed to publish any stories" unless @stories;

  # write the index
  foreach $s(@stories) {
    $pi->add_story(@$s);
  }

  die "Could not publish story index (" . $pi->error . ")" unless $pi->publish();

  print "Published story index as " . $pi->target . "\n";
}

sub usage {

  return <<USAGE;
publish_dir.pl story_dir target_dir [-p index page template] [-i index item
template]

USAGE
}

sub full_path {
  my $dir = shift;

  return $dir if ($dir =~ m|^/|);

  my $cwd = cwd();

  return "$cwd/$dir";
}
```

publish_dir.pl (continued)

```perl
sub relative_path {
  my $dir  = shift;
  my $file = shift;

  # if file is an absolute path, remove $dir from it
  if ($file =~ m|^/|) {
    $file =~ s|^$dir(/?)||;
  } else {

    # file is a relative path -- presumably from
    # the current working directory.
    # make it absoulte, then cut $PUB_DIR
    $file = full_path($file);
    $file =~ s|^$dir(/?)||;
  }

  # if $file is still a full path,
  # make it relative to $WWW_ROOT,
  # then make it look absolute, so the
  # URL will be correct.
  $file = '/' . relative_path($WWW_ROOT,$file) if ($file =~ m|^/|);

  return $file;
}
```

To run the script, simply type the following from the command line:

```
publish_dir.pl story_dir target_dir [-p index page template]
[-I index item template]
```

The script will now read each individual story in the story directory, and publish it to the target directory. Then it will use the Publisher::Index.pm module to create an index.html file in the target directory. It is this file that will contain the list of linked stories successfully published.

What's Up Next

If you've been thinking of creative ways to use this Perl-based automation system, hang on to your hats! In Chapter 9 we'll show you how to build on the automation process and allow your site visitors to customize the pages they want to see.

Creating Your Own Portal

Personalized, user-driven content has become a mainstay of contemporary sites. Many of these large, customizable sites are referred to as *portals*, and are offered up by such well-known sites as Yahoo!, Netscape, MSN, and Excite. The appeal of these sites is largely due to the fact that people can add the items of interest to them—be it stories on entertainment, world news and views, weather information, or their daily horoscope.

Creating user-driven content can be quite complex, and that's no exception when using CGI and Perl. However, Chapter 8, "Designing with Templates," quietly lead you up to this point, showing you how to set up a publishing method behind the scenes.

Now, we'll step up the intensity of your work with the scripts. We're going to show you a bit more details regarding object inheritance, dive into more complex combinations of templates, and demonstrate how you can use CGI and Perl to access data from SQL (Structured Query Language) databases.

Introduction to DBI

The next step in the evolution of our template-based publishing system requires that we move our data from flat text files to a more structured type of storage. Text files simply aren't fast or flexible enough for what we want to do. We'll use the DBI.pm module to facilitate storing our data in a SQL database.

DBI.pm is one of the most complex and powerful Perl modules around. It provides easy and portable access to many SQL database servers, from open source database servers such as PostgreSQL and MySQL, to enterprise products such as Oracle, to simple text file-based databases.

For our examples in this chapter, we have used MySQL, an open source, freely available SQL server that is very fast, stable, and full-featured.

Files You Need

We're going to start by installing MySQL. It's interesting to note that MySQL (pronounced "My S, Q, L" not "My Sequel"), although freely available, is a database server with profoundly powerful features. It can be used for simple applications, as well as very complex, large-scale operations. As mentioned, one of its greatest features is its speed.

To install MySQL:

1. MySQL is available on the CD-ROM accompanying this book. Or, for the most recent version , visit http://mysql.com and find a mirror site close to you where you can download it.

2. Download the recent, recommended MySQL version for your Web server.

3. Install to your server according to the instructions. Make sure to set a root password.

Now you'll need to download and install the DBI.pm module from CPAN, if you haven't already done so. You'll also want to download a specialty module called Msql-MySql-DBD from CPAN.

To download these files:

1. Visit http://www.perl.com/cpan/ and find the DBI.pm module, then download it to your computer.

2. Download and install Msql-MySql-DBD module from CPAN (and the modules it depends on) on your sever, making sure to select MySQL as the database you want to use.

Setting Up the Database Tables in MySQL

When you have the files you need set up on your server, you're ready to create the database and its necessary information tables, stories, and story sets. Here's how:

1. Create the database

   ```
   mysqladmin create story_database -u root -p
   ```

2. Create the database tables

   ```
   /path/to/mysql -uroot -ppassword story_database \
   < /path/to/story_tables.sql
   ```

3. Add users with appropriate permissions for creating the data-base tables, and for using them. Please remember to change the fake passwords in the story-permissions.sql file below (`'auth_pass'`) to a strong password of your own choosing. A strong password includes both upper and lower case letters, and numbers or punctuation, is not a word or a name, or a common numeralization of a word or name. For example, "j@s0n" is not a strong password.

   ```
   /path/to/mysql -uroot -ppassword mysql \
   < /path/to/story_permissions.sql
   mysqladmin -u root -p password reload
   ```

Here's the tables script:

story_tables.sql

```
# create the tables

# uncomment these if you need to recreate the tables
#drop table stories;
#drop table story_sets;
#drop table story_fields;
#drop table users;
#drop table user_sets;

#
# stories table
#
create table stories (
        id                      int not null auto_increment,
        set_id                  int not null,
    created     datetime not null,
    story           char(128),
    template    char(50),
    target          char(255),
    published_as        char(255),
    published_on        datetime not null,
    title           char(255) not null,
    author      char(255) not null,
    summary         text,
    text            text,
    ts          timestamp,
    key (set_id),
    key (created),
```

story_tables.sql (continued)

```
        key (published_on),
        key (title),
        key (author),
        primary key (id)
)\g


#
# story_sets table
#
create table story_sets (
    id              int not null auto_increment,
    name            char(50) not null,
    pub_dir         char(128),
    created         datetime not null,
    published_on    datetime not null,
    idx_needs_upd   tinyint,
    idx_template    char(50),
    idx_set_tmpl    char(50),
    idx_item_tmpl   char(50),
    idx_thresh_type char(5),
    idx_threshold   int,
    dflt_tmpl    char(50),
    dflt_target  char(128),
    dflt_title   char(255),
    dflt_author  char(255),
    dflt_summary text,
    ts           timestamp,
    unique (name),
    key(published_on),
    key (created),
    primary key (id)
)\g


#
# story_fields table (keeps non-standard fields for stories)
#
create table story_fields (
    id           int not null auto_increment,
    story_id     int not null,
    field_name   char(128) not null,
    field_content   text,
    ts           timestamp,
    key (story_id),
    key (field_name),
    primary key (id)
)\g


#
# users table (add your own fields if you want to keep more info about each user)
#
create table users (
    id           int not null auto_increment,
    ts           timestamp,
    primary key(id)
)\g
```

story_tables.sql (continued)

```
#
# user_sets table (keeps each user's preferences)
#
create table user_sets (
    id          int not null auto_increment,
    user_id     int not null,
    set_id      int not null,
    display     int not null,
    ts          timestamp,
    key(user_id),
    key(set_id),
    key(display),
    unique user_set(set_id,user_id),
    primary key (id)
)\g


#
# create some example sets
# (you can replace these with your own story sets)
#
insert into story_sets values ( '',
    'food_stories',
    '/usr/local/htdocs/perlbook/chap_11/food',
    NOW(),
    '',
    0,
    'food_page_tmpl',
    'food_tmpl',
    'food_item_tmpl',
    '',
    0,
    '',
    '',
    '',
    '',
    'A delicious romp!',
    NULL)\g

insert into story_sets values ( '',
    'art_stories',
    '/usr/local/htdocs/perlbook/chap_11/art',
    NOW(),
    '',
    0,
    'art_page_tmpl',
    'art_tmpl',
    '',
    0,
    '',
    '',
    '',
    '',
    '',
    'A beautiful romp!',
    NULL)\g
```

story_tables.sql (continued)

```
insert into story_sets values ( '',
    'music_stories',
    '/usr/local/htdocs/perlbook/chap_11/music',
    NOW(),
    '',
    0,
    'music_page_tmpl',
    'music_tmpl',
    '',
    0,
    '',
    '',
    '',
    '',
    '',
    'An harmonious romp!',
    NULL)\g

insert into story_sets values ( '',
    'other_stories',
    '/usr/local/htdocs/perlbook/chap_11/other',
    NOW(),
    '',
    0,
    '',
    'basic_index',
    '',
    '',
    0,
    '',
    '',
    '',
    '',
    'A romp!',
    NULL)\g
```

The permissions script, in this case, will create two MySQL users.
One has the ability to update stories and sets, and the other is
allowed to read stories and sets, and to update users and user sets. In
the context of this system, a story is the file that contains the actual
story text, and story sets are sections of related stories, such as all
stories under "movies" or "food" sections within a given publication.

story_permissions.sql

```
# the 'author' can update stories
# replace the user name, database (test.) and password with
# values appropriate to your site
```

story_permissions.sql (continued)

```
GRANT select, insert, update, delete ON test.*
TO author@localhost IDENTIFIED by 'auth_pass';

GRANT select, insert, update, delete ON test.*
TO author@"%" IDENTIFIED by 'auth_pass';

# the 'user' can read everything, but only update user & user_sets
GRANT select ON test.*
TO user@localhost IDENTIFIED by 'user_pass';
GRANT insert, update ON test.users
TO user@localhost IDENTIFIED by 'user_pass';
GRANT insert, update ON test.user_sets
TO user@localhost IDENTIFIED by 'user_pass';

GRANT select ON test.*
TO user@"%" IDENTIFIED by 'user_pass';
GRANT insert, update ON test.users
TO user@"%" IDENTIFIED by 'user_pass';
GRANT insert, update ON test.user_sets
TO user@"%" IDENTIFIED by 'user_pass';
```

Now you'll need to set the modules in place.

Adding the Modules

You've either downloaded—or already have—the following modules that we'll be working with in this section. We're going to take a much more microscopic look at what's going on with them this time around.

Story::DBI.pm

The first place we'll make use of DBI for data storage is with our site's stories. A story is basically text, so isn't it best to store it as a text file? Not always—especially not when you need speed and flexibility, and the ability to update and edit data at will.

Also, if you keep in mind the fact that the story texts we've read have all been in a fairly rigid format, and we've spent a decent amount of time parsing and interpreting them, you'll see the benefit to be had from letting a database do some of that structural work for us.

At this time, we also add the concept of story sets, which are related stories that you can choose to group together. *Story sets are the foundation of the personalization scheme in this chapter.* Essentially, we are taking the stories and dividing them into organized topics.

Story::DBI.pm is therefore quite different from Story::Text: which we used earlier, in Chapter 8. We don't have to parse stories, but we do have to deal with the complexities of dealing with our database management via MySQL. Because this is a fairly long module, we'll take it in pieces.

Story::DBI.pm

```perl
package Story::DBI;

# for security
$ENV{'PATH'}  = '/bin:/usr/bin:/usr/local/bin';
$ENV{'SHELL'} = '/bin/sh';
$ENV{'ENV'}   = '';
$ENV{'IFS'}   = '';

use DBI;
use strict;
use vars qw($AUTOLOAD @ISA $DBH);
```

These are the primary story fields—the ones that are in the stories table in the database. For other fields, we'll need to store the name and contents in a separate table, so we need to treat these two kinds of fields differently. To do that, we need to define which is which.

```perl
my @MAIN_FIELDS = qw(TITLE AUTHOR SUMMARY TEXT TEMPLATE STORY
  TARGET SET_ID PUBLISHED_AS PUBLISHED_ON CREATED TS);
```

This Story class has fewer top-level fields than Story::Text—we use a cool AUTOLOAD trick instead, to make the fields we load from the database look real. We'll explain this in greater detail at the end of the module.

```perl
my %fields = ( 'story'        => {},
               'story_id'     => undef,
               'story_set_id' => undef,
               'dirty'        => undef,
               'error'        => undef, );

sub new {
  my $proto     = shift;
  my $story_id  = shift;
  my $story_flds = shift;

  my $class = ref($proto) || $proto;
  my $self  = { %fields };
```

```
    bless $self, $class;
    $self->_initialize($story_id,$story_flds);
    $self->{'dirty'} = 0;

    return $self;
}
```

Actually, **new()** is a class method that can also be used as an object method. We've used it as a class method in our scripts.

db_connect() is a class, not an object, method. All the Story::DBI objects created in one session will share the same database connection. You've seen class methods before: **new()**, in each of the classes where we've used it, is a class method.

```
sub db_connect {
    my $class          = shift;
    my $dbi_connect_str = shift;
    my (@dbi_args)      = @_;

    my $dbh = DBI->connect($dbi_connect_str,@dbi_args);

    return unless $dbh;

    $DBH = $dbh;
    return $DBH;
}

sub _initialize {
    my $self       = shift;
    my $story_id   = shift;
    my $story_flds = shift;

    unless ($DBH) {
        $self->error("Story::DBI: no database connection\n");
        return;
    }

    if ($story_flds) {
        $self->add_story($story_id,$story_flds);
        return;
    }

    if ($story_id) {
        $self->read_story($story_id);
    }
}
```

You'll notice that the **read_story()** method in this class is quite different from those we've seen previously. Here, instead of reading and parsing a text file, we use two SQL queries to retrieve the primary and secondary fields of each story directly, with no need to parse.

```
sub read_story {
  my $self     = shift;
  my $story_id = shift;

  my ($sth, $rc, $story_fields, %story, $a, $fn, $fc);

  $story_id ||= $self->story_id;
  unless ($story_id) {
    $self->error("Story::DBI: read_story: no story id specified");
    return;
  }

  # as with the 'main' function wrapper in CGIs,
  # we use eval here to trap any errors that
  # come up -- during database access, in this case
  eval {

    # read the main story info
    $sth = $DBH->prepare("select * from stories where id='$story_id'");
    die $DBH->errstr unless ref $sth;

    $rc = $sth->execute;
    die $sth->errstr unless $rc;

    $story_fields = $sth->fetchrow_hashref;

    # read the other story fields
    $sth = $DBH->prepare("select * from story_fields where story_id='$story_id'");
    die $DBH->errstr unless $sth;

    $rc = $sth->execute;
    die $sth->errstr unless $rc;
```

Here's where things get meaty in this version of read_story. For each row returned (each story field), we need to add the value of the story field (story_fields.field_content) to the item in the story hash keyed by story_fields.field_name.

If there's already an array of values in there, we add the new one at the end of the array. If there's only one value, we make a new array with the old and new values. If there's no value at all, we just set the value to story_fields.field_content.

What's the point, you might be wondering? This way we can store multiple values for each field. If you wanted to provide random *or* user-defined content within a story, this would be a great place to start. You'd write your own subclass of Story::DBI with methods to select one of the multiple values to return, and you're most of the way there.

```
while($a = $sth->fetchrow_arrayref) {

    $fn = $a->[2];
    $fc = $a->[3];

    if ($story_fields->{$fn}) {

        if (ref $story_fields->{$fn}) {
          push @{$story_fields->{$fn}}, $fc;
        } else {
          $story_fields->{$fn} = [ $story_fields->{$fn}, $fc ];
        }

    } else {
        $story_fields->{$fn} = $fc;
    }
  }
};

if ($@) {
  $self->error("Story::DBI: read_story: $@");
  return;
} else {

  # make all story fields uppercase
  foreach my $k(keys %$story_fields) {
    $story{uc($k)} = $story_fields->{$k};
  }

  $self->story(\%story);
  $self->story_id($story_id);
  ($story{'SET'}) && ($story{'SET_ID'} =
    $self->story_set_to_id($story{'SET'}));
  $self->story_set_id($story{'SET_ID'});

  return 1;
  }
}
```

Because our data doesn't come out of files that can be edited by hand, we need to offer some means of entering data. The add_story() method does just that. It takes a standard story hash and creates whatever database records are needed to save that story. Of course, using this method, it's quite easy to convert stories from text to DBI format. And you guessed it! We've provided a utility script at the end of the chapter that does just that.

```
sub add_story {
  my $self     = shift;
  my $story_id = shift;
  my $story    = shift;

  my ($f,$v,$rc,$sth,$sql,@flds,@vals,$created_id);
```

```
# build a SQL statement to create the new story record
$sql = 'REPLACE INTO stories ';

# look up the set id if we got SET field
($story->{'SET'}) && ($story->{'SET_ID'} =
  $self->story_set_to_id($story->{'SET'}));
delete $story->{'SET'};

# process the main story fields
foreach $f (@MAIN_FIELDS) {
  if ($story->{$f}) {

    push @flds, lc($f);
    push @vals, $DBH->quote($story->{$f});
  }

  # remove the field from the story hash
  # so that we don't see it again below
  delete $story->{$f} if exists $story->{$f};
}

# put in the id field --
# this way, we can update an existing record
# (we need to make sure that this value is not
# overridden, so we knock it out of the $story hash
# first)
delete $story->{'ID'};
unshift @flds, 'id';
unshift @vals, $DBH->quote($story_id);

# set the created date if it's new
unless ($story_id) {
  push @flds, 'created';
  push @vals, 'NOW()';
}

$sql .= '(' . join(', ', @flds) .
        ') VALUES (' . join(', ', @vals) .')';

# catch any errors
eval {
  $sth = $DBH->prepare($sql) || die $DBH->errstr;
  $sth->execute()            || die $sth->errstr;

  # get the id of the story we just
  # created.
  # NOTE: this is not portable code. It will only
  # work with MySQL. If you use some other
  # database server, consult the docs of DBD driver
  # for that database to find an equivalent function
  $created_id = $story_id || $sth->{'mysql_insertid'};

  die "Unable to determine whether story was created"
  unless $created_id;
};
```

```perl
    if ($@) {
      $self->error("Story::DBI: add_story: $@");
      return;
    }

    # clean out any story fields belonging to me
    eval {
      $DBH->do("DELETE FROM story_fields WHERE id=$created_id")
        || die $DBH->errstr;
    };

    if ($@) {
      $self->error("Story::DBI: add_story: " .
                   "error while cleaning out story fields: $@");
      return;
    }

    # now add any other fields as story_field records
    if (keys %$story) {
      eval {
        foreach $f(keys %$story) {
          $v = $DBH->quote( $story->{$f} );
          $f = $DBH->quote($f);
          $sql = "INSERT INTO story_fields " .
                 "VALUES ( '', $created_id, $f, $v,NULL)";

          $DBH->do($sql) || die $DBH->errstr;
        }
      };

      if ($@) {
        $self->error("Story::DBI: add_story: " .
                     "error while adding extra story fields: $@");
        return;
      }

    }

    $self->story_id($created_id);

    # since the 'dirty' mechanism hinges on autoload,
    # we've got to be careful declaring our cleanliness.
    $self->{'dirty'} = 0;

    # finally, read the newly created story into my story field
    $self->read_story($created_id);

    # and return the id of the created story
    return $created_id;
}

sub delete_story {
  my $self     = shift;
  my $story_id = shift;
```

```
my ($sql,$rc);

$sql = "DELETE FROM stories WHERE id='$story_id'";

eval {
    $DBH->do($sql) || die $DBH->errstr;
};

if ($@) {
    $self->error("Story::DBI: delete_story: $@");
    return;
}

$self->{'dirty'} = 0;

return 1;
}
```

Most humans (perhaps Perl programmers are exempt from this),
strangely enough, find it easier to remember words than to
remember strings of numbers. So, we provide the **story_set_to_id()**
function to convert story set names to the id numbers we need for
quick access to the **story_sets** table in the database. This way, you
can, for example, use **$LOCAL_NEWS** in your templates instead of
$SET_1267.

```
sub story_set_to_id {
    my $self     = shift;
    my $set_name = shift;

    my ($sth, $rc, $r, $n);
    $n = $DBH->quote($set_name);

    eval {
        $sth = $DBH->prepare("SELECT id FROM story_sets " .
                             "WHERE name=$n");
        die $DBH->errstr unless ref $sth;
        $sth->execute() || die $sth->errstr;

        $r = $sth->fetchrow_arrayref;
    };

    if ($@) {
        $self->error("Story::DBI: could not determine " .
                     "id of story set '$set_name': $@");
        return;
    }

    return $r->[0];
}
```

```perl
# set the local field, and
# the story field
sub story_set_id {
  my $self = shift;
  my $id   = shift;
  return $self->{'story_set_id'} unless $id;

  # set my obj. field
  $self->{'story_set_id'} = $id;

  # and the field in my story hash
  $self->story->{'SET_ID'} = $id;

  # now update the db
  $self->dirty(1);
}

# convert set id to set name
sub story_set {
  my $self = shift;

  return unless $self->set_id;

  my ($sql, $sth, $sid, $r);

  $sid = $self->set_id;
  $sql = "SELECT name FROM story_sets WHERE id=$sid";

  eval {
    $sth = $DBH->prepare($sql);
    die $DBH->errstr unless ref $sth;

    $sth->execute || die $sth->errstr;

    $r = $sth->fetchrow_arrayref;

    return unless ref $r;
  };

  return $r->[0];
}

sub story_id {
  my $self = shift;
  my $id   = shift;

  return $self->{'story_id'} unless $id;

  die "Cannot override story id!"
    if (($self->{'story_id'}) &&
        ($id != $self->{'story_id'}));

  $self->{'story_id'} = $id;
  $self->dirty(1);
  return $id;
}
```

Here's an "object" lesson in why you should always use accessor functions instead of directly accessing the fields of an object. To a caller, these functions look no different than those in Story::Text, but they are implemented in a completely different way, and do a lot more than just return a predetermined value. If we had been accessing story values by saying **$story->{'field'}** instead of **$story->field()**, we couldn't do this.

```
# return the story template, or the default template
# for the story's story_set, if the story tmpl is
# not defined
sub template {
  my $self = shift;
  return $self->_get_field_or_dflt('template','dflt_tmpl');
}

sub target {
  my $self = shift;
  return $self->_get_field_or_dflt('target','dflt_target');
}

sub title {
  my $self = shift;
  return $self->_get_field_or_dflt('title','dflt_title');
}

sub author {
  my $self = shift;
  return $self->_get_field_or_dflt('author','dflt_author');
}

sub summary {
  my $self = shift;
  return $self->_get_field_or_dflt('summary','dflt_summary');
}

# a generalized routine to get a field value, if present,
# or the corresponding story_set field
sub _get_field_or_dflt {
  my $self      = shift;
  my $story_fld = shift;
  my $set_fld   = shift;

  my ($set_id,$sql,$sth,$rc,$set);

  $story_fld = uc($story_fld);

  return $self->story->{$story_fld} if $self->story->{$story_fld};

  $set_id = $self->story_set_id;

  $sql = "SELECT * FROM story_sets WHERE id='$set_id'";
```

```
eval {
  $sth = $DBH->prepare($sql);
  die $DBH->errstr unless ref $sth;

  $rc = $sth->execute;
  die $sth->errstr unless $rc;

  $set = $sth->fetchrow_hashref;
};

if ($@) {
  $self->error("Story::DBI: _get_field_or_dflt: $@");
  return;
}

return $set->{$set_fld};
}
```

Another "object" lesson: a modification of our regular AUTOLOAD function looks for unknown fields in the story hash before giving up. This makes it possible to say, for example, **$story->text()**, and actually get the value of **$story->story->{'TEXT'}**.

We examine the function that the caller has tried to call. If the name matches an object field, we access that field. If not, we check the name against the fields in the story hash, and if it matches any of those, we access that value. AUTOLOAD is just *so* cool Jason can hardly stand it. Molly just figures it's one of those programmer things—but if he thinks it's cool, well, it *must* be cool.

```
sub AUTOLOAD {
  my $self = shift;
  my $type = ref($self) || ( die "$self is not an object" );
  my $name = $AUTOLOAD;
  my $ptr  = $self;
  my $dirt = $self->{'dirty'};
  $name =~ s/.*:://;

  unless (exists $self->{$name}){

    $ptr = $self->{'story'};
    $name = uc($name);

    #
    # if we're going to set a value
    # in the story fields, make sure we
    # save our state when we die
    #
    $dirt = 1;
    unless (exists ($self->{'story'}->{$name})) {
```

```
      die "Can't access '$name' field in object of class $type";
    }
  }

  if (@_) {
    $self->{'dirty'} = $dirt;
    return $ptr->{$name} = shift;
  } else {
    return $ptr->{$name};
  }
}
```

Here's where all those **$self->{'dirty'}** statements pay off. If any story hash data has been changed, we'll update the database automatically before going away. This makes the Story::DBI object's data storage totally transparent to a script that uses it—you can just use it as if it were a magical object that knows when to save its state between sessions, never worrying about when or how that happens.

```
sub DESTROY {
  my $self = shift;

  warn "wrong type" unless ref $self;

  # sync our local data, if any, with the database
  if (($self->dirty) && ($self->story_id) && ($self->story)) {
    $self->add_story( $self->story_id, $self->story );
  }
}
```

Okay, you made it! Time to move on to our next module!

Publisher::Index::Multi.pm

This module is an extension of Publisher::Index that handles multi-part indexes. In real language, this means if we have a news page with sections for Top Stories, World News, Local News, Sports, and so forth, this module can manage that topical breakdown.

If you're thinking this sounds like what we described earlier as *story sets*, you're right on target! In this package, each of those sections would in fact be a story set. This is why the story sets we say in Story::DBI come in handy—we can use a story's set to determine which section of the index it should go in. We'll show you shortly how to use Netscape cookies to allow users to determine which index sections they'd like to see at all.

All of this totals up to some pretty powerful user-driven content.
Here's the module:

Publisher::Index::Multi.pm

```perl
package Publisher::Index::Multi;

# for security
$ENV{'PATH'}  = '/bin:/usr/bin:/usr/local/bin';
$ENV{'SHELL'} = '/bin/sh';
$ENV{'ENV'}   = '';
$ENV{'IFS'}   = '';

# modules
use lib '/path/to/library';
use Publisher::Index;

use Cwd;
use CGI;                    # for the function &escape()
use CGI::FastTemplate;
use strict;
use vars qw(@ISA $AUTOLOAD);

@ISA = qw(Publisher::Index);

my %fields = ( 'tpl'         => undef,
               'tmpl_dir'    => undef,
               'item_tmpl'   => undef,
               'set_tmpl'    => undef,
               'page_tmpl'   => undef,
               'story_sets'  => undef,
               'page'        => undef,
               'target'      => undef,
               'www_root'    => undef,
               'error'       => undef, );

sub new {
  my $proto = shift;
  my $class = ref($proto) || $proto;
  my $self  = { %fields };

  bless $self, $class;
  $self->_initialize();

  return $self;
}

sub _initialize {
  my $self = shift;
  my $tpl  = new CGI::FastTemplate;
  $self->tpl($tpl);
}
```

Let's break in here with a comment about data storage. We use a
fairly complex data structure to keep the stories and story sets in
line. The **story_sets** field is a hash of hashes of arrays and hashes.
Yikes! If you were to blow it up it would look like this:

```
story_sets->{'SET_1'}->{'set_tmpl'  =>'template',
                        'item_tmpl' =>'another_template',
                        'stories'   =>
                           [0]->{'story'=>story, 'url'=> }
                           [1]->{'story'=>story, 'url'=> }
                           [2]->{'story'=>story, 'url'=> } }
              {'SET_2'}->{'set_tmpl'  =>'template',
                        'item_tmpl' =>'another_template',
                        'stories'   =>
                           [0]->{'story'=>story, 'url'=> }
                           [1]->{'story'=>story, 'url'=> } }
```

. . . and so on. It's harder to explain than it is to use, luckily!

```perl
sub add_story {
  my $self  = shift;
  my $set   = shift;
  my $story = shift;
  my $url   = shift;

  $set ||= 'DEFAULT_SET';

  unless (ref $story) {
    $self->error("Publisher::Index::Multi: add_story: " .
                 "no story specified");
    return;
  }

  # create a hash with the story fields, and url of the story's
  # HTML page, defaulting to using the value of the story's
  # published_as field as the url, if none is specified

  my %st = ( 'story' => $story,
             'url'   => $self->make_abs_url( ($url
                            || $story->published_as() )) );

  # make sure the set for this story is defined
  $self->add_story_set( $set );

  # get the list of stories for the set
  my $tmp = $self->story_sets->{$set}->{'stories'};
  $tmp ||= [];

  # add the story to the set's list of stories
  push @$tmp, { %st };
  $self->story_sets->{$set}->{'stories'} = $tmp;
```

```perl
    return 1;
}

sub add_story_set {
  my $self     = shift;
  my $set      = shift;
  my $set_tmpl  = shift;
  my $item_tmpl = shift;

  $self->{'story_sets'}     ||= {};

  # don't define it twice...
  return if ref $self->story_sets->{$set};

  $self->story_sets->{$set} ||= { ( 'set_tmpl'  => undef,
                                    'item_tmpl' => undef,
                                    'stories'   => undef,
                                    'html'          => undef, ) };

  # NOTE that these are template NAMES not template FILE names --
  # you must make the templates you want to use known to the
  # publisher with use_template before using them!
  ($set_tmpl) &&
    ($self->story_sets->{$set}->{'set_tmpl'} = $set_tmpl);
  ($item_tmpl) &&
    ($self->story_sets->{$set}->{'item_tmpl'} = $item_tmpl);
}

sub publish {
  my $self      = shift;
  my $target_fl = shift;
  my $page_tmpl = shift;
  my $set_tmpl  = shift;
  my $item_tmpl = shift;

  my $published;

  unless ($self->build_page($page_tmpl,$set_tmpl,$item_tmpl)) {
    my $err = $self->error;
    $self->error("Publisher::Index::Multi: " .
                 "unable to build page: $err");
    return;
  }

  unless ($published = $self->write_file($target_fl)) {
    $self->error("Publisher::Index::Multi: ".
                 "unable to write file $target_fl");

    return;
  }

  return $published;
}
```

Because we're dealing with more than one set of stories, building the page is more complex than it was in Publisher::Index. We have to step through the **story_sets** hash, building for each a template object constructed of rows for each story (formatted by **item_tmpl**). Each must contain the full formatting of the HTML block from **set_tmpl**.

Then we assign those HTML blocks to variables in the main page template, using the name of the set as the variable name. It's a mouthful to explain, but we promise it's easy to use. Simply put, the name of a story set in your index page template, and the set's story links will appear at that spot in the final page.

```perl
sub build_page {
  my $self      = shift;
  my $page_tmpl = shift;
  my $set_tmpl  = shift;
  my $item_tmpl = shift;

  my $tpl = $self->tpl;
  my ($set_html, $p);

  $page_tmpl ||= $self->page_tmpl;

  # build each story set
  foreach my $st(keys %{$self->story_sets}) {
    unless ($set_html = $self->build_story_set($st,
                                               $set_tmpl,
                                               $item_tmpl)) {
      $self->error("Publisher::Index::Multi: ".
                   "failed to build story set $st");
      return;
    }

    # Assign the result to a template variable with the
    # same name as the set. Use this variable in the main
    # page template to place the story set.
    $tpl->assign( uc($st)=>$set_html );
  }

  # build the whole page
  $tpl->parse( 'MAIN', $page_tmpl );
  $self->page( $tpl->fetch('MAIN') );

  $p = $self->page;

  if ((ref $p) && ($$p)) {
    return $p;
  } else {
    $self->error("Publisher::Index::Multi: failed to build page");
    return;
  }
}
```

In this case, we have to take into account the likelihood that the method will be called several times in succession. So, we have to clean out the old template assignments before we do anything else.

The **build_story_set()** method in this class is pretty similar to the **build_page()** function in **Publisher::Index()** – as you'd expect, because they both take a single group of stories and produce a block of HTML with links to those stories.

The big difference? In your page templates for **Publisher::Index**, you included **<html>** and **<body>** tags.

```perl
sub build_story_set {
  my $self     = shift;
  my $set      = shift;
  my $set_tmpl     = shift;
  my $item_tmpl     = shift;

  my $tpl = $self->tpl;

  my ($s,$p,$st);

  # return a single space, NOT the empty string, otherwise
  # the names of empty story sets will appear in the output page!
  return ' ' unless $self->story_sets->{$set}->{'stories'};

  $st = $self->story_sets->{$set}->{'stories'};

  # these rather hideous constructions allow a cascading override
  # of the default values for templates -- use what we're told,
  # or what the story set wants, or, last resort, the default
  $set_tmpl  ||= $self->story_sets->{$set}->{'set_tmpl'}
    || $self->set_tmpl;
  $item_tmpl ||= $self->story_sets->{$set}->{'item_tmpl'}
    || $self->item_tmpl;

  # clean up a bit -- this is needed so that the stories from
  # the first set won't get tacked on to the second
  $tpl->clear('STORIES');

  # build the STORIES item for insertion into set tmpl
  foreach $s(@$st) {

    $tpl->assign( 'ST_TITLE'   => $s->{'story'}->title,
          'ST_URL'     => $s->{'url'},
          'ST_AUTHOR'  => $s->{'story'}->author,
          'ST_SUMMARY' => $s->{'story'}->summary, );

    $tpl->parse( 'STORIES' => ".$item_tmpl" );
  }

  # pass the set name, in clear and HTML escaped form,
  # to the template
  $tpl->assign( 'SET_NAME' => $set,
      'ESC_SET'   => CGI::escape($set), );

  # build the html block for this set
  $tpl->parse( uc($set) => $set_tmpl );
  $p = $tpl->fetch( uc($set) );
```

```
  if ((ref $p) && ($$p)) {
    $self->story_sets->{$set}->{'html'} = $$p;
    return $$p;
  } else {
    $self->error("Publisher::Index::Multi: " .
      "failed to generate html block for story set '$set'");
    return;
  }
}
```

Finally, two functions that help us make the links we produce actually point to the story pages, and our old friend AUTOLOAD.

```
# Take a file path, make it into a URL
# that is absolute (from the root of $self->www_root)
sub make_abs_url {
  my $self = shift;
  my $file = shift;
  my $dir  = $self->www_root;

  $file = &_full_path($file);
  $file =~ s|^$dir(/?)|/|;

  # Note that if the filename was a full path to a file
  # outside of www_root, we haven't changed it
  # at all!
  return $file;
}

sub _full_path {
  my $file = shift;
  return $file if ($file =~ m|^/|);

  my $cwd = cwd();
  return "$cwd/$file";
}

sub AUTOLOAD {
  my $self = shift;
  my $type = ref($self) || (die "$self is not an object" );
  my $name = $AUTOLOAD;

  $name =~ s/.*:://;
  unless (exists $self->{$name}){
    die "Can't access '$name' field in object of class $type";
  }

  if (@_) {
    return $self->{$name} = shift;
  } else {
    return $self->{$name};
  }
}
```

Okay, you're through that step. But there's miles to go before you rest. We promise it will be worth it, and we'll even serve up cookies along the way. Next in line, the CGI you'll need.

CGI

Naturally, you're going to need to use CGI to help shuttle all of the information around. Here's a look at the script that pulls it all together.

my.cgi

This CGI implements the basic personalization for a portal style "newsy" Web site. It uses a cookie to track users, storing user id and preferences in a SQL database using DBI. A user can pick which sets of stories he or she wants to see regularly on the index page (Figure 9.1).

Users are tracked silently, and don't need to register or sign up to enable the page.

Figure 9.1

Pick the stories you want!

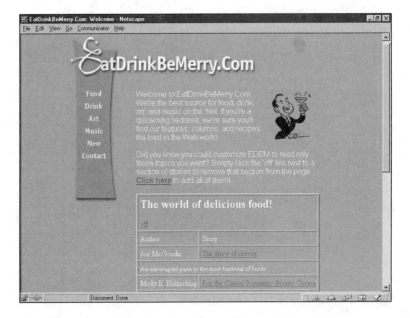

my.cgi

```perl
#!/usr/bin/perl -wT

# local libraries
use lib '/path/to/library';
use Story::DBI;
use Publisher::Index::Multi;
use Taintcheck;

use CGI;
use DBI;

use strict;
use vars qw($__START__ $CGI $AGE_LIMIT $DBH $DSN $USER $PASSWD
            $TMPL_DIR $PAGE_TMPL $SET_TMPL $ITEM_TMPL);

# DBI connection settings. Replace the driver, hostname, database,
# user, and user password file with values
# appropriate to your site
$DSN     = 'dbi:mysql:hostname=localhost:database=test';
$USER    = 'web_user';
$PASSWD  = `cat /path/to/web_user/passwd_file`;
chomp($PASSWD); # remove newline that cat appends

$CGI     = 'my.cgi';

# number of days 'young' a story must be to
# be included.
$AGE_LIMIT = 7;

# replace with real path to template directory
$TMPL_DIR = '/path/to/templates';

# required template
$PAGE_TMPL = 'idx_page';

# optional templates
$SET_TMPL = 'basic_set';
$ITEM_TMPL = 'basic_item';

eval { main(); }; $__START__ = __LINE__;

if ($@) {
  chomp($@);

  $@ =~ s/\(eval\) line (\d+)/${CGI} . " line " .
    ($__START__-$1-1)/e;
  $@ =~ s/( at ).*( line )/$1${CGI}$2/;

  my $error_message = $@;

  print <<ERR;
Content-type: text/html
```

my.cgi (continued)

```
<HTML>
  <HEAD><TITLE>Error</TITLE></HEAD>
  <BODY>
    <H1>Error</H1>
    <code>$error_message</code>
  </BODY>
</HTML>
ERR

}

exit(0);

sub main {
  my ($q, $user, $set, %sets, $pub, $page);
  my ($set_tmpl, $item_tmpl, $stories, $story, $cookie);

  # uncomment this if you're having trouble debugging
  # problems with database access
  #DBI->trace(2);

  # connect to the database
  $DBH = Story::DBI->db_connect($DSN, $USER, $PASSWD);
  die "Could not connect to database" unless (ref $DBH);

  # get and untaint input
  $q = new CGI;
  untaint_params($q);

  # get the user record associated with the cookie
  # if there is no cookie, or if the user record
  # is invalid, a new user record will be created
  # and returned.
  $user = get_user($q);
  die "Could not get user record" unless $user;

  $pub = new Publisher::Index::Multi();
  die "Could not initialize publisher: " .
    $pub->error if $pub->error;


  # set up the template & publishing environment
  # replace the path with the real path to your www root directory
  # (for redhat linux users, for example, /home/httpd/html)
  $pub->www_root('/path/to/www/root');
  $pub->template_dir($TMPL_DIR);
  $pub->use_template('MAIN', $PAGE_TMPL, 'page');
  $pub->use_template('SET', $SET_TMPL, 'set');
  $pub->use_template('ITEM', $ITEM_TMPL, 'item');

  # select stories, according to user prefs
  foreach $set (@{$user->{'sets'}}) {
```

my.cgi (continued)

```
    # define any templates used in the set
    $set_tmpl  = '';
    $item_tmpl = '';

    if ($set->{'set_tmpl'}) {
      $set_tmpl = ($set->{'name'}) . '_set_tmpl';
      $pub->use_template( $set_tmpl, $set->{'set_tmpl'} );
    }

    if ($set->{'item_tmpl'}) {
      $item_tmpl = ($set->{'name'}) . '_item_tmpl';
      $pub->use_template( $item_tmpl, $set->{'item_tmpl'} );
    }

    # add the set
    $pub->add_story_set( $set->{'name'}, $set_tmpl, $item_tmpl );

    # get the set's stories
    $stories = select_stories($set);

    # add those stories
    if (ref $stories) {
      foreach $story(@$stories) {
        $pub->add_story( $set->{'name'}, $story );
      }
    }
  }

# make the page -- here we don't use the
# publish method, which saves a file to disk,
# because we're going to send the created page
# right to the browser.

my $p = $pub->build_page();

if (ref $p) {
  $page = $$p;
} else {
  die "Could not generate page: " . $pub->error;
}

# finally, send the page to the browser,
# and set the cookie, so that the user's preferences will
# 'stick' for her next visit
$cookie = $q->cookie(-name=>'my.cgi_userid',
                     -value=>$user->{'id'});
print $q->header(-cookie=>$cookie), $page;
}
```

There are three scenarios we have to deal with when trying to get a user's preferences: the new user; the repeat visitor whose cookie correctly picks out her user record; and the user with a bad cookie (or our site with a bad database) that isn't associated with a user record.

```perl
sub get_user {
  my $q = shift;

  my ($uid,$user);

  # get or create a user id
  unless (($q->cookie('my.cgi_userid')) &&
      ($user = user_prefs($q->cookie('my.cgi_userid'),$q))) {
    $user = user_prefs(new_user());
  }

  return $user;
}
```

When we create a new user record, we don't store much information—just the user id and a timestamp, both of which are generated automatically. If you want to store more information, you'll have to update both the **users** table definition, and this function.

```perl
sub new_user {
  my ($uid,$sth);

  # insert a new user record
  $sth = $DBH->prepare("INSERT INTO users VALUES(NULL,NULL)")
    || die $DBH->errstr;
  $sth->execute() || die $sth->errstr();

  # this is MySQL specific -- if you use an different
  # database, you'll have to look in its documentation
  # for an equivalent function.
  $uid = $sth->{'mysql_insertid'};
  die "Failed to create new user" unless $uid;

  return $uid;
}

sub user_prefs {
  my $uid = shift;
  my $q   = shift;

  return unless $uid;

  my (@updates, $sth, $r);

  if ($q) {
    @updates = map { /^update_(.*)$/ ? $1 : () } $q->param;

    if (@updates) {
```

To update a user's preferences in the database, we make a **user_set** record for each **update_[set name]** parameter in the CGI parameter list. You make this work by submitting form fields like: **<input name="update_localnews" value="0">** to turn off the section with stories from the localnews set, or **<input name="update_localnews" value="1">** to turn it on.

```perl
      foreach my $set(@updates) {

        # get the id of the user_set for this
        # story_set/user combo
         $sth = $DBH->prepare("SELECT us.id FROM
                    user_sets as us, story_sets as s
                        WHERE us.user_id=$uid AND
                        s.name='$set' AND us.set_id=s.id");

        die $DBH->errstr unless ref $sth;

        $sth->execute() || die $sth->errstr;
        $r = $sth->fetchrow_arrayref;

        # update the user set setting
        $DBH->do("UPDATE user_sets SET display=" .
              $q->param("update_$set") .
              " WHERE id=" . $r->[0])
          || die $DBH->errstr;
      }
    }

  } else {
    # no input to work from - fall back on the default, and
    # get all sets, making a user_set record for each
    $sth = $DBH->prepare("SELECT id FROM story_sets");
    die $DBH->errstr unless ref $sth;

    $sth->execute() || die $sth->errstr;

    while(my @r = $sth->fetchrow_array) {
      $DBH->do("INSERT INTO user_sets VALUES(NULL,$uid," .
            $DBH->quote($r[0]) .
            ",1,NULL)")
        || die $DBH->errstr;
    }

  }

  return read_user($uid);
}

sub read_user{
  my $uid = shift;
  my ($sth, $u, $tmp, $r);

  die "read_user: No user id submitted" unless $uid;
```

```perl
    # get the user record from the database
    $sth = $DBH->prepare("SELECT * FROM users WHERE id=$uid");
    die $DBH->errstr unless ref $sth;

    $sth->execute || die $sth->errstr;

    # fetch the whole user record, with field names
    $u = $sth->fetchrow_hashref;
    return unless ref $u;

    # then build the $u->{'sets'} field
    # from the user_sets table in the db
    $sth = $DBH->prepare("SELECT s.id, s.name, s.idx_set_tmpl,
                          s.idx_item_tmpl, us.display
                          FROM user_sets as us, story_sets as s
                          WHERE us.user_id=$uid
                          AND s.id=us.set_id");

    die $DBH->errstr unless ref $sth;

    $sth->execute || die $sth->errstr;

    while ($r = $sth->fetchrow_arrayref) {

      my %h = ( 'id'        => $r->[0],
                'name'      => $r->[1],
                'set_tmpl'  => $r->[2],
                'item_tmpl' => $r->[3],
                'display'   => $r->[4], );

      $tmp = $u->{'sets'};
      $tmp ||= [];

      push @$tmp, { %h };
      $u->{'sets'} = $tmp;
    }

    return unless ref $u->{'sets'};
    return $u;
}

# get the stories in each set
# that are younger than $AGE_LIMIT
sub select_stories {
  my $set    = shift;
  my $set_id = $set->{'id'};

  my ($sql, $sth, $r, @stories);

  # only load stories for the sets the user wants
  return @stories unless $set->{'display'};

  $sql = "SELECT id FROM stories
          WHERE set_id='$set_id'
          AND (TO_DAYS(CURRENT_DATE) - TO_DAYS(created)
          <= $AGE_LIMIT)";
```

```
$sth = $DBH->prepare($sql);
die $DBH->errstr unless ref $sth;

$sth->execute || die $sth->errstr;

while( $r = $sth->fetchrow_arrayref ) {
  my $s = new Story::DBI( $r->[0] );
  push @stories, $s;
}

return \@stories;
}
```

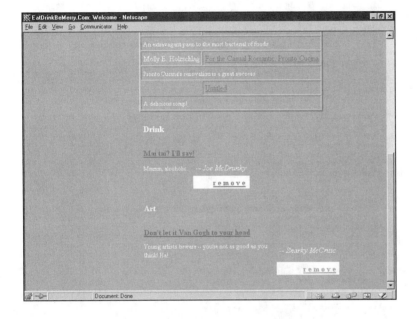

Figure 9.2

Don't like the way the results look? Change your preferences via the page options.

Now let's take a look at some utilities that will help you get down to the nitty-gritty publishing and management of the user-driven content you're creating.

Utilities

The following Perl scripts will help you write, add, and publish your stories on your site.

Perl Web Site Workshop

story_txt2dbi.pl

Ok, so this is all lovely, you say, but what about all of those story text files I so laboriously created in the last chapter? Do I throw them out?

Nope. You pop them into the database, very easily, by reading them with **Story::Text**, and copying them into **Story::DBI** objects, with this short script.

```perl
#!/usr/bin/perl

use lib '/path/to/library';
use Taintcheck;
use Story::Text;
use Story::DBI;
use strict;
use vars qw($DSN $USER $PASSWD $DBH);

# globals
# replace these with values appropriate to your site
$DSN    = 'DBI:mysql:database=stories:host=localhost';
$USER   = 'user';
$PASSWD = 'secret';

# usage
die usage() unless $ARGV[0];

# connect to the database
$DBH = Story::DBI->db_connect($DSN,$USER,$PASSWD);

die "Could not connect to database with DSN $DSN, " .
    "user $USER and passwd [hidden]" unless ref $DBH;

# convert each story passed on the command line
# you can easily convert whole directories by using wildcards
foreach my $st(@ARGV) {
  convert_story(untaint($st) );
}

# subroutines

# read the submitted text file and submit it to the database
sub convert_story {
  my $story_file = shift;

  my ($text_story, $db_story, $st, $ti);

  $text_story = new Story::Text( $story_file );
  die $text_story->error if $text_story->error;

  # the first parameter is the id of the story to
  # read or update; since we're creating a new story,
```

```
    # we send an empty string.
    $db_story = new Story::DBI( '', $text_story->story );

    die $db_story->error if $db_story->error;

    $ti = $db_story->title || 'untitled';
    $st = $db_story->story->{'STORY'} || '(unnamed)';


    print "Story '$ti' was successfully converted " .
          "from text file $st.\n";
}

sub usage {
  return <<USAGE;
story_txt2dbi.pl story_file [story_file …]
USAGE
}
```

add_story_set.pl

The addition of story sets to the database provides more flexibility
and power, but it's also one more thing to maintain. If you don't
want to set up your sets when you create your tables, or want to add
more later, you can use this utility script.

We also take this opportunity to introduce the **GetOpt::Long** module
(part of the standard Perl distribution), which is very useful in
command-line scripts. This module makes it possible for your
program to accept verbose options on the command line, so that
users of the script can say script –option instead of script –o.

In this case, we make use of it to save some work by naming our
options with the names of database fields. We can then pipe input
directly into the right places, without having to do any guessing
about what goes where.

add_story_set.pl

```
#!/usr/bin/perl -w
#
#
# add_story_set.pl
#
# creates story set record

use DBI;
use Getopt::Long;
```

add_story_set.pl (continued)

```perl
use strict;
use vars qw($DBH $DSN $USER $PASS %OPTS);

# globals
# replace these with values appropriate to your site
$DSN  = 'dbi:mysql:hostname=localhost:database=test';
$USER = 'user';
$PASS = 'secret';

# get command line options
%OPTS = ();
GetOptions(\%OPTS, 'idx_set_tmpl:s', 'idx_item_template:s', 'dflt_tmpl:s',
'dflt_target:s', 'dflt_title:s', 'dflt_author:s', 'dflt_summary:s');

die usage() unless $ARGV[0];

$DBH = DBI->connect($DSN, $USER, $PASS);
die "Could not connect to database" unless ref $DBH;

add_set($ARGV[0], \%OPTS);

# subroutines

sub add_set {
  my $set_name = shift;
  my $opts     = shift;

  my ($sql, @flds, @vals);

  #
  # build the sql statement that will add the set
  #
  $sql = "INSERT INTO story_sets ";

  # add the one required field
  push @flds, 'name';
  push @vals, $DBH->quote($set_name);

  # and any of the optional fields that are set
  foreach my $f(keys %$opts) {
    push @flds, $f;
    push @vals, $DBH->quote($opts->{$f});
  }
  $sql .= '(' . join (', ', @flds) .
    ') VALUES (' . join (', ', @vals) . ')';

  #
  # execute the SQL statement, and report the results
  #
  $DBH->do($sql) || die $DBH->errstr;
```

add_story_set.pl (continued)

```perl
  print "Story set $set_name was added succesfully.\n";
}

sub usage {

return <<USAGE;
add_story_set.pl set_name [--idx_set_tmpl template] \
 [--idx_item_template template] \
 [--dflt_tmpl template] \
 [--dflt_target target_file | target_dir] \
 [--dflt_title 'story title'] \
 [--dflt_author 'author'] [--dflt_summary 'summary']USAGE}
```

publish_dbi.pl

Our last utility is more of an example of how to use Story::DBI, than it is a real utility. Nobody remembers the ID numbers of database records—so how is this useful? First, it demonstrates the power of object-oriented programming. The differences between this script, which accesses a SQL database for its data, and publish.pl, which only uses flat-text files, are minimal. The pages are actually produced by exactly the same code, the Publisher module.

Second, you should take a good look at this module because you'll see this code again in Chapter 10, "Web Site Publishing Wizard." In that chapter, we show you a completely Web-based publishing system that uses Story::DBI, and code just like this, to take all the command lines and text files out of this publishing business, and lets you run your whole site from a browser.

publish_dbi.pl

```perl
#!/usr/bin/perl
use lib '/path/to/library';
use Publisher;
use Story::DBI;
use Taintcheck;

use Getopt::Std;
use strict;
use vars qw($opt_f $opt_d $STORY $TEMPLATE $TARGET
            $TEMPLATE_DIR $DBH $DSN $USER $PASSWD);

die usage() unless @ARGV;

getopt('fd');
```

publish_dbi.pl (continued)

```perl
$STORY        = untaint($ARGV[0]);
$TEMPLATE     = untaint($ARGV[1]);
$TARGET       = untaint($ARGV[2]);
$TEMPLATE_DIR = untaint($opt_d) ||
  '/path/to/templates';

$DSN    = 'DBI:mysql:database=test:host=localhost';
$USER   = 'root';
$PASSWD = 'potato';

$DBH = Story::DBI->db_connect($DSN,$USER,$PASSWD);

die "Could not connect to database with DSN $DSN, " .
    "user $USER and passwd [hidden]" unless ref $DBH;

if ($opt_f) {

  my $s;
  my @stories = read_opts_file(untaint($opt_f) );

  foreach $s(@stories) {
    &publish_page(@$s);
  }

} else {

  die usage() unless $STORY;
  publish_page( $STORY, $TEMPLATE, $TARGET );

}

sub read_opts_file {
  my $file = shift;
  my ($story, $tmpl, $targ, @stories);

  # option file format is:
  # story [template] [target]
  open (OPTS, "<$file")
    || die "publish.pl: could not read options file $file";

  while (<OPTS>) {
    chomp;
    push @stories, [ split(/[\s\t]+/, $_) ];
  }

  close OPTS;

  return @stories;
}

sub publish_page {
  my $story    = shift;
```

publish_dbi.pl (continued)

```
  my $template = shift;
  my $target   = shift;

  my ($s, $p);

  $s = new Story::DBI($story);
  die "Could not read story $story" unless ref $s;

  $p = new Publisher($s);
  die "Could not create publisher for " . $story->story_file
    unless ref $p;
  $p->template_dir( $TEMPLATE_DIR ) || die $p->error;
  $p->use_template( 'MAIN', $template ) || die $p->error;
  ($target)   && ($p->target( $target ));

  $p->publish() || die $p->error;
}

sub usage {

  return <<USAGE;
usage:
publish_dbi.pl [-d template_dir] story_id [template] [target_file]
 | -f file
Use -f file to read story/template/target triplets from a file
USAGE

}
```

What's Up Next

By now you should be able to see that Perl is an intense part of making Web sites do amazing things. In this chapter, perhaps more than others that have come before, you've put a variety of powerful technologies to work including CGI, Perl, and databases.

In Chapter 10, we're going to take you to the next level and demonstrate, in great detail, exactly how you can use these techniques to manage a Web site.

Web Site Publishing Wizard

In this chapter, we'll use the skills you've built through this book to create a complete browser-based, Web site management system. Imagine sitting at your desk simply entering in text stories and images and having an easy-to-use Web interface that leads you and your coworkers through the daily management of your site.

Sounds great, right? It is. But, it takes organization and structure to put this Wizard into place. To that end, this chapter will require a little more intense study of where and how each script and module works to achieve the end goal.

The centerpiece of this system is the Site Manager script, siteman.cgi—affectionately termed "Siteman." It builds on the modules, scripts, and concepts from earlier chapters. When you use and understand the script in this chapter, you'll be able to create and update a complete, dynamic, customizable Web site directly from your Web browser (Figure 10.1).

Figure 10.1

A publishing interface built with Siteman.

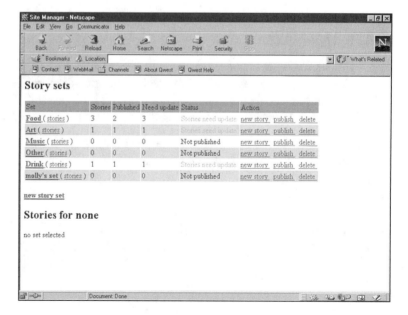

Be forewarned—if you have already set up the needed modules and helper scripts, setting up siteman.cgi is fairly straightforward. However, if you haven't already set these up, you will likely find the setup phase of this process somewhat complex—because it is! Begin by checking to see that the following modules are in place and working properly:

- Publisher

- Publisher::Index

- Story::DBI

- Publisher::Index::Multi (Only if you want to use the my.cgi front end. See Chapter 9, "Creating Your Own Portal.")

After you've ascertained that everything is functioning properly, you'll need to add a few tables to your stories SQL database. You can do that by following these steps:

1. Create the following file auth.sql and save it to your root direc-tory.

2. Type `mysql -u[root user] -p[password] stories < auth.sql` on the command line. This will generate the tables for your database.

auth.sql

```
drop table if exists auth_users\g
drop table if exists session\g

create table auth_users (
    id          int not null auto_increment,
    login       char(16) not null,
    passwd      char(16) not null,
    active      int not null,
    key (active),
    unique (login),
    key (passwd),
```

auth.sql (continued)

```
    primary key (id)
)\g

create table sessions (
    id          int not null auto_increment,
    login       char(16) not null,
    ts          timestamp not null,
    key (ts),
    key (login),
    primary key (id)
)\g

# replace the login and password here
# with unique settings of your own.
INSERT INTO auth_users VALUES (NULL, 'admin',
   PASSWORD('bingo'), 1)\g
```

In the last portion of the database, you'll notice the function for login (Figure 10.2). This is our first step in user authentication and security, which will remain a constant, important issue throughout this chapter.

Figure 10.2

Authorization entryway.

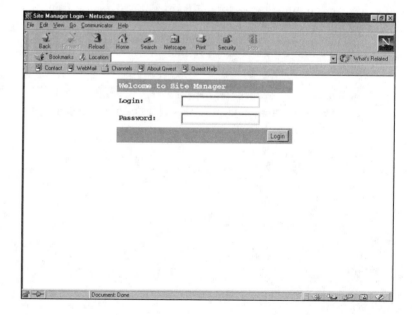

The Siteman script needs two SUID scripts. Remember, these are your Set User ID scripts, which gives the person running the script privilege levels based *on the script*—no matter who they are. One of these, publish_dbi.pl, is available in Chapter 9. You should have it up and running properly—if not, go back to Chapter 9 and set it up. The second script you'll create now.

You'll be placing Publish_set.pl in your user utility directory, and set permissions by typing CHMOD +xs publish_set.pl.

Publish_set.pl

```perl
#!/usr/bin/perl -wT

$ENV{'PATH'}  = '/bin:/usr/bin:/usr/local/bin';
$ENV{'SHELL'} = '/bin/sh';
$ENV{'IFS'}   = '';
$ENV{'ENV'}   = '';

use lib '/path/to/library';
use Taintcheck;
use Story::DBI;
use Publisher;
use Publisher::Index;

use Getopt::Long;
use strict;
use vars qw(%OPT $DBH $DSN $USER $PASSWD $TMPL_DIR $PAGE $ITEM);

$DSN    = 'dbi:mysql:hostname=localhost:database=stories';
$USER   = 'author';
$PASSWD = 'auth_pass';

# defaults for templates
$TMPL_DIR = '/path/to/templates';
$PAGE     = 'basic_index_page';
$ITEM     = 'basic_index_item';

$DBH = DBI->connect($DSN, $USER, $PASSWD);
die "Could not connect to database" unless ref $DBH;

# use the same database connection for stories
$Story::DBI::DBH = $DBH;
```

As we continue, let's look at some of the technical concepts used by this script. In the following sequence, we use the Getopt::Long module. This is part of the standard Perl distribution, and is used to read command-line options.

Because SUID scripts give over the permission of the script, they require a bit more tender care! If you put an SUID inside the cgi-bin directory, you create a serious security problem. SUID scripts should be placed in a separate utility directory, clearly outside of the cgi-bin directory.

Getopt::Long is a good choice for scripts that are called from other scripts (known as *cron jobs*). The long option names are much easier to interpret six months down the line when you're trying to figure out what that script you once wrote is supposed to be doing!

```
# get command-line options
GetOptions(\%OPT, "noindex", "nostories", "template-dir:s");

die usage() unless @ARGV;
```

Next, we process all of the rest of the arguments passed to the script, which are the id numbers of the story sets to be published.

```
foreach my $set(@ARGV) {
  eval {
    publish_set($set);
  };

  if ($@) {
    print "publish_set failed: $@\n";
    exit(1);
  }
}
```

For each set, the publish set function is called.

```
sub publish_set {
  my $id = shift;
  die "No set id submitted"  unless $id;

  my $set = get_story_set($id);
  die "Set does not exist" unless (ref $set);
  die "No stories in set" unless @{$set->{'stories'}};

  my (@stories, $now, $tmpl_dir, $page_tmpl,
      $item_tmpl, $p, $pi, $s);

  # the time we'll set published_on to
  $now = _sql_datetime(time);

  # create pub_dir if it doesn't already exist
  mkdir (untaint($set->{'pub_dir'}), oct '755')
    unless (-d $set->{'pub_dir'});

  # make sure pub_dir is there
  die "Could not create set publication directory"
    unless (-d $set->{'pub_dir'});

  # make a publisher & publisher::index
  $p  = new Publisher();
  $pi = new Publisher::Index();
```

```
# set pi story/page templates
$tmpl_dir  = $OPT{'template_dir'}     || $TMPL_DIR;
$page_tmpl = $set->{'idx_template'}   || $PAGE;
$item_tmpl = $set->{'idx_item_tmpl'}  || $ITEM;

$p->template_dir($tmpl_dir);
$pi->template_dir($tmpl_dir);

die $pi->error
  unless $pi->use_template( 'page_template',
            $page_tmpl, 'page' );
die $pi->error
  unless $pi->use_template( 'item_template',
            $item_tmpl, 'item' );

$pi->target( $set->{'pub_dir'} . '/index.html' );
```

We have to respect the -noindex and -nostories options. So, if the -nostories option has been passed, we only build a list of the stories we would have published, without actually publishing them. If -noindex is in effect, the stories will be published, but the index page will not.

Publishing a set means publishing the set's stories, as well as the index page that links to them all. The ID numbers, by the way, relate to the story *set*. Each set is then identified uniquely.

```
foreach $s(@{ $set->{'stories'} }) {
  $p->use_template($s->template);
  $p->story($s);
  $p->target($set->{'pub_dir'} . '/' . $s->target);

  if ($OPT{'nostories'}) {

    # just record the story, so we know to put it in  the index
    push @stories, [ $s,
                &relative_path($set->{'pub_dir'},
                      $s->published_as) ];

  } else {

    if ($p->publish()) {
        push @stories, [ $s,
                  &relative_path($set->{'pub_dir'},
                        $s->published_as) ];
        $s->published_on($now);

    } else {
        warn "Could not publish story " .
        $s->story_file . " (" . $p->error . ")";
    }

  }
}

die "Failed to publish any stories" unless @stories;
```

```perl
  foreach my $st(@stories) {
    $pi->add_story(@$st);
  }

  unless ($OPT{'noindex'}) {

    # write the index

    die "Could not publish story index (" . $pi->error . ")"
      unless $pi->publish();

    set_published($set, $now);
  }

  print "Story set $set published ok\n";
}

sub usage {
  return <<USAGE;
publish_set.pl set_id [--noindex] [--nostories] [--template_dir template_dir]
USAGE
}
```

Now comes our first example of how using a wrapper class like Story::DBI can make programming easier. Essentially, a wrapper class creates an easy interface for a more complex structure—in this case, a database table.

```perl
sub get_story_set {
  my $set_id = shift;

  my ($sql, $sth, $set, $r, $s, @stories);

  #
  # first get the set itself
  #
  $sql = "SELECT * FROM story_sets WHERE id=$set_id";
  $sth = $DBH->prepare($sql);
  die $DBH->errstr unless ref $sth;

  $sth->execute || die $sth->errstr;
  $set = $sth->fetchrow_hashref;

  die "No set with id $set_id" unless ref $set;

  #
  # now get the stories that fall under its threshold
  #
  $sql = "SELECT id FROM stories WHERE set_id=$set_id";
```

```
  if ($set->{'idx_threshold'}) {
    if ($set->{'idx_thresh_type'} eq 'age') {

      $sql = "SELECT id FROM stories WHERE set_id=$set_id " .
             "AND TO_DAYS(created) > (TO_DAYS(NOW()) - " .
             $set->{'idx_threshold'} .
             ") ORDER BY created DESC";

    } elsif ($set->{'idx_thresh_type'} eq 'count') {

      $sql = "SELECT id FROM stories WHERE set_id=$set_id " .
             "ORDER BY created DESC LIMIT " .
             $set->{'idx_threshold'};

    }
  }

  $sth = $DBH->prepare($sql);
  die $DBH->errstr unless ref $sth;

  $sth->execute || die $sth->errstr;

  while ($r = $sth->fetchrow_arrayref) {
    $s = new Story::DBI($r->[0]);
    push (@stories, $s) if (ref $s);
  }

  $set->{'stories'} = \@stories;
  return $set;
}
```

We need to update the database with publication information for the
set we just published, which is done in the following function:

```
sub set_published {
  my $set = shift;
  my $ts  = shift;

  my ($sql);

  $sql = "UPDATE story_sets SET published_on='$ts' " .
         "WHERE id=" . ($set->{'id'});

  $DBH->do($sql) || die $DBH->errstr;
}


sub relative_path {
  my $root = shift;
  my $file = shift;

  $file =~ s|^$root/?||;
```

```
  return $file;
}

#
# If you use a database other than MySQL, you may have to
# change this function
#
sub _sql_datetime {
  my $unixtime = shift;

  my ($sec, $min, $hour, $mday, $mon, $year, $wday, $yday, $isdst)
    = localtime($unixtime);

  # clean up a bit: add decimals, etc.
  $year += 1900;
  $mon++;
  ($mon < 10)     && ($mon = "0$mon");
  ($mday < 10)      && ($mday = "0$mday");
  ($sec < 10)     && ($sec = "0$sec");
  ($min < 10)     && ($min = "0$min");
  ($hour < 10)      && ($hour = "0$hour");

  return  "$year-$mon-$mday $hour:$min:$sec";
}
```

Okay! You've got your publish_set.pl ready to roll. Make sure it's placed in the same directory as the publish_dbi.pl. We're preparing you to set this up as the $SCRIPT_DIR for Siteman so that all these scripts will eventually work together smoothly.

Because these are SUID scripts, we have to give them special permissions. To do this:

Making these, or any, scripts SUID root is a very bad idea. If someone does manage to crack the script, and it is SUID root, they have just gained access to your whole system. For similar security reasons, it's best to keep all SUID scripts somewhere outside of your HTML directories. If the root of your HTML tree is in /home/httpd, for example, you might put all of your SUID scripts into /home/scripts, or in ~/bin (the bin directory in your home directory).

1. Log in to your server. You should have write privileges to the directories in which you're storing your site.

2. Make sure each script is located with the other. This must be in a proper, safe utility directory and *not* the cgi-bin.

3. From the command line, enter the command chmod +sx publish_dbi.pl to set the permissions for publish_dbi.pl

4. To set permissions for the other SUID Perl script, type chmod +sx publish_set.pl

When you have all of the modules and helper scripts set up, and have added the new tables to your stories database, you're ready to setup Siteman. The siteman.cgi script is the main brain of the entire

Web creation wizard, pulling all these management and development processes together with the modules to create the management interface.

The first block of code should be looking very familiar to you by now. We set things up to keep Perl's taint mechanism happy, and point the way to the modules and other files that the script will need.

Siteman.cgi

```perl
#!/usr/bin/perl -wT

$ENV{'PATH'}  = '/bin:/usr/bin:/usr/local/bin';
$ENV{'SHELL'} = '/bin/sh';
$ENV{'IFS'}   = '';
$ENV{'ENV'}   = '';

use lib '/path/to/library';
use Taintcheck;
use Story::DBI;
use Publisher;
use Publisher::Index;

use CGI;
use CGI::FastTemplate;
use strict;
use vars qw($DBH $DSN $USER $PASS $CGI $__START__
            $WWW_ROOT $SCREEN_DIR $SCRIPT_DIR $TMPL_DIR);

# GLOBALS
$DSN        = 'dbi:mysql:hostname=localhost:database=stories';
$USER       = 'author';
$PASS       = 'auth_pass';

$CGI        = 'siteman.cgi';

$WWW_ROOT   = '/path/to/www/root';
$SCREEN_DIR = '/path/to/screens';
$SCRIPT_DIR = '/path/to/scripts';
$TMPL_DIR   = '/path/to/templates';

# MAIN
eval { main(); }; $__START__ = __LINE__;

# ERRORS
if ($@) {
  chomp($@);
```

Siteman.cgi (continued)

```
$@ =~ s/\(eval\) line (\d+)/${CGI} .
  " line " . ($__START__-$1-1)/e;
$@ =~ s/( at ).*( line )/$1${CGI}$2/;

my $error_message = $@;

print <<ERR;
Content-type: text/html

<html>
  <head><title>Error</title></head>
  <body>
    <h1>Error</h1>
    <code>$error_message</code>
  </body>
</html>
ERR

}
```

Next comes main, which is primarily a dispatcher function. This helps us figure out whether a user attempting to work with the Siteman interface to publish stories is authorized. With this function, we also determine which screen he or she is coming from, and what function to call to handle the input from that screen.

In this version of main, we've avoided the usual huge if .. elsif .. elsif construction by using references to functions. Just as you can take a reference to a hash, array, or scalar value (See Chapter 11, "Getting Ready to Learn Perl"), you can take a reference to a function, pass that reference around just as you would any other variable, and then use it to call the function it points to. This is very convenient for a case like this, where what input we get determines how we want to process that input.

So the first thing we do is set up a hash, keyed on the parameter "screen" (which is present in each HTML page that makes up the Siteman interface), with the record value being a reference to the function that handles input from that screen. Thus, after making sure the user is authorized to use the system, all we have to do is figure out what screen we're coming from, and then hand off to the function associated with that screen, and we're done.

```perl
sub main {
  my $q = new CGI;
  my $screen;

  &untaint_params($q);

  # we use function references to connect
  # each screen in the CGI to the function that
  # processes input from that screen
  my %screen_funcs = ( 'begin'        => \&draw_login,
                       'login'        => \&handle_login,
                       'index'        => \&handle_index,
                       'info'         => \&handle_info,
                       'story_detail' => \&handle_story_detail,
                       'set_detail'   => \&handle_set_detail, );

  # make sure $SCREEN_DIR, $WWW_ROOT, and $SCRIPT_DIR exist
  die "Required directory not found"
    unless ((-d $SCREEN_DIR)    &&
            (-d $WWW_ROOT)      &&
            (-d $SCRIPT_DIR));

  # connect to database
  $DBH = DBI->connect($DSN,$USER,$PASS);
  $Story::DBI::DBH = $DBH;

  die "Could not connect to database"
    unless ref $DBH;

  #
  # determine which screen we're on, defaulting to  the first
  #
  $screen = $q->param('screen') || 'begin';

  # authenticate & authorize the user
  # using session_id parameter, unless she's trying to
  # log in, in which case the login screen handler will
  # take care of the authentication.
  unless ($screen eq 'login') {
    unless (&authorized( $q->param('session_id'),
                         $q->param('login')))
    {
      # user is not authorized - present login screen
      $screen = 'begin';
    }
  }

  #
  # process the screen, return results to browser
  #
  print $q->header,
        &{$screen_funcs{$screen}}($screen,$q);

}
```

Some of the screen handler functions are very simple—just drawing another screen, or checking the user's login and password.

```perl
#
# screen handlers
#
sub draw_login {
  my $screen = shift;
  my $q      = shift;

  return draw_screen('login',$q);
}

sub handle_login {
  my $screen = shift;
  my $q      = shift;
  my $session_id;

  #
  # authenticate login & password,
  #
  $session_id = &authorized(undef,
                       $q->param('login'),
                       $q->param('passwd'));

  #
  # create new session id and present index
  #
  if ($session_id) {
    $q->param('session_id',$session_id);

    return draw_index($q);
  } else {

    # the login was incorrect, deny access
    return draw_screen('bad_login');
  }
}


# info screens don't accept any input, so we don't have to
# do anything beyond go back to the index.
sub handle_info {
  my $screen = shift;
  my $q      = shift;

  draw_index($q);
}
```

But some functions are not simple at all. The most complex screen handler function deals with input from the main ('index') screen of the site manager. The index screen (see Figure 10.1) lists all the defined story sets and the individual stories for the selected story set. It allows the user to create, edit, delete, and publish stories and sets. It has to deal with a wide range of possible actions on stories and sets, so it has a lot of options.

```perl
# The index screen has a large number of options,
# so this is the most complicated handler.
sub handle_index {
  my $screen = shift;
  my $q      = shift;

  #
  # the 'do' param sets the action to take
  #
  my $do = $q->param('do');

  if ($do eq 'story_detail') {              # show story page

    # not new
    $q->param('new_record',0);

    # get the story
    &prep_story($q);

    # and show the detail screen
    return &draw_screen('story_detail',$q);

  } elsif ($do eq 'set_detail') {           # show set page

    # not new
    $q->param('new_record',0);

    # get the set
    prep_set($q);

    # and show the screen
    return draw_screen('set_detail',$q);

  } elsif($do eq 'new_story') {             # create new story

    # create a new story
    my $story = new Story::DBI('',
                        {'TITLE'  => 'Untitled',
                         'SET_ID' => $q->param('set_id')}});
    my $story_id = $story->id;

    # kill the created story object, which calls DESTROY which
    # writes it to db
    undef $story;

    # set story_id param to story's id
    $q->param('story_id',$story_id);
```

```perl
  # net new_record to true
  $q->param('new_record',1);

  # get it
  prep_story($q);

  # show its detail screen
  return &draw_screen('story_detail',$q);

} elsif($do eq 'new_set') {                    # create new set

  # create a new record in the database
  my $set_id = new_set();

  # save the id of the new rec
  $q->param('set_id',$set_id);

  # net new_record to true
  $q->param('new_record',1);

  # prep & show the detail screen
  prep_set($q);
  draw_screen('set_detail',$q);

} elsif ($do eq 'delete') {                    # delete something

  if ($q->param('set_id')) {
    return delete_set($q->param('set_id'));
  } elsif ($q->param('story_id')) {
    return delete_story($q->param('story_id'));
  } else {
    die "Cannot delete: no story or set specified";
  }

} elsif ($do eq 'publish') {                   # publish something

  if ($q->param('story_id')) {

    my $story = new Story::DBI($q->param('story_id'));
    die $story->error if $story->error;

    my $set = get_story_set($story->story_set_id);

    # pass along info to info sceen
    $q->param('TITLE', $story->title);
    $q->param('PUBLISHED_AS',
      $set->{'pub_dir'} . '/' . $story->target);
    $q->param('SELECT_SET', $set->{'id'});

    # call the SUID wrapper to actually publish the page
    return publish_story($q,
                         $story->id,
                         $story->template,
                         $set->{'pub_dir'} .
                           '/' . $story->target);

  } elsif ($q->param('set_id')) {
```

```
        # sets don't need as much 'set' up -- just called the
        # wrapper function and publish the set.
        return publish_set($q,
                 $q->param('set_id'));

    }

} elsif ($do eq 'list_stories') {            # list set's stories

    # draw index will do all the work for us
    draw_index($q);

} else {

    # If you see this, you've probably got a typo in one of your
    # links or form fields. Or someone is having fun with you.
    die "Unknown command ($do) from index screen";
}
}
```

The two detail screen handlers act on the data submitted on a detail screen. Detail screens (Figure 10.3) show all of the information about a story or a set, allowing you to edit any of that, and publish the story or set.

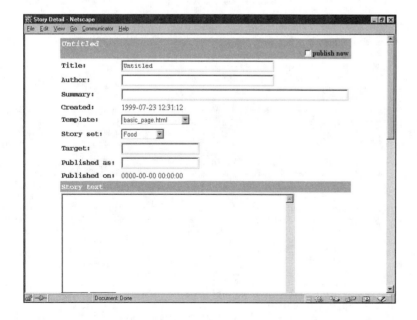

Figure 10.3

Story Detail screen.

This means the handler must handle saving any changes to the database (or not, if the form was cancelled), publishing the item (if requested), and returning to the index screen in a readable state.

```perl
#
# update database with new story info, return to index
#
sub handle_story_detail {
  my $screen = shift;
  my $q      = shift;
  my ($story, %story_flds);

  if ($q->param('cancel')) {

    #
    # Don't save, and undo anything we did in the background
    #

    if ($q->param('new_record')) {

      # delete the new record
      return delete_story($q->param('ID'));

    } else {
      return draw_index($q);
    }

  } else {

    #
    # store updated data
    #
    foreach my $fld($q->param) {
      next unless ($fld eq uc($fld));
      $story_flds{$fld} = $q->param($fld);
    }

    # convert text to nice paragraphs
    $story_flds{'TEXT'} =~ s|\n\s*\n|\n<p>|g;

    $story = new Story::DBI( ($q->param('ID')), \%story_flds );
    die $story->error if $story->error;

    #
    # publish, if pub_now checked,
    # with the right template, in the right place
    #
    if ($q->param('pub_now')) {
      my $set = get_story_set($story->story_set_id);

      # pass along info to info sceen
      $q->param('TITLE', $story->title);
      $q->param('PUBLISHED_AS',
              $set->{'pub_dir'} . '/' . $story->target);
      $q->param('SELECT_SET', $set->{'id'});
```

```
      # publish the story
      return publish_story($q,
                        $story->id,
                        $story->template,
                        $set->{'pub_dir'} .
                          '/' . $story->target);
    }
  }

  #
  # go back to the index
  #
  # we don't want to gum up the works with random
  # story fields, so we create a clean new CGI object,
  # with only the values we need.
  #
  my $nq = new CGI( { 'session_id' =>$q->param('session_id'),
                    'login'      =>$q->param('login'),
                    'do'         =>'list_stories',
                    'select_set' =>$story->set_id } );

  return draw_index($nq);
}
```

Now we come to the set detail handler (Figure 10.4). This is very
similar to handle_story_detail—except that it shows off how helpful
the Story::DBI object really is.

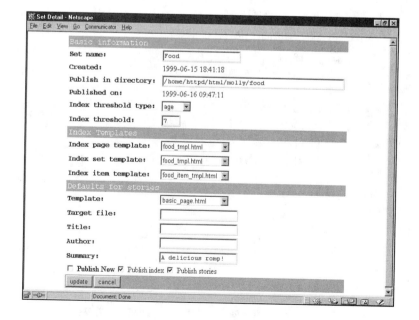

Figure 10.4
Story Set Detail screen.

We have to do a lot more work here to save the set's updated fields than we have to do to save a story. For example, the previous function never explicitly saves any data to the database—we just create a new story object and assign values to its fields. The Story::DBI object we create takes care of saving itself when the time comes.

```perl
sub handle_set_detail {
  my $screen = shift;
  my $q      = shift;

  my (%set_flds, $sql, $sth, @flds, @vals);

  if ($q->param('cancel')) {

    if ($q->param('new_record')) {

      # delete the new record
      return delete_set($q->param('ID'));

    } else {
      return draw_index($q);
    }

  } else {

    #
    # store updated info
    #

    # set fields are in uppercase
    foreach my $fld($q->param) {
      next unless ($fld eq uc($fld));

      push @flds, lc($fld);
      push @vals, $DBH->quote($q->param($fld));
    }

    # store the data in the db
    $sql = "REPLACE INTO story_sets (";
    $sql .= join(', ', @flds);
    $sql .= ") VALUES (";
    $sql .= join(', ', @vals);
    $sql .= ")";

    $sth = _exec_query($sql);

    if ($q->param('pub_now')) {

      # we'll need this value when we get to the output page
      $q->param('SET_ID', $q->param('ID'));

      my @opts;

      push (@opts, '--noindex') unless $q->param('pub_index');
      push (@opts, '--nostories') unless $q->param('pub_stories');
```

```
      return publish_set($q, $q->param('ID'), @opts);
   }

   my $nq = new CGI( { 'session_id' =>$q->param('session_id'),
                       'login'      =>$q->param('login'),
                       'do'         =>'list_stories',
                       'select_set' =>$q->param('ID') } );

   draw_index($nq);
 }
}
```

The authentication handler tests whether a submitted session ID is
still valid. It also checks whether login and password are valid.
When validated, the authentication handler starts a new session and
returns the ID. If it is given a valid session ID, it updates the timestamp for that session's record. This pushes forward the time when
the session will "time out" and force the user to log in again.

```
#
# data processing & publishing routines
# some of these call secondary SUID scripts!
#
sub authorized {
  my $session_id = shift;
  my $login      = shift;
  my $passwd     = shift;

  my ($sql, $sth, $h, $r);

  return unless $login;

  # if $session_id is supplied, find that id, match
  # $login with login field in session record, and make
  # sure it's not more than 20 minutes old.

  if ($session_id) {

    $sql = "SELECT * FROM sessions WHERE id=$session_id ".
           "AND login='$login' " .
           "AND UNIX_TIMESTAMP(NOW()) - UNIX_TIMESTAMP(ts) " .
           " < (20 * 60)";

    $sth = _exec_query($sql);
    $h   = $sth->fetchrow_hashref;

    if (ref $h) {

      # touch the session timestamp, so
      # that it won't time out
      &continue_session($session_id);
```

```perl
      # return the session id
      return $session_id;
    } else {
      return;
    }
  }

  # otherwise, if login & password were supplied,
  # look for the pair in auth_users table,
  # make new session record if login & passwd found

  if (($login) && ($passwd)) {

    $sql = "SELECT id FROM auth_users " .
           "WHERE login='$login' " .
           "AND passwd=PASSWORD('$passwd') AND active=1";

    $sth = _exec_query($sql);
    $r   = $sth->fetchrow_arrayref;

    if ((ref $r) && ($r->[0])) {

      # create a new session record
      # and return the session id
      return &new_session($login);
    }
  }

  return;
}
```

The following functions set and call the SUID wrapper, and look for the right response. If they don't get the one they want, they assume that something went wrong—a bad UID for example. The function will, in that case, echo the response back as an error.

```perl
# The next two functions set up and call the SUID wrapper,
# which in turn executes SUID scripts to publish the pages
# that need publishing.
sub publish_story {
  my $q      = shift;
  my (@args) = (@_);

  my $result = _suid_wrapper("$SCRIPT_DIR/publish_dbi.pl",
                             "-d $TMPL_DIR",
                             @args);


  die "Failed to publish story: $result"
    unless $result =~ /published ok/;

  return &draw_screen('story_published',$q);
}
```

```
sub publish_set {
  my $q      = shift;
  my $id     = shift;
  my (@args) = (@_);

  my $result =  _suid_wrapper("$SCRIPT_DIR/publish_set.pl",
                              "-d $TMPL_DIR",
                              $id,
                              @args);

  die "Failed to publish story set: $err"
    unless $result =~ /published ok/;

  #
  # clear the idx_needs_upd bit
  #
  my $sql = "UPDATE story_sets SET idx_needs_upd=0 WHERE id=$id";
  &_exec_query($sql);

  #
  # get some set info for the results screen
  #
  my $set = get_story_set($id);
  if (ref $set) {
    foreach my $sf (%$set) {
      $q->param($sf, $set->{$sf});
    }
  }

  return draw_screen('set_published',$q);
}
```

The following data access functions are utility routines that make it easy to grab information about stories and story sets in many places in the script.

```
#
# get a story and prep it for output on the detail page
#
sub prep_story {
  my $q = shift;

  my $story = new Story::DBI($q->param('story_id'));
  die $story->error if $story->error;

  #
  # set params in $q from story fields
  #
  foreach my $fld (keys %{$story->story}) {
    $q->param($fld, $story->story->{$fld});
  }

  #
  # make popups for set and template,
```

```perl
  # and select current value  for each
  #
  my ($set,$tmpl);

  # set selected item only if it's not a new story
  if ($q->param('story_id')) {
    $set = $story->story_set;
    $tmpl = $story->template;
  }

  $q->param('TMPL_SELECT', &draw_tmpl_select($tmpl));
  $q->param('SET_SELECT', &draw_set_select($set));

  # since we're working with the master CGI object, we
  # don't need to return anything
}

#
# get a story set and prep it for output
#
sub prep_set {
  my $q = shift;
  my $set = get_story_set($q->param('set_id'));

  return unless ref $set;

  foreach my $fld(keys %{$set}) {
    $q->param(uc($fld), $set->{$fld});
  }

  #
  # story sets have quite a few templates
  #
  $q->param('IDX_TMPL_SEL',
            &draw_tmpl_select($set->{'idx_template'},
                              'IDX_TEMPLATE'));
  $q->param('IDX_SET_TMPL_SEL',
            &draw_tmpl_select($set->{'idx_set_tmpl'},
                              'IDX_SET_TMPL'));
  $q->param('IDX_ITEM_TMPL_SEL',
            &draw_tmpl_select($set->{'idx_item_tmpl'},
                              'IDX_ITEM_TMPL'));
  $q->param('DFLT_TMPL_SEL',
            &draw_tmpl_select($set->{'dflt_tmpl'},
                              'DFLT_TMPL'));

  # since we're working with the master CGI object, we
  # don't need to return anything
}


#
# get list of .html and .tpl files in $TMPL_DIR
#
sub get_templates {
  my @tmpl;
```

```perl
opendir (TD, $TMPL_DIR)
  || die "Could not open dir $TMPL_DIR: $!";

# look for files we can read (-r), that don't start with .,
# and that do end with .html or .tpl

@tmpl = grep { (-r "$TMPL_DIR/$_") &&
              (!/^\./) &&
              (/(\.html|\.tpl)$/) } readdir TD;
closedir TD;
return @tmpl;
}


#
# get story set names from db
#
sub get_story_sets {
  my ($sql, $sth, $r, @sets);

  $sql = "SELECT id FROM story_sets";
  $sth = _exec_query($sql);

  while($r = $sth->fetchrow_arrayref) {
    push @sets, get_story_set($r->[0]);
  }

  return @sets;
}
```

Okay, ready for the big one? Here it is. This function gets the story set record from the database.

```perl
#
# get a story set record from the db, and set some additional
# info about it's status
#
sub get_story_set {
  my $set_id = shift;

  my ($sql, $sth, $h, $r);

  $sql = "SELECT * FROM story_sets WHERE id=$set_id";
  $sth = _exec_query($sql);
  $h   = $sth->fetchrow_hashref;

  if (ref $h) {

    #
    # get status -- do I need an update?
    #
    my $sid = $h->{'id'};

    #
    # total number of stories
    #
```

```perl
undef $r;
$sql = "SELECT count(id) FROM stories WHERE set_id=$sid";
$sth = _exec_query($sql);

$r = $sth->fetchrow_arrayref();

if (ref $r) {
  $h->{'total_stories'} = $r->[0];
}


#
# stories whose published_on is earlier than their timestamp
#
$sql = "SELECT count(id) FROM stories " .
  "WHERE set_id=$sid " .
  "AND published_on < ts";

$sth = _exec_query($sql);
$r   = $sth->fetchrow_arrayref();

if (ref $r) {
  $h->{'need_update'} = $r->[0];
}


#
# stories updated since index published
#
undef $r;
$sql = "SELECT count(s.id) FROM stories as s, " .
       "story_sets as st " .
       "WHERE st.id=$sid AND s.set_id=st.id " .
       "AND s.published_on > st.published_on";

$sth = _exec_query($sql);
$r   = $sth->fetchrow_arrayref();

if (ref $r) {
  $h->{'newer_than_index'} = $r->[0];
}


#
# number of published stories
#
undef $r;
$sql = "SELECT count(id) FROM stories WHERE set_id=$sid " .
       "AND NOT ISNULL(published_as)";
$sth = _exec_query($sql);
$r   = $sth->fetchrow_arrayref();

if (ref $r) {
  $h->{'published_stories'} = $r->[0];
}


#
# summarize my status, for the index listing
#
```

```perl
    if ($h->{'idx_needs_upd'}) {
      $h->{'status'} =
        '<font color="red"><b>Needs Update</b></font>';
    }

    if ($h->{'published_stories'} > 0) {

      if (&_num($h->{'published_on'}) < $h->{'ts'}) {
        $h->{'status'} =
          '<font color="red"><b>Needs Update</b></font>';
      } else {
        $h->{'status'} = '<font color="darkgreen">Ok</font>';

        if ($h->{'need_update'} > 0) {
          $h->{'status'} =
            '<font color="orange">Stories need update</font>';
        } else {

          if ($h->{'newer_than_index'} > 0) {
            $h->{'status'} =
              '<font color="orange">Index Needs Update</font>';
          }
        }
      }

    } else {
      $h->{'status'} = 'Not published';
    }

    return $h;
  } else {
    return {};
  }
}

sub get_stories_for_set {
  my $set_id = shift;
  return [] unless $set_id;

  my ($sql, $sth, $h, @stories);

  $sql = "SELECT id, title, created, " .
         "published_as, published_on, ts " .
         "FROM stories WHERE set_id=$set_id";
  $sth = _exec_query($sql);

  while ($h = $sth->fetchrow_hashref) {
    push @stories, $h;
  }

  return \@stories;
}

sub new_set {
  my ($sql, $sth);
```

```perl
$sql = "INSERT INTO story_sets (created) VALUES (NOW())";
$sth = _exec_query($sql);

return $sth->{'mysql_insertid'};
}
```

Alas, sometimes even stories and story sets must die!

```perl
sub delete_story {
  my $id = shift;

  my ($sql, $sth, $r, $set_id);

  # save the story's set id
  $sql = "SELECT set_id FROM stories WHERE id=$id";
  $sth = &_exec_query($sql);
  die "Could not delete story" unless ref $sth;

  $r = $sth->fetchrow_arrayref;
  if (ref $r) {
    $set_id = $r->[0];
  }

  $sql = "DELETE FROM stories WHERE id=$id";
  $sth = _exec_query($sql);

  if (ref $sth) {

    # alert the set that it probably needs to update it's index
    if ($set_id) {
      $sql = "UPDATE story_sets " .
             "SET idx_needs_upd=1 WHERE id=$set_id";
      $sth = _exec_query($sql);

      die "Story was deleted, but could not update story set!"
        unless ref $sth;
    }

    return alert("Story has been deleted");
  } else {
    die "Could not delete story: " . $sth->errstr;
  }
}

#
# Note that this DOES NOT delete the stories in the set!
# (Maybe you want to move them to another set?)
#
sub delete_set {
  my $id = shift;

  my ($sql, $sth);

  $sql = "DELETE FROM story_sets WHERE id=$id";
  $sth = _exec_query($sql);
```

```
  if (ref $sth) {
    return alert("Set has been deleted");
  } else {
    die "Could not delete story set: " . $sth->errstr;
  }
}
```

As you can see from the script, once you've deleted a story or story set, you'll receive a delete alert (Figure 10.5).

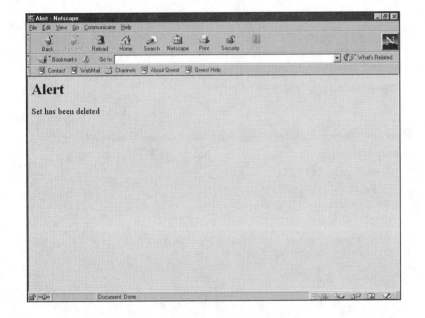

Figure 10.5

Story set delete alert.

Now we'll move to the script portion that controls session management. This allows us to keep Siteman secure, without demanding a login and password before every action, or passing that information around in hidden fields. We do this to avoid security problems—any time login and password information is requested and passed around, we run a potential security risk, so we try to always keep actions of that nature to an absolute minimum.

```
#
# Session management
#
sub new_session {
```

```perl
  my $login = shift;
  my ($sql, $sth, $created_id);

  $sql = "INSERT INTO sessions (login) VALUES ('$login')";
  $sth = _exec_query($sql);

  $created_id = $sth->{'mysql_insertid'};
  die "Could not determine id of created session"
    unless $created_id;

  return $created_id;
}

sub continue_session {
  my $session_id = shift;

  # setting ts to NULL resets it to now
  my $sql = "UPDATE sessions SET ts=NULL WHERE id=$session_id";

  $DBH->do($sql) || die $DBH->errstr;
}
```

Next up? Output handlers. These are the routines that handle the actual drawing of interface screens. Index needs a lot of special stuff, so it gets its own.

```perl
#
# output handlers
#

# the main index screen has complex lists and such,
# and so needs its own output handler
sub draw_index {
  my $q = shift;

  my ($tpl, %q_flds, $set, @sets, @stories, $p, $c);

  # set up template environment
  $tpl = new CGI::FastTemplate;
  $tpl->set_root($SCREEN_DIR);

  $tpl->define('MAIN', 'index_tmpl.html');
  $tpl->define('set_row', 'index_set_row.html');
  $tpl->define('story_row', 'index_story_row.html');

  # assign vars from $q
  foreach my $k($q->param) {
    $q_flds{uc($k)} = $q->escape($q->param($k));
  }

  $tpl->assign(%q_flds);

  # display list of sets, with status for each.
  @sets = get_story_sets();
```

```perl
foreach $set (@sets) {
  $tpl->clear_href;

  # alternate row bg colors
  if ($c eq 'white') {
    $c = '#DDDDDD';
  } else {
    $c = 'white';
  }
  $set->{'bg_color'} = $c;

  # make set fields recognizable template variables
  $set = _uc_keys($set);
  $tpl->assign($set);
  $tpl->parse('SET_LIST' => '.set_row');
}

# show stories list for selected set
if ($q->param('select_set')) {
  $set = get_story_set($q->param('select_set'));
  @stories = get_stories_for_set($q->param('select_set'));

  $tpl->assign('SELECTED_SET' => $set->{'name'},
               'STORY_LIST'   =>
                  draw_story_list($q->param('select_set'),
                                  $q));

} else {
  $tpl->assign('SELECTED_SET' => 'none',
               'STORY_LIST'   => 'no set selected');
}

$tpl->parse('PAGE'=>'MAIN');
$p = $tpl->fetch('PAGE');

die "Could not create index page" unless  ((ref $p) && ($$p));

return $$p;
}
```

This portion of the script addresses the needs of any page that has a form on it. It uses some cool regular expression tricks to fill the form in with any values in the CGI object for the same fields, which makes it very easy to do detail screens for items. This cuts down on hand-coded HTML or Perl functions to fill in fields. Don't you like it when we make life easier for you?

```perl
# detail pages all operate on the same principle:
# they're big forms, that have default values, if
# you're editing a pre-existing record.
sub draw_screen {
```

```perl
my $screen = shift;
my $q      = shift;

my $file = $screen;
my ($tpl, %params, $p, $page, $sc,
    $match, $orig, $type, $v, $pos);

unless (-r $file) {
  if (-r "$SCREEN_DIR/$file.html") {
    $file .= '.html';
  } elsif (-r "$SCREEN_DIR/$file.tpl") {
    $file .= '.tpl';
  } else {
    die "No screen '$screen' found in $SCREEN_DIR";
  }
}

#
# set up template environment
#
$tpl = new CGI::FastTemplate;
$tpl->set_root($SCREEN_DIR);

$tpl->define('tmpl', $file);

if (ref $q) {

  #
  # one field we don't want to set the value for: screen
  # save the value in a different parameter, just in case
  #
  $sc = $q->param('screen');
  $q->delete('screen');
  $q->param('last_screen',$sc);

  #
  # build CGI:FastTemplate-useable hash of param values
  # and substitute those into the page
  #
  foreach my $pn($q->param) {
    $params{uc($pn)} = $q->unescape($q->param($pn));
  }

  $tpl->assign(%params);
  $tpl->parse('SCREEN'=>'tmpl');
  $p = $tpl->fetch('SCREEN');

  if ((ref $p) && ($$p)) {
    $page = $$p;
  } else {
    die "Unable to process template vars in $file";
  }

  #
  # fill in any form fields whose names
  # match CGI params with the value of
```

```
# the matching param.
#

my ($name, $type, $tag);

# go through page, grabbing up each form field
while ($page =~
    /(<(input|select|textarea)[^>]+>(?:.*?<\/\2>)?)/isg)
{

    $match = $1;
    $tag   = lc($2);
    $orig  = $match;

    #
    # remember where the match left off
    #
    $pos = pos $page;

    if ($match =~ /type="([^"]+)"/) {
      $type = $1;
    }

    if ($match =~ /name="([^"]+)"/) {
        $name = $1;
    }

    #
    # If the form field corresponds to a parameter...
    #
    if ($q->param($name)) {

        $v = _html_safe($q->param($name));

        if ($tag eq 'input') {
          if ($type =~ /check/i) {

            #
            # for checkboxes, set checked if value is true
            #
              if ($v) {
                $match =~ /checked/i
              || $match =~ s|>| checked>|i;
            } else {
                $match =~ s|\s*checked\s*||i;
            }

          } elsif ($type =~ /radio/i) {

            #
            # for radiogroups, set checked
            # if value matches param value
            #
            if ($match =~ /value="?$v"?/i) {
              $match =~ /checked/i
            || $match =~ s|>| checked>|i;
```

```perl
          } else {
            $match =~ s|\s*checked\s*||i;
          }

        } elsif ($type =~ /text|hidden|password/i) {

          #
          # for text, hidden, and passwd,
          # set value to param value
          #
          $match =~ s|value=".*?"|value="$v"|i
            || $match =~ s|>| value="$v">|i;
        }

      } elsif ($tag eq 'textarea') {

        #
        # for textarea, fill in value
        #
        $match =~ s|>.*?</textarea>|>$v</textarea>|is;

      } elsif ($tag eq 'select') {

        #
        # for select, set the option whose value
        # matches $v to 'selected'
        #
        $match =~ s|\s*selected\s*||isg;
        $match =~ s|(<option.*?value="$v".*?)>|$1 selected>|is
          || $match =~ s|<option>(\s*$v\s*)</option>
                        |<option selected>$1</option>
                        |isx;
      }

      #
      # put new tag back into page
      # and reset matching to just before
      # end of the new tag
      #
      $page =~ s|$orig|$match|i;
       pos $page = $pos + (length($match) - length($orig)) - 2;
    }
  }

} else {

  #
  # No params... just output the screen
  #
  $p = $tpl->fetch('SCREEN');

  if ((ref $p) && ($$p)) {
    $page = $$p;
  }

}
return $page;
}
```

Let's add some "helper" functions that draw complex tables or
widgets.

```perl
#
# draw the list of stories in the selected set
#
sub draw_story_list {
  my $set_id = shift;
  my $q      = shift;

  return unless $set_id;

  my ($tpl, %q_flds, $stories, $s, $p, $c);

  # get my stories
  $stories = get_stories_for_set($set_id);

  # set up template environment
  $tpl = new CGI::FastTemplate();
  $tpl->set_root($SCREEN_DIR);

  $tpl->define('story_list' => 'story_list_tmpl.html');
  $tpl->define('story_row'  => 'story_row_tmpl.html');

  # assign vars from $q
  foreach my $k($q->param) {
    $q_flds{uc($k)} = $q->escape($q->param($k));
  }
  $tpl->assign(%q_flds);

  if (@$stories) {

    # make all of the story keys UC (for template inclusion)
    $stories = [ map(&_uc_keys($_), @$stories) ];

    foreach $s(@$stories) {
      $tpl->clear_href;

      # alternate row bg colors
      if ($c eq 'white') {
          $c = '#DDDDDD';
      } else {
          $c = 'white';
      }
      $s->{'BG_COLOR'} = $c;

      # set status item
      if ($s->{'PUBLISHED_AS'}) {

          if (&_num($s->{'PUBLISHED_ON'}) < $s->{'TS'}) {
            $s->{'STATUS'} =
              '<font color="red"><b>Needs update</b></font>';
          } else {
            $s->{'STATUS'} =
              '<font color="darkgreen">Up to date</font>';
          }
```

```
        } else {
            $s->{'STATUS'} = 'Not published';
            $s->{'PUBLISHED_AS'} = '-';
        }

        $tpl->assign($s);
        $tpl->parse('ROWS' => '.story_row');
    }

    } else {
      $tpl->assign('ROWS'=>
                    '<tr><td>No stories for this set</td></tr>');
    }

    $tpl->parse('PAGE'=>'story_list');

    $p = $tpl->fetch('PAGE');

    if ((ref $p) && ($$p)) {
      return $$p;
    } else {
      return '<p>Error: could not generate story list!</p>';
    }
}
```

We do a lot of template selection.

```
sub draw_tmpl_select {
  my $selected    = shift;
  my $name        = shift;
  my @tmpl        = get_templates();

  $name ||= 'TEMPLATE';
  my $tmpl_select = "<select name=\"$name\">";

  foreach my $t (@tmpl) {

    if ($t =~ /^$selected(\.html|\.tpl)?$/) {
      $tmpl_select .= "\n  <option selected>$t</option>";
    } else {
      $tmpl_select .= "\n  <option>$t</option>";
    }
  }
  $tmpl_select .= "\n</select>";

  return $tmpl_select;
}

sub draw_set_select {
  my $selected    = shift;
  my @sets        = &get_story_sets();
  my $set_select  = '<select name="SET">';
```

```
foreach my $s(@sets) {
  if ($s->{'name'} eq $selected) {
    $set_select .= "\n <option selected>"
  . ($s->{'name'}) . "</option>";
  } else {
    $set_select .= "\n <option>" . ($s->{'name'}) . "</option>";
  }
}
$set_select .= "\n<select>";

return $set_select;
}
```

And add one more full-screen handler, for non-error alerts.

```
sub alert {
  my $msg = shift;

  return <<ALRT;
<html>
<head><title>Alert</title></head>

<body bgcolor="#DDDDCC">

<h1>Alert</h1>

<font size=+1>$msg</font>

</body>
</html>
ALRT
}
```

Of course, Jason insists on adding some utility functions here. First is the SUID wrapper, which we use to run scripts whose UID bit is set. This allows us to do things (like writing HTML pages to disk) that we ordinarily couldn't do from a CGI. The wrapper allows us to do this securely. It makes sure that we don't start a shell, making it much harder for someone to crack our server by sending carefully composed data to the CGI.

```
#
# utility functions
#

#
# Run SUID helper script securely,
# using piped open() and exec();
#
sub _suid_wrapper {
```

```
  my $script = shift;
  my (@args) = (@_);

  my ($pid, $result);

  return unless (-x $script);

  #
  # open -| forks a new process
  #
  defined($pid = open(SCRPT, '-|')) ||
    die "Could not run $script securely (no fork): $!";

  if ($pid) {              # parent - read output from script

    while (<SCRPT>) {
      $result .= $_;
    }

    close SCRPT;
    return $result;

  } else {                # child - run the script
    exec($script,@args);
  }
}
```

Now we'll run a whole lot of SQL queries.

```
#
# prepare and exec a sql query
#
sub _exec_query {
  my $sql = shift;
  my $sth;

  $sth = $DBH->prepare($sql);
  die $DBH->errstr unless ref $sth;

  $sth->execute || die $sth->errstr;

  return $sth;
}


#
# convert the keys of a hash to upper case
#
sub _uc_keys {
  my $h = shift;
  my ($k, %out);

  return unless ((ref $h) =~ /HASH/);
```

```
  foreach $k(%$h) {
    $out{uc($k)} = $h->{$k};
  }

  return \%out;
}

#
# convert a MySQL-style date value into a number
#
sub _num {
  my $ds = shift;

  $ds =~ s/\D//g;

  $ds;
}

#
# convert field values into something safe for
# inclusion in <input value=""> tags
#
sub _html_safe {
  my $val = shift;

  $val =~ s|\n*<p>\n*|\n\n|ig;      # replace <p> with \n\n
  $val =~ s|"|\&quot;|g;            # replace quotes with &quot;
  $val =~ s|\&|\&amp;|g;            # replace & with &amp;

  return $val;
}
```

And that's Siteman! Using these scripts—and the templates, modules and scripts from earlier chapters—you can now publish, update, and manage an entire Web site directly from your Web browser window.

What's Up Next

We've come to the end of the prepared CGI programs that you can use to publish your Web content. In the next chapter, you'll be introduced to resources to help you modify these programs, and write your own to fully customize your Web site.

Getting Ready to Learn Perl

So, you enjoyed working with Perl so much you want to learn it. That's great! We want to help you get off to a strong start. This chapter takes a look at some of the basic syntax—all of which you've encountered when actually working with the code in the book. We'll provide definitions and give you some frame of reference to understand what important syntax structures do.

We then provide you with some invaluable tips to help you get prepared to learn Perl—wisdom that will certainly help you to avoid pitfalls and frustrations along the way. Finally, we offer up a number of resources for furthering your Perl education.

Arrays, Expressions, Scalars, Oh My!

Throughout this book, a variety of programming terms have been put to use. We talk a lot about these in the tips section (as well as throughout the book), so you'll want to read this stuff to get the most out of the tips.

Knowing the basic terminology also helps take some of the mystique out of the programming language—neatly packaging individual concepts into logical blocks instead of having to figure out long strings of seemingly undecipherable code.

The following list gives a brief explanation of what these common concepts are

Array

An array is an ordered list of values. To get to a value, arrays require an index—to show which of the elements you're interested in. For example, `@links` is an array, and `$links[3]` is an element in the array.

Expression

An expression is a piece of code that has a value. Like `2+5` is an expression, and so is `@foo=grep ! /^.{1,2}$/, readdir DIR`.

An expression that does an entire bit of work on its own is called a *statement*. Statements in Perl are followed by a semicolon.

Function

A function is a block of code that optionally takes input and produces some kind of output. A Perl function is the same as a math function in math, technically mapping input to output.

Hash

A hash is a special kind of array which is accessed in key-value pairs instead of numerically. For example, `%fields` is a hash and `$fields{'From'}` is an individual element of a hash.

Variable

A variable is a storage area for a value or a group of values. The label attached to the variable is the *variable name*.

Scalars

A scalar is a single value, one number or one string, within your Perl script. Scalar values in Perl are preceeded by a dollar sign. `$links[1]`, `$fields{'To'}` and `$name` are all scalar values, and `$name` is a scalar variable.

Seven Tips for Making Perl Fun

Or should that read "Making Fun of Perl?" Either way, We offer the following guidelines to ensure that you get learning Perl off to a good start. The final objective, however, no matter your intermediate goals—is to have fun.

Start Small

Programming can be difficult to learn, and frustration born of having to deal with too much information at once doesn't make it any easier. Start with small scripts and programs, and work your way up.

Working on a script that provides immediate output helps a lot, so try to make your first scripts ones that do something—the famous "hello world" is a good start. After you've begun with a simple script like that, or like the ones in our chapter on CGI forms, and gotten that working, you can expand it. Then, you can work on its features one by one, and build up to something much cooler.

Don't Let the Syntax Scare You

The first time you see something like this

```
@hits = grep { !/^\./ && -d $_ } readdir PWD;
die "Nothing found" unless @hits;
```

it's likely to have you seeing halo effects and feel the onslaught of a vicious migraine approach. Perl is a language that has been cultivated more than planned, and as a result it doesn't have the cleanest-looking syntax around. But after you get used to a few of Perl's idiosyncrasies, things begin make a lot more sense.

Here are a couple of the most important syntax concerns to keep in mind:

- Variable names always start with a variety of characters: $ for scalars (things with only one value), @ for arrays, % for hashes, & for functions, and * for typeglobs (which are a kind of super-reference)

- When you're accessing a member of an array or a hash, you're really asking for a scalar value, and that's why you write $a[1] and $h{'this'} instead of @a[1] or %h{'this'}

- You don't have to use forward slashes (/) in **s///** or **m//** statements. You can use any character you want as the separator—a convenient thing to remember when the pattern you're searching for is a directory path, or a closing html </tag>. Which is easier to read:
  s/http:\/\/www.perl.com\/stuff\/things\.html/http:\/\/ www.perl.com\/things\/stuff\.html/
  or
  s|http://www.perl.com/stuff/things\.html|http://www.perl .com/things/stuff\.html| ?

- Perl defines a lot of special global variables, too many to go into here. The important ones to remember are **$_**, **@_**, **@ARGV**, **$!** and **$@**.

- **$_** is the default scalar variable. If you see an operation that doesn't appear to be acting on anything (e.g., **while(<>) { print; }**, it's really using **$_**.

- **@_** is the list of parameters passed to a function. When the first line of a function is something like my **$var = shift;**, **@_** is the array you're taking the top value from. We've used the shift syntax in all of our scripts, but you can just as well say **my ($var1, $var2, $var3) = @_;**

- **@ARGV** is the array of command-line arguments passed to a script called from the command line

- **$!** is used for system error strings; if **open(FILE, ">$file-name")** fails, **$!** will tell you why

- **$@** is set for errors that occur inside **eval{}** blocks. We use this variable extensively in our CGI scripts, to catch errors and display them to the user

Read the &%$& Manual!

This section can also be referred to as "perldoc is my new best friend!"

Even if you don't have any Perl books, and can't find any other outside sources of reference and examples, you have plenty of documentation close at hand. Perl has built-in documentation in POD ("Plain Old Documentation") format, which can be read with the **perldoc** command.

You can get help with built-in Perl functions and operators with the **perldoc perlfunc** and **perldoc perlop** commands, and get documentation for just about any module with **perldoc [module name]**, where [module name] is entered exactly as in a use statement. (for example, for **CGI::Carp**, you'd say **perldoc CGI::Carp**). The manual page **perldoc perl** contains a table of contents for the Perl manual pages and is a good starting place.

Many people find perldoc difficult and not at all user-friendly. You may wish to choose a good resource book. We've listed several to choose from later in this chapter.

For help with the perldoc system itself, you can type **perldoc perldoc**.

There's More Than One Way to Do It

Just because you see `die "Nothing found" unless @hits` in a book doesn't mean you can't write it as `unless(@hits) { die "Nothing found"; }`, or even `if (!@hits) { die "Nothing found"; }`, if you like one of those better. The upside of Perl's wacky syntax is that you have a lot of freedom to make your code readable for yourself. The downside is that everybody else has that freedom too, and a lot of them don't agree with you, or each other, about what "readable" really means!

For almost any programming problem you'll come across, you'll find a multitude of solutions in Perl; you're free to choose the one that works best for you, or just the one that you like best. You don't have to accept anybody else's solutions if you don't like them because there's always another way. Which brings us to...

Know When to Reinvent a Wheel or Two

And of course, when *not* to. It's your call. I've had to write (among other things) an SMTP relay server, a proprietary encryption-enabled beta authorization system, and a Perl client for a proprietary online gaming service. Each in less than a few hours.

This not a testament to the power of Perl, or to my programming skills, as much as it is to the power of the Perl community. In each of these examples, the solution was built by gluing together blocks of code that others had written and donated to the community!

So you don't always have to reinvent the wheel, nor should you try. Check the upcoming section, "Resources You Want, Stuff You Need."

On the other hand, sometimes you really want your own darn wheel, and nobody else's will do. That's fine—Perl is a great wheel-invention language because it makes experimentation easy. The important thing is to know when you need to go it alone, and when you don't.

Use the Debugging Tools

Perl has a number of built-in debugging helpers, all of which can make your life a whole lot easier. The most useful are the `-w` and `-d` command line arguments, and the modules strict, Carp, and CGI::Carp for use within scripts.

The -w and -d switches are best used for command-line debugging. -w prints helpful warnings to the console when you run your script— for example, it can catch common errors such as typos in variable names and using = when you mean ==, and it will tell you exactly where in your script it sees a problem. There's no reason not to use -w in every Perl script you write.

The -d switch invokes a full debugger, that will allow you to step through your code line by line, to catch those really intractable bugs.

Carp and CGI::Carp make finding runtime bugs much easier, especially, in the case of CGI::Carp, runtime bugs in CGI scripts. No CGI author should even think of starting a new script without these modules close at hand.

The strict module's usefulness is a lot less obvious, but if anything, it's even more powerful than the Carp twins. Strict forces you to use good programming practices: declaring all variables before using them, not using named references or bare words, among others. It can catch a lot of bugs that don't look like bugs to the naked eye, and prevent a lot of bugs before they happen. You should make it a practice to include use strict in every script you write. It may seem like a chore, but it will save you much more work in the end.

Get Help

What do you do when your script isn't working, the debugging tools aren't helping, everything looks fine, but it *just doesn't work*? Who do you call when you've read all the documentation, but you can't figure out what the heck it's talking about? These are important questions because Perl, as an open source product, does not come bundled with a 1-800 support hotline. So where can you turn for answers?

As the astute reader has probably already guessed, the same Perl community that works together to maintain CPAN and Perl itself, is the best place to go for answers to your Perl questions. If you have a question that you think is probably quite common, look for the FAQ first. A helpful list is provided for you in the upcoming section, "Resources You Want, Stuff You Need."

Resources You Want, Stuff You Need

We've compiled a list of what we think are the best ways to get help using and learning Perl. We've included books, Web sites, Newsgroups, and FAQs. As mentioned several times in this book, the Perl community is an extremely tight one—and it's there for you.

Books

There are several books that we keep on our desktops and use regularly. They include:

- *Sams Teach Yourself Perl in 24 Hours* by Clinton Pierce. This is the book you want to get next if you're serious about learning to program Perl. It will start you with the true basics: history, concepts, and the "Hello, World" program. From there, you'll learn how to work with the concepts mentioned at the beginning of this chapter, as well as a variety of others Perl programming methods. The book contains exercises so you can practice. The end of the book approaches CGI programming as a set of small building-blocks so that you can construct larger programs like those presented here.

- *Programming Perl* by Larry Wall, Tom Christiansen, and Jon Orwant. Also referred to as the "Camel" book, once you've worked your way through the basics, this book is akin to jumping into the deep end of the pond. Larry Wall, as the principle architect of Perl, explains his motives and wishes for the language as well as provides a thorough reference. You'll learn to see, and use, Perl like a programmer does. *Programming Perl* provides a lot of detail, and includes an excellent glossary of terms.

- *Perl 5: Desktop Reference* by Johan Vromans. This palm-size reference includes syntax, modules, and debugging information that you'll find invaluable when working with Perl.

Another, non-Perl-specific book that we use is

- *Unix in a Nutshell* by Daniel Gilly. This desktop reference is a very comprehensive and handy book to have around when trying to work with those complex Unix commands. Molly's copy was never far from her fingertips while working through Jason's scripts.

If you have a code question that you want to post to a newsgroup, post the code and question in the message, and be as specific as possible about what's wrong, the platform and Perl version you're using, and any other information that might be pertinent. Then, wait patiently for an answer. Remember that the people who answer your question do it out of the goodness of their hearts, and are under no obligation to help you, and certainly *won't* if you act anything but respectful.

Web Sites

These days, Web sites provide the detailed support that is necessary for any budding programmer, and certainly for Web designers. Here's a selection of our favorites for both general and specific development information.

O'Reilly's Perl site is a good stop for information on new Perl books and products, modules, as well as upcoming conventions and conferences, http://www.perl.com/.

The Perl community is a very active and motivated group, and their official Web site is **http://www.perl.org**. There you'll find job listings, pointers to help and mailing lists, code, and information on local community groups called Perl Mongers.

Several efforts by the Perl community at educating new programmers are noteworthy. Among them, **http://learn.perl.org** has the best quality moderated mailing list traffic for answering questions.

For general design information and resources try these great sites:

- Builder.Com. This site from C|NET is a terrific resource for Web developers. It offers regular features and columns as well as a variety of newsgroups, **http://www.builder.com/**.

- Ziff-Davis' DevHead. A favorite of Molly's, this site offers up scripts galore. There's a nice, punchy section for Perl fans, http://www.devhead.com/.

- WebReview. This site specializes in providing thoughtful articles and resources for Web developers, http://www.webreview.com/.

- Developer.Com. A large technology-oriented site, Developer.Com offers news, discussion, and training with a good section on Perl. They also have an "Ask the Experts" section that can be quite helpful, **http://www.developer.com/**.

Newsgroups

Perl newsgroups are abundant. The following are widely available via most Internet Usenet news services:

- Comp.lang.perl.announce—Perl authors use this group to announce new modules or scripts that have become available.

- Comp.lang.perl.misc—The most active of Perl newsgroups within the "comp" hierarchy, this newsgroup offers you the opportunity to ask any Perl question and discuss general Perl topics. The topics generally are mid-to-high level and very varied in scope.

- Comp.lang.perl.moderated—This newsgroup offers moderation in order to help focus in on relevant Perl questions from both novice and high-level programmers. Posters must be registered— if you post to the newsgroup, you'll automatically be sent details on how to do just that. All posts are reviewed, so this is a good place to go if you have very specific questions.

- Comp.lang.perl.modules—If you're looking specifically for Perl modules or module solutions, you can use this newsgroup.

- Comp.infosystems.www.authoring.cgi—If you have questions specific to CGI programming, but aren't necessarily about the Perl language itself this is the place to ask.

Please use proper newsgroup etiquette when participating in any newsgroup. If you have questions about etiquette, check out *http://unix1.sncc.lsu. edu/internet/usenet/ usenet-etiquette.html*

Web discussion groups for Perl abound. One such group is PerlMonks (**http://perlmonks.org**) that specializes in teaching Perl development skills through interaction among its users. There's a large amount of working code and discussion on the site—a great deal of which concerns CGI programming.

Helpful FAQs

Use the following FAQ offering for quick Perl references.

The Perl FAQ—For a comprehensive list of Perl FAQs, begin at http://www.perl.com/CPAN/doc/manual/html/pod/perlfaq.html. A copy of the FAQ is shipped with every installation of Perl. To get to the FAQ, type **perldoc perlfaq** at a command prompt.

All We Want to Do Is Have Some Fun

Writing a program can be a bit like doing a crossword puzzle. If you know the language it's written in, and have a couple of clues to work with, it can be fun, challenging, and downright rewarding to get it done right.

On the other hand, if you don't know the language, and the clues don't make any sense, it's just an exercise in frustration and futility. Any American who's tried a British crossword can tell you what that's all about.

The key to learning a new programming language, and learning how to program in general, is to stick with the fun and challenging puzzles as much as possible. You'll find, in time, that the puzzles that at first seemed frustrating and intractable will become much clearer as you solve some easier ones.

If you start out with stuff that doesn't make a lick of sense to you, you'll have a hard time getting anywhere. But wherever you begin, the point is to enjoy yourself. The process will be more exciting and the results of your labors will be much more gratifying as a result.

INDEX

Symbols

A

B - C

E - F

Q - R

Hey, you've got enough worries.

Don't let IT training be one of them.

Get on the fast track to IT training at InformIT,
your total Information Technology training network.

 | **www.informit.com** | **SAMS**

■ Hundreds of timely articles on dozens of topics ■ Discounts on IT books from all our publishing partners, including Sams Publishing ■ Free, unabridged books from the InformIT Free Library ■ "Expert Q&A"—our live, online chat with IT experts ■ Faster, easier certification and training from our Web- or classroom-based training programs ■ Current IT news ■ Software downloads ■ Career-enhancing resources

Other Related Titles

Sams Teach Yourself Macromedia Dreamweaver 4 in 24 Hours
Betsy Bruce
ISBN: 0-672-32042-8
$24.99 US/$37.95 CAN

How to Use Dreamweaver 4 and Fireworks 4
Lon Coley
ISBN: 0-672-32041-X
$29.99 US/$44.95 CAN

Sams Teach Yourself HTML and XHTML in 24 Hours, Fifth Edition
Dick Oliver
ISBN: 0-672-32076-2
$24.99 US/$37.95 CAN

Sams Teach Yourself JavaScript in 24 Hours, Second Edition
Michael Moncur
ISBN: 0-672-32025-8
$24.99 US/$37.95 CAN

Sams Teach Yourself Dreamweaver UltraDev 4 in 21 Days
John Ray
ISBN: 0-672-31901-2
$39.99 US/$59.95 CAN

How to Use Macromedia Flash 5
Denise Tyler and Gary Rebholz
ISBN: 0-672-32004-5
$29.99 US/$44.95 CAN

Sams Teach Yourself DHTML in 24 Hours
Michael Moncur
ISBN: 0-672-32302-8
$24.99 US/$37.95 CAN

Sams Teach Yourself LiveMotion in 24 Hours
Molly E. Holzschlag
ISBN: 0-672-31916-0
$24.99 US/$37.95 CAN

Sams Teach Yourself SVG in 24 Hours
Micah Laaker
ISBN: 0-672-32290-0
$29.99 US/$44.95 CAN

Sams Teach Yourself Perl in 24 Hours
Clinton Pierce
ISBN: 0-672-32276-5
$29.99 US/$44.95 CAN

Sams Teach Yourself Flash 5 in 24 Hours
Phillip Kerman
ISBN: 0-672-31892-X
$24.99 US/$37.95 CAN

SAMS
www.samspublishing.com

All prices are subject to change.

What's on the CD-ROM?

The book companion CD-ROM contains all the project files used in the book, Perl for Linux/Unix, Macintosh, and Windows platforms, and Perl modules.

Installation Instructions

Windows

1. Insert the disc into your CD-ROM drive.

2. From the Windows desktop, double-click the My Computer icon.

3. Double-click the icon representing your CD-ROM drive.

4. Double-click on start.html. All the CD-ROM files can be accessed by the HTML interface.

Macintosh

1. Insert the disc into your CD-ROM drive.

2. Double-click the PERLWORKSHOP icon when it appears on your desktop.

3. Double-click on start.html. All the CD-ROM files can be accessed by the HTML interface.

Linux/Unix

These installation instructions assume that you have a passing familiarity with Unix commands and the basic setup of your machine. Because Unix has many flavors, only generic commands are used. If you have any problems with the commands, please consult the appropriate manual page or your system administrator.

1. Insert the disc into your CD-ROM drive.

2. If you have a volume manager, mounting of the CD-ROM will be automatic. If you don't have a volume manager, you can mount the CD-ROM by typing

   ```
   mount -tiso9660 /dev/cdrom /mnt/cdrom
   ```

   NOTE: /mnt/cdrom is just a mount point, but it must exist when you issue the mount command. You may also use any empty directory for a mount point if you don't want to use /mnt/cdrom.

3. Open the start.html file. All of the CD-ROM files can be accessed by the HTML interface.